HOW TO RECOGNIZE GOOD POLICING

Books Under the General Editorship of
DANIEL CURRAN

CRIME AS STRUCTURED ACTION
by James W. Messerschmidt

EMERGING CRIMINAL JUSTICE
Three Pillars for a Proactive Justice System
by Paul H. Hahn

CRIME CONTROL AND WOMEN
Implications of Criminal Justice Policy
edited by Susan L. Miller

HOW TO RECOGNIZE GOOD POLICING
Problems and Issues
edited by Jean-Paul Brodeur

HOW TO RECOGNIZE GOOD POLICING

Problems and Issues

Edited by

Jean-Paul Brodeur

POLICE EXECUTIVE
RESEARCH FORUM
WASHINGTON, DC.

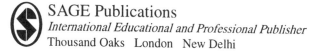

SAGE Publications
International Educational and Professional Publisher
Thousand Oaks   London   New Delhi

For information:

SAGE Publications, Inc.
2455 Teller Road
Thousand Oaks, California 91320
E-mail: order@sagepub.com

SAGE Publications Ltd.
6 Bonhill Street
London EC2A 4PU
United Kingdom

SAGE Publications India Pvt. Ltd.
M-32 Market
Greater Kailash I
New Delhi 110 048 India

Printed in the United States of America

Library of Congress Cataloging-in-Publication Data

Main entry under title:

How to recognize good policing: Problems and issues / editor,
  Jean-Paul Brodeur.
    p. cm.
  Includes bibliographical references and index.
  ISBN 0-7619-1613-X (cloth: acid-free paper)
  ISBN 0-7619-1614-8 (pbk.: acid-free paper)
    1. Police—United States—Evaluation. 2. Police
administration—United States—Evaluation. 3. Police-community
relations—United States. 4. Community policing—United States.
I. Brodeur, Jean-Paul.
  HV8141.H68   1998
  363.2′0973—ddc21   98-9032

This book is printed on acid-free paper.

              01   02   03   10   9   8   7   6   5   4   3

Acquiring Editor: C. Terry Hendrix
Production Editor: Astrid Virding
Editorial Assistant: Lynn Miyata
Indexer: Will Ragsdale
Designer/Typesetter: Janelle LeMaster
Cover Designer: Candice Harman

CONTENTS

PART III   Issues in Organizational Change

PART IV   Perspectives and Conclusions

INTRODUCTION

Jean-Paul Brodeur

Since the early 1970s, a wealth of books and articles on the reform of policing, written both by police professionals and by academic researchers, has appeared. The phrases "community-oriented policing" and "problem-oriented policing" are found in an early report by Sherman, Milton, and Kelly (1973) on team policing. Since then, the pioneering work of Goldstein (1977, 1979, 1987, 1990) and of numerous other authors (e.g., Eck & Spelman, 1987b) have put community and problem-oriented policing at the top of the policing reform agenda.

The first spate of these works focused on clarifying what was presented as a new paradigm for policing. This "new" paradigm was usually called community policing and was incidently referred to as problem-oriented policing; the latter designation has gained increasing currency over the years.[1] The second wave of research literature, epitomized by the work of Greene and Mastrofski (1988), asked whether community policing was merely a new form of rhetoric or whether it actually influenced the daily operations of police departments. This second wave was characterized by the production of the first assessments of the impact of community and problem-oriented policing (Rosenbaum, 1994). The most recent research concerns the evaluation process itself, a process no longer taken for granted. Evaluating policing as performed by individual police, by police organizations, and by their partners is now seen as raising complex questions that are both theoretical and practical.

This critical recognition—that the evaluation of policing in itself raised unresolved issues—was to a large extent a predictable outcome of the development of research in this field. It was also spurred on in no insignificant way by the unforeseen decline in crime rates observed in most Western countries, particularly in large cities. In certain major U.S. cities the decline in serious crime during the past few years has been hailed as nothing short of spectacular.[2] For instance, the homicide rate has dropped by more than 50% in New York City between 1992 and 1996. The drop in crime rates was so sudden and so steep that criminologists and other social scientists have yet to agree on an explanation. Contending that policing had been hastily dismissed as a major determinant for the downward trends in crime, senior managers of large police departments were quick to claim credit, with the support of many researchers, on behalf of their organizations.[3] Their claims were all the more convincing given that the decline in reported crime was the outcome of processes that are still very largely unaccounted for by evaluation research. The drop in reported crime is a success story in search of an acknowledged author.

THE RESEARCH BACKGROUND

These developments make the publication of studies on the evaluation of policing very timely. Although the authors of the chapters in this book have different backgrounds, there are a number of common threads running through their work and more generally through the research literature on the evaluation of policing.

To begin with: Why is there now such interest in evaluating police performance? There are two main answers to this question. First, large claims were made by police reformers for community policing and problem-oriented policing. Whether these claims were just rhetoric or were based on actual results was an unavoidable question. Second, there is a strong demand for police accountability and for getting value for money in these times of budgetary constraint. Performance assessment is a crucial tool for achieving accountability and for verifying how well tax dollars are spent. Another reason why we should be involved in program evaluation began to emerge as researchers proceeded farther in the evaluation of programs. It was found that evaluation was a powerful instrument for revealing the assumptions underlying policing programs. Furthermore, the belief that the underpinnings of these programs were known was shown to be wrong once thorough assessment began.

It can be asked next whether there are many kinds of program evaluation and, if so, what they are. There are essentially two kinds of evaluation. First, there is day-to-day monitoring by the police of their operations. This kind of evaluation is performed internally and is part of the routine of police organizations, although there are very significant differences from one force to another in how thoroughly the assessment is performed. A second kind of evaluation is based on an explicit methodology and uses the resources of the social sciences. These *research evaluations* are generally performed by external consultants who do not belong to the police organizations that call on them. Such evaluations are both costly and time-consuming, and generally performed in relation to a special program of policing. In addition to these two kinds of evaluation, it has been suggested that the same kinds of instruments applied in corporate studies of how well a private company is performing in the market can be used in assessing policing.

A third cluster of issues concerns the objects of an assessment. There are generally thought to be three kinds of objects that can be submitted to an evaluation in the field of policing. The first is a program of intervention. Most of the programs so far selected for evaluation have been community policing and problem-oriented policing programs. In most cases, these were submitted to *research evaluations*. There is, however, a crucial distinction in respect to programs. They can be assessed from the standpoint of process or of outcome; the same distinction can be made by using the terminology of implementation as opposed to that of impact. So far, evaluations have focused on outcome and impact, and many of them may have entirely missed the point. Recent research on implementation (see, in this volume, McElroy, Chapter 4; Greene, Chapter 8; and Mastrofski, Chapter 9) shows that the proper and complete implementation of a program raised very serious difficulties. Unless it can be demonstrated that a program was in fact implemented as designed, there can be no valid reason for crediting it with producing a specific effect. An impact on a neighborhood may be identified and measured, even though its precise cause cannot be attributed with certainty. There is an additional problem regarding the distinction between implementation and outcome: There must be a reasonable guarantee that a program was in fact implemented as it was originally conceived—notwithstanding the necessary adjustments that always have to be made during implementation—before it can be credited with the production of a given outcome. Yet one of the practical findings of evaluation research as it is discussed in this book is that the obstacles to measuring both implementation and impact in the course of the same assessment are very difficult to overcome. It often happens that going through one of the two main phases of an evaluation generally overshadows and even inhibits the realization of the other, with unfortunate consequences for the evaluation's validity.

The two other objects of evaluation are people and partnerships. As with programs, the assessment of people may focus on two different aspects of behavior. Persons first behave individually. Consequently, the assessment of the performance of individual police is important. This kind of evaluation is performed both internally, often for the purposes of promotion, and externally, when individual police involved in a community or problem-oriented program are questioned about how they implement the program and about their level of job satisfaction in performing their tasks. Persons also behave collectively. An evaluation of their collective performance is far-reaching and generally encompasses the position of the whole organization in regard to the program under scrutiny. Organizations are of prime concern for evaluation research that strives to find and explain resistance to change. Finally, because community policing rests in theory on establishing partnerships with segments of the community for the co-production of security, the operation of such partnerships can be assessed from different standpoints. Evaluations of programs, of people and the organizations to which they belong, and of partnerships are not mutually exclusive; they generally overlap.

More needs to be said about the distinction between assessing a process (implementation) and assessing impact (outcome). Implementation can be assessed with a view to finding whether it factually matches the design and the goals of a program. It can also be assessed with regard to the quality of process and of the provision of services to the community. Questions regarding quality go beyond asking whether the right moves were actually performed; they raise the issue of how well they were accomplished. Researchers looking at implementation—whether in terms of its correspondence to plan or in terms of the quality of the service delivered—have often complained that it was very difficult to collect from the police implementing a program the data necessary to perform a thorough evaluation. The reason for this is not that the police were trying to hide something, but rather that they became weary of filling in all the forms used to collect data on implementation.

There are many different ways to measure impact. Two strings of distinctions recur in the research literature. The first has to do with the type of measurement: aggregate figures that cover a large geographical entity, such as a whole city, are contrasted to disaggregated numbers that are more locally relevant. It is frequently argued that there is more need for micro-indicators reflecting local situations than for the macro-indicators that make for good media headlines but are less useful in devising effective intervention strategies. The nature of the impact being measured is in part determined by the kind of measurement used. Generally speaking, aggregate measurements focus on the traditional trinity of crime, disorder, and fear of crime. Disaggregated local data are more sensitive to the character of the relationships among the different ethnic or age groups that may constitute a neighborhood and are generally more revealing of local problems. In much the same way that there is a call for more locally relevant measurements, voices are increasingly heard demanding that the impact of community and problem-oriented policing be assessed at a deeper level than the general occurrence of crime and disorder and the intensity of fear of crime. Specific data on the impact of policing on particular crimes and forms of disorder may then be collected; the extent to which local community problems, such as racial conflict, have been solved or alleviated may also be explored.

Measuring the impact of police action on crime, disorder, and fear of crime remains the central concern of impact studies. Nevertheless, it is now increasingly urged that these studies reach beyond crime, disorder, and fear of crime. This recommendation comes from two opposite directions: a demand for assessing the impact of policing at the micro-level of local community programs, and, at the same time, a strong bid for contextualization, that is, for impact studies that take into consideration the larger social, economic, political, and cultural forces that jointly define the whole context in which police action takes place. Impact studies, then, tend to split between the micro/local and the macro/aggregate levels, and they also shift between law enforcement and its broader context. There is finally an unfortunate tendency to isolate the impact of policing on the reduction of serious crime from everything else. The New York Comstat program is an instance of focusing most if not all police resources on the struggle against crime, with little consideration for any undesirable side-effects, such as the deepening of racial conflict and the growing alienation of youth, that may spring from this single emphasis.

One last general issue is raised by evaluation research: the issue of the criteria to be used in assessing the success of an intervention. The first criteria to be discussed were effectiveness, efficiency, and equity.[4] These factors are mostly germane to the measurement of program *outcomes*. Other criteria, such as faithfulness to the specifications of a program, program awareness, levels of public participation, quality of service delivery, and job satisfaction, are being developed to gauge the process of program implementation.

AN OVERVIEW OF THE CONTENT

The book is divided into four parts. The first provides a general overview of community and problem-oriented policing, on which most of the evaluation research on policing has so far focused.[5] Chapter 1, by Dennis P. Rosenbaum, briefly reviews the historical context in which community policing was born and defines it through five key elements. The main purpose of Rosenbaum's chapter is to dispel current misunderstandings about the nature of community policing and to provide up-to-date information on its implementation. One of the chapter's goals is to contrast community policing with enforcement policing and to stress that the community model does not call for different goals that would, for instance, supplant crime reduction efforts; rather, the community suggests alternative *means* of achieving the goals of policing. Rosenbaum recognizes that community policing faces widespread problems in implementation, particularly given the current budgetary crunch. For him, the most serious implementation problem is the cost overrun that may be incurred if police managers add new police functions without remarketing police services to the public in a way that would permit cutbacks in some police responsibilities (e.g., dispatching a patrol car to the scene of every burglary reported through 911).

In Chapter 2, Jean-Paul Brodeur makes three points. Through an examination of the literature published on police reform in several countries, he concludes that reforming the police has been a continuing trend since the end of World War II, and that the different labels used to designate the new programs—team policing, unit beat policing, Neighborhood Watch, community-oriented policing, problem-oriented policing—refer, with one exception, to practices (e.g., foot patrol) that have similar limitations. The one exception is problem-oriented policing. His main thesis is that problem-oriented policing is significantly different from community policing. Although they can be packaged under the same label for strategic reasons, problem-oriented policing does not belong in the same paradigm. Finally, Brodeur stresses the difficulty of evaluating policing that involves the kind of multiagency action that both community and problem-oriented policing should. The problems of evaluating the implementation and outcomes of community and problem-oriented policing are presently so formidable that the idea of undertaking a multiagency evaluation fades into the distant future.

The second part of the book consists of five chapters concerned with several issues in the assessment of police performance. Chapter 3 was written by Robert Reiner, the foremost British expert on policing. Reiner discusses the assessment of *individual* police performance and the numerous obstacles in the way of making such an assessment successfully. He first notes that traditional assessments of individual police performances targeted police misconduct. Later, when attempts were made to measure good individual performance, evaluation centered on the outcome of criminal investigations. Such assessments may have been suited to detectives but did not do justice to the actual work performed by patrol officers, who were usually involved in peacekeeping. Reiner's main position regarding the assessment of peacekeeping and related police work is that the assessment must focus on the process and the quality of the service provided rather than on its outcome, of which we do not have a clear conception. However, assessing the quality of a process is currently very difficult because of our lack of knowledge about how peacekeeping and the maintenance of order are actually conducted and because the nature of this work involves conflict arbitration. Assessments of the success of conflict-solving tend to reflect the biases of the parties involved in the conflict and to yield contradictory results. Naked rates of reported crime and police clearance rates are unsuited for this kind of *process* evaluation, since they essentially measure outcomes and are vulnerable to manipulation. Finally, Reiner discusses the meaning of the intense police resistance to reform in the United Kingdom, reform that purports to increase the efficiency of police by subjecting them to market disciplines.

Chapter 4 was written by Jerome E. McElroy who, with his colleagues Colleen Cosgrove and Susan Sadd, evaluated the Community Patrol Officer Program (CPOP) experienced in New York from 1985 to 1988. The purpose of McElroy's chapter is not to discuss the results of the CPOP evaluation, which are contained in a substantial report,[6] but to reflect on the problems that are raised when an evaluation is made. McElroy begins by challenging the belief that the traditional tools of evaluation research can be applied in the evaluation of a policing program such as CPOP. The methods of evaluation research assume that the program to be assessed was actually implemented as it was designed. This requirement was not really met by the CPOP program, and a great deal of effort had to be devoted to evaluating the extent to which the program was faithfully implemented. If a program is not correctly implemented, evaluation cannot provide a "bottom-line" assessment of its worth. What is needed is to identify the assumptions underlying the program and to collect data to describe how these assumptions were translated into the reality of policing, and then to assess whether the assumptions were sound (e.g., was the public genuinely interested in entering into a partnership with the police in order to solve the community's problems?). Not only was it difficult to collect such data, but their quality did not allow the researchers to measure the impact of the problem-solving strategies provided by the CPOP program. Because the implementation of the program varied so much from one beat to another, aggregate measures of the program's impact on street crime were not reliable. It was also found that the greater proportion of people in the public sample did not have specific knowledge of the changes in police operations brought about by the program. The overall conclusion drawn from McElroy's detailed discussion is that a substantial number of painstaking preconditions need to be fulfilled before rushing to assess the impact of a policing program.

The next three chapters examine different aspects of the role of the public in community policing. In Chapter 5, Wesley G. Skogan presents his findings on public participation in beat meetings in two Chicago areas. In implementing its community policing program, the Chicago Police Department wanted to increase the effectiveness of the patrol by targeting issues of public concern, and it wanted to mend the very strained relations between the police and racial and ethnic communities in the city. Beat meetings were regular gatherings of small groups of residents and police intended to be the forum for identifying and prioritizing local problems, as well as for finding ways to tackle them. The researchers tried first to learn whether the beat meetings created a new opportunity for citizen participation. Although awareness of organized activity increased in both prototype areas, the people who got the message belonged mostly to the more privileged groups (white home owners with higher incomes and higher education). It is doubtful that at this level of awareness the program contributed to healing the breach between police and racial and ethnic minorities as was originally intended. Yet despite the fact that sequential surveys showed that participation trends did not significantly increase, it seems that actual participation was "mildly redistributive" in the prototype areas; this meant that the program was partly successful in mobilizing new elements in the community. Interestingly enough, despite an initial finding that what happened in the beat meetings did not fit a community policing model, a later survey showed that the participants responded very favorably to the meetings: 50% said that the meetings were very useful for improving the community's relations with the police, and 38% said that the meetings were very useful for finding solutions to neighborhood problems. These findings confirm Skogan's earlier statement—that the public is eager to meet the police and to talk to them.[7]

There are many references by the U.K. police to the philosophy of community policing, and there are more than 100,000 Neighborhood Watch schemes in England and Wales. So, we are not on uncharted ground with respect to community policing in the United Kingdom. In Chapter 6, Trevor Bennett evaluates what is reported in research literature about how effective both the police and the public consider the delivery of police services to be. There is a sharp decline in public satisfaction with the delivery of routine policing services, the level of satisfaction being lowest among the segments of the British population that appear to be most in need of traditional police protection. No great improvement is likely to come from the adoption of community policing, for Bennett found in conducting a national survey of community constables that the younger officers were inclined to perceive community police work as less important. All the other indicators measuring the implementation of community policing, whether at the organizational or operational levels, showed negative results. The same unfortunate situation appears to prevail when the public's involvement in community policing is assessed. Meetings of the consultative committees appointed on the advice of the Home Office were poorly attended. When they do attend, people are generally passive, limiting their role to receiving information from the police. Moreover, Neighborhood Watch schemes, despite their number, have only minimal impact. Bennett completes this rather bleak picture by voicing his concern over the apparent lack of commitment on the part of both the police and the public to improving the quality of service delivery in general and to community policing in particular.

In Chapter 7, Vincent F. Sacco reflects on public surveys as a measure of satisfaction with policing services. Relying on his own research conducted in Canada and on an extensive review of the research literature, he asserts that surveys are better indicators of police performance under community-based models of policing than are such traditional indicators as response time or crime, arrest, and clearance rates. The latter measures fail to speak to the role of the public as the consumer of police services. Although Sacco believes that surveys are more revealing of the attitudes of police service consumers than media coverage or the complaints received by specially appointed boards, he is aware of their limitations, and it is on the limitations that he focuses his analysis. His study agrees with the general findings of Skogan in his work for the British Home Office[8] and with the findings of Trevor Bennett (Chapter 6 in this book). Public satisfaction with policing reflects general contentment with the order of things rather than approval of the action of a specific group of professionals (the police). Although generally high in Canada, public satisfaction with the police is lowest among those who have the most contacts with the police, either as complainants and victims or as suspects and offenders. There is a paradox that stems from this finding. Sacco rightly observes that, on the one hand, higher levels of public satisfaction with the police can be achieved through programs like community policing that increase the number of noncoercive contacts with the police. Yet he also notes that high levels of public satisfaction are of limited utility for determining optimal policing strategies, because those who rely on police services for their own protection express less satisfaction. It would seem to follow that community policing programs mainly serve to enhance the police image through public relations, but have little connection with their core mandate.

The third part of the book addresses organizational change and its assessment. In Chapter 8, Jack R. Greene confronts the multifaceted difficulties of implementing community and problem-oriented policing at the level of a police organization. The main obstacle to translating the rhetoric of change into policing reality is the intractability of police organizations in their resistance to change and their capacity to minimize and eventually defeat reform movements. The most obvious indication of this imperviousness to change is the enduring character of the core technology of policing—basic patrol and criminal investigation services—a technology that has evolved only slightly over the past half century. In order to assess the dimensions of change, Greene proposes a comprehensive model that distinguishes between the nature and the agent of the policing intervention. With respect to the nature of intervention, Greene makes use of the classical distinctions (borrowed from medical research) between primary, secondary, and tertiary intervention found in the literature on crime prevention. Such distinctions imply that evaluations do not rely only on measures of crime, disorder, and fear of crime reduction, but also involve issues such as community cohesion, individual attitudes toward criminal behavior, victim readjustment, and a broader scope of problem solving. Evaluation research on the agent of change should be extended to the outcomes of interventions that stem from networks established in the larger environment and that imply multiagency linkages; it should also measure the impact of police organizations, subgroups, or units within the organization and of individual police officers. In order to make these measure-

ments, monitoring should be paired with feedback. Greene's chapter ends with
five core questions that as a minimum should be addressed in evaluating
policing programs and police innovation.

   In Chapter 9, Stephen D. Mastrofski examines whether structural reforms
patterned on the community policing model enjoy strong prospects of implementation in police organizations. In order to conduct this examination,
Mastrofski draws a key distinction between two perspectives on organizational structures. When following a *technical model,* organizations are goal
oriented, and they try to produce a specific and measurable impact on a
situation through the implementation of rational strategies. When operating
in conformity with an *institutional model,* an organization does not so much
strive to be efficient in the production of outcomes, as it tries to respond to
current beliefs about what it should be and what it should accomplish. When
an organization seeks to conform to a set of preconceived and untested notions
about how it should appear rather than to a set of external goals, it is very
difficult—if not impossible—to assess what it actually produces. For Mastrofski, these models are not mutually exclusive: All organizations operate within
both technical and organizational environments.

   Having made this basic distinction between organizational structures,
Mastrofski assesses the consequences for police organizations of four elements of reform that are entailed by the implementation of community
policing: delayerization (thinning the hierarchy), professionalization (increasing the discretion of the problem-solving practitioner), democratization (seeking more public input and striking partnerships with nonpolice agencies), and
service integration. His general finding is that all these elements of reform fit
well within the institutional model, but are fraught with serious difficulties
when interpreted in their technical sense. Mastrofski concludes his chapter by
examining the implication of his analyses for the future of reform. He is
critical of leaders who are quick to claim technical competence in a time of
declining crime rates but who are opposed to tying down their job security to
such results in the long run. Mastrofski suggests that police should end the
search for the holy grail of the "right structures" and have the boldness to
experiment and progress through trial and error.

   The last part of the book is devoted to conclusions and perspectives. Les
Johnston, who is a British expert on private security, was invited to provide a
perspective that would encompass the production of security in its broader
aspects. Despite the differences in their theoretical background and tools,
Johnston and Mastrofski share to a certain extent a common outlook. Whether
considering the implications of community and problem-oriented policing, as

Mastrofski does, or the implications of the growing penetration of the private and the civil sector in policing, as does Johnston, they both take seriously the fact that policing is no longer the monopoly of public police departments, and they both attempt rigorously to draw the consequences of this fact.

In Chapter 10, Johnston begins by asserting that the definition of policing should be functional rather than focused on the action of a particular kind of personnel. Security being increasingly perceived as a market commodity, this commodification of policing implies that the police function is not the monopoly of any one group of professionals whose legitimacy is provided by the State. Johnston then provides an overview of the social changes that led to important transformations in policing in our late modern societies. Two fundamental transformations are addressed. The first is identified as "sectoral" and involves a restructuring of the field of policing, spurred on by the growing role played by such new actors as private security agencies, hybrid agencies that blend public and private dimensions, and members of the community involved in "civil policing" (in a later section of his chapter, Johnston develops six models for articulating the relationships between the different agents performing a police function). The second major transformation Johnston describes concerns the spatial distribution of policing agencies. The main point of his analysis is to remind us that there are two opposite kinds of forces at play here. There are, on the one hand, forces of decentralization and of localization; on the other hand, there are marked tendencies toward centralization and concentration. The latter tendencies do not receive the attention they deserve in discussions of community and problem-oriented policing.

In his concluding comments, Johnston underlines the meaning of his analyses for the evaluation of policing. Significant evaluation should take into consideration the movement from public and client-based policing toward individual- and consumer-based modes of service delivery; it should also take stock of a shift from crime-oriented policing toward individually focused risk-oriented policing. The proliferation of the actors functionally involved in policing call for a rethinking of who and what is evaluated—whole security networks may be substituted for single and compact public agencies. Johnston finally raises what he believes to be the crucial question: whether the changes that have taken place imply that the evaluation of policing will essentially be governed by the satisfaction of the individual customer or whether it will still be underpinned by wider collective concerns. The advent of collective concerns is seen as profoundly detrimental to policing and to justice.

In the Conclusions, Brodeur presents some of the exchanges that took place at a workshop in Montréal in 1994 that was attended by the book's contributors, police professionals, and others involved in the production of security. The importance of two issues in particular, police unionization and interagency cooperation, is discussed.

ACKNOWLEDGMENTS

We thank the ministry of the Solicitor General of Canada for providing the funds for the workshop during which the authors of the chapters of this book presented their papers and exchanged ideas among themselves and with other invited guests. Special thanks are addressed to Mr. Barry Leighton of the Ministry, who co-hosted the workshop with the International Centre for Comparative Criminology of the Université de Montréal. I also acknowledge the financial help provided for my own research by the Social Sciences and Humanities Council of Canada. I express my gratitude to Kristin Bergstad for her work on this book. Last but not least, I express my most sincere thanks to Dale Grenfell, formerly of Sage Publications, for her continuous support, which was crucial for bringing this project to a happy ending.

NOTES

1. Between 1988 and 1990 a series of pioneering papers on community policing was published by the National Institute of Justice and by the Program in Criminal Justice Policy and Management of the John F. Kennedy School of Government, Harvard University. This series, titled *Perspectives on Policing,* consisted of 13 short papers in point form that addressed all aspects of community policing. It targeted a very broad audience of police professionals and was meant to introduce them to what was being presented as a new paradigm for policing. For many police and police researchers, this new paradigm was to a significant extent a rediscovery of Sir Robert Peel's principles of preventive policing. Some objections were therefore voiced against calling community policing a new paradigm. These objections are weaker when they are directed against problem-oriented policing, which implies a systematic use of information technology. This aspect of problem-oriented policing may be viewed as an innovation.

2. The drop in reported crime in New York City has sparked great interest from the media and was the object of intensive coverage. See, for instance, "Better Cops, Fewer Robbers," by James Lardner, in the *New York Times Magazine,* February 9, 1997, Section 6. In this same issue of the *NYT Magazine,* also see "Why Crime Is Down," by David C. Anderson. In the past few months, there is hardly an issue of *Law Enforcement News* that does not report on the NYPD and its Comstat program.

3. See the remarks of former New York police chief, William Bratton, as quoted in *Measuring What Matters, Part One: Measures of Crime, Fear and Disorder,* by Thomas V. Brady, p. 11 (1996, December), Washington, DC: National Institute of Justice, Research in Action. Also see "Mapping Change: How the New York City Police Department Re-Engineered Itself to Drive Down Crime," by Eli B. Silverman, *Law Enforcement News,* A Publication of John Jay College of Criminal Justice/CUNY, Vol. XXII, No. 457, December 15, 1996, pp. 10-12. Silverman identifies as a "predominant theme" in previous research on policing that *"traditional police practices have little impact on crime"* (p. 10).

4. See Eck and Rosenbaum (1994).

5. Needless to say, evaluation research has not focused exclusively on community and problem-oriented policing. All kinds of traditional police strategies have been reviewed in order to find out which of them "really worked" (e.g., Sherman, 1986). Traditional law enforcement programs directed against particular crimes such as spousal abuse have also been the object of extended evaluation research. See Sherman (1992b) and Sherman and Berk (1984).

6. See McElroy, Cosgrove, and Sadd (1993).

7. ". . . there is evidence in many evaluations that a public hungry for attention have a great deal to tell police and are grateful for an opportunity to do so" (Skogan, 1994a, p. 180).

8. See Skogan (1990b, 1994b).

PART I

POLICING AND EVALUATION RESEARCH
Overview

1

THE CHANGING ROLE
OF THE POLICE

Assessing the Current Transition
to Community Policing

Dennis P. Rosenbaum

This is an exciting and challenging time in the world of policing. The winds of change are moving through the hallways of many police organizations in Northern America. For some, these winds are like a summer breeze that opens the door to new possibilities. For others, they signal the onset of a cold, uncertain winter. Regardless of how one experiences it, something is happening, and this "something" is an attempt to rethink and restructure the role of police in society.

This reform movement is both promising and threatening; it promises to improve public safety, yet it offers no simple formula or road map to get there; it promises to reform police agencies and stimulate community involvement in public safety, yet police officers and community residents are often left to imagine how this will happen. In any event, there is no debate about the magnitude of this push to create a new model of policing. The concept of community policing has spread rapidly in many countries and is touted highly by police executives in Canada and the United States (Leighton, 1991; Normandeau & Leighton, 1990; Wycoff, 1995). In the United States, community policing is the centerpiece of the 1994 national crime bill, which provides funding for 100,000 new community policing officers over 6 years (see 42 USC 3796dd, Sec. 1701; Office of Community Oriented Policing Services, 1994). In Canada, community policing has been promoted aggressively by the federal government through official publications and conferences (e.g., Normandeau & Leighton, 1990; Solicitor General of Canada, 1990).

Although this reform movement may seem mature and well advanced to those who have been advocating such change over the past few years, in the larger picture it is (at best) only the beginning of what is likely to be a long and arduous journey down a new road. The future is very uncertain, the tasks ahead are complex, and the obstacles are numerous. Community policing is still in what might be called the conceptualization phase of development. At this stage, we are still grappling with some very basic questions, such as: What is the appropriate role for the police in society, and do we really want to move in a new direction without reservation? What are the central elements of community policing, and how is it different from what police have traditionally done under the "reform era" (Kelling & Moore, 1988)? What is the theory that provides the foundation and justification for changing the role of police in society? If community policing sounds good in theory, what about when the "rubber meets the road"?—what implementation problems can be expected? What evidence exists to suggest that community policing will be more effective than the current model of policing? At this point, there are more questions than answers, but we should expect this state of affairs during the conceptualization phase. Police administrators, government officials, academics, and community leaders are struggling with the concept of community policing and are experimenting with a wide range of operational translations.

The task here is to explore the changing role of police in North America. Because community policing is the only real alternative to the traditional model (at this point in time), comparisons between these two approaches can be found throughout this analysis. First, this chapter offers a brief historical account of the forces driving this latest reform movement. Second, and more important, some key components of community policing theory are developed and analyzed. Third, the question of whether community policing is a cost-effective investment in times of budget austerity is explored. Finally, some concerns about the future of this reform movement are examined.

THE CONTEXT OF REFORM

A full historical account of this reform movement is beyond the scope of this chapter and would include a reexamination of a century and a half of organized policing (see Fogelson, 1977; Kelling & Moore, 1988; Sparrow, Moore, & Kennedy, 1990; Walker, 1983). Suffice it to say that over the past 20 years, the traditional model (present in the United States since the 1930s) has been under serious attack. Several factors have contributed to this latest round of criticism and to a rethinking of the police role in the United States and Canada. The growing violence and civil unrest in the United States during the 1960s led the President's Commission on Law Enforcement and Administration of Justice (1967) to recommend "team policing" in 1967 as a means of closing the physical and psychological distance between the beat officer and the community. This precursor to community policing was attempted in many U.S. police departments in the 1970s, but serious implementation problems were encountered when management resisted plans for decentralization (see Anderson, 1978; Bloch & Specht, 1972; Schwartz & Clarren, 1977; Sherman, Milton, & Kelly, 1973). This opposition delayed any future community-oriented reforms for a full decade, but research in the 1970s and 1980s continued to highlight the limitations of the traditional model. Although cities have their own reasons for pursuing community policing, a growing dissatisfaction with "business as usual" can be attributed, at least in part, to two decades of research that suggest that the traditional model is ineffective, inefficient, and inequitable (see Eck & Rosenbaum, 1994).

Meanwhile, community crime prevention initiatives were receiving substantial publicity during the 1980s in both Canada and the United States (Lavrakas, 1985; Linden, Barker, & Frisbie, 1984; Rosenbaum, 1986, 1988), and the concept of community involvement became especially attractive as the level of government funding began to decline.[1] Furthermore, as violence, drugs, gang activity, and police brutality received growing media attention in the late 1980s and early 1990s, police chiefs and politicians in the United States were under growing pressure to develop more effective response strategies. By this point, several demonstration programs had been developed and tested through the National Institute of Justice, and were ready to be marketed—Foot patrol in Newark, New Jersey (Pate, 1986), and Flint, Michigan (Trojanowicz, 1986); problem solving in Newport News, Virginia (Eck & Spelman, 1987a); and a variety of community-oriented initiatives in Newark and Houston (Pate, Wycoff, Skogan, & Sherman, 1986), including storefront

mini-stations, newsletters, door-to-door contacts, and the creation of voluntary community organizations. Meanwhile, throughout the 1980s, hundreds
of police departments were experimenting independently with various community-oriented initiatives, the most popular being foot patrol.

Community policing in Canada did not emerge from the same conditions
of urban crisis, but nevertheless followed a similar pattern of development.
Some Canadian scholars have suggested that, in the absence of other political
pressures, the pursuit of community policing in Canada has followed recent
trends in the United States, where a larger body of experimental programs and
scientific evaluations is available (Murphy, 1988). Others have suggested that
Canadian police "simply returned to their 19th century origins" (referring to
Robert Peel's Metropolitan London Police Bobbies) after "a few decades of
flirting with the professional policing model" (Leighton, 1994, p. 211). In any
event, what is clear to the observer is that Canadian scholars have worked very
closely with the federal government and local police officials throughout
Canada to help establish a clear agenda for police reform and to evaluate
promising initiatives.

Changing the Role of Police: Community
Versus Enforcement-Oriented Policing

What is "community policing" and what, if anything, is so special about
it? *Community policing* is a very popular term but one that has a multitude of
definitions. The popularity and ambiguity of this concept are both a blessing
and a curse. On the positive side, the term is something that everyone can
identify with (after all, who is opposed to the concept of "community," or to
"mother" and "apple pie," for that matter?), thus providing the popular support
that is needed to engender police reform in the long run. On the negative side,
the concept has been badly abused by police chiefs and politicians who use
this nebulous term to justify any and every program of their liking. Granted,
programs must be tailored to local circumstances, but the label of community
policing can produce a "halo effect" around pet programs and prevent outside
observers from being able to distinguish true police innovation from traditional policing. The question is whether "community policing" in practice is
truly innovative, or, as Bayley (1988) put it, simply "another attempt to put
old wine into new bottles?" In addition, Goldstein (1993) warns us that the
popularity of the community policing concept increases public expectations
and "create[s] the impression that, somehow, on implementation, community
policing will provide a panacea for not only crime, disorder, and racial tensions, but many of the other acute problems that plague our urban areas" (p. 1).

Hence, one of the challenges that we face today is to figure out what community policing is and is not, and how to distinguish it from the current model. Providing such a clarification will help to set the stage for a critical discussion of the merits and limitations of this reform movement. Unfortunately, criminal justice scholars and police administrators have yet to articulate the full theory behind community policing with all of its assumptions and implications.[2] This theoretical imprecision has contributed to the criticism of community policing by many police researchers (see, for example, Klockars, 1988; Manning, 1988; Mastrofski, 1988).

While definition problems abound, it would be a mistake to leave the impression that this reform movement is all rhetoric and no substance, or that there exists no consensus as to what constitutes the core elements of this new model of policing. Although community policing has been operationalized through a variety of programs and practices, the concept appears to be supported by a common set of guiding principles and assumptions (see Eck & Spelman, 1987a; Goldstein, 1990; Greene & Mastrofski, 1988; Leighton, 1991; McElroy, Cosgrove, & Sadd, 1993; Murphy & Muir, 1984; Rosenbaum, 1994; Skogan & Hartnett, 1997; Skolnick & Bayley, 1986; Sparrow et al., 1990; Toch & Grant, 1991; Trojanowicz & Bucqueroux, 1990). Some of the commonly cited elements of this model include: (a) a broader definition of police work; (b) a reordering of police priorities, giving greater attention to "soft" crime and disorder; (c) a focus on problem solving and prevention rather than incident-driven policing; (d) a recognition that the "community," however defined, plays a critical role in solving neighborhood problems; and (e) a recognition that police organizations must be restructured and reorganized to be responsive to the demands of this new approach and to encourage a new set of police behaviors. More and more, these shared concepts and assumptions are being translated into common practices, such as decentralized organizational structures, permanent beat assignments, new mechanisms for community participation and problem solving, new training programs, and revised performance evaluation systems. (Nevertheless, the tendency to call nearly everything "community policing" is also a widespread practice.)

To explore some of these changes in policing, community policing can be compared to the current model on the key dimensions of police effectiveness, equity, and efficiency (Eck & Rosenbaum, 1994). The public expects the police to be *effective* in the services they provide; to offer services in a manner that is *equitable and fair* to the community; and to make every effort to see that these equitable and effective services are provided at *minimal cost* to society (i.e., efficiency). The community policing model turns the spotlight on police effectiveness in a way that previous approaches do not. Consequently, this chapter will give disproportionate attention to the issue of effectiveness. Furthermore, given the current fiscal concerns in Canada and the United States, this chapter also gives considerable attention to the question of police efficiency.

Police Effectiveness

When someone asks whether the police are "effective," the first thought that comes to mind is—"effective at doing what?" The proper role of police in society has been a debated subject for many years, but there can be little doubt that the job of controlling crime is considered the highest priority of the police under the traditional model (other key functions include providing emergency services, administering justice by means of arrest, and offering a wide range of nonemergency services). The traditional methods used to fight crime include deterrence (through preventive patrol and arrest), incapacitation, and rehabilitation. Several major studies have questioned the effectiveness of these general strategies for controlling or preventing crime (Blumstein, Cohen, & Nagin, 1978; Blumstein, Cohen, Roth, & Visher, 1986; Sechrest, White, & Brown, 1979). Furthermore, research on the police in particular has failed to support the hypothesis that random patrols, rapid response, and follow-up investigations—practices at the core of enforcement-oriented policing—would produce more arrests and less crime (Greenwood, Petersilia, & Chaiken, 1977; Kelling, Pate, Dieckman, & Brown, 1974b; Spelman & Brown, 1984). Nevertheless, police have fully adopted (and, over the years, have promoted) the image of "crime fighter," while taxpayers continue to demand that crime control (via law enforcement) is the primary function of the police.

Under the community policing model, traditional police functions have not been discontinued; rather, the priorities have been rearranged to give greater attention to some functions and less to others. Moreover, additional police functions have been added under the new model. Most important, the manner in which these functions are executed is entirely different under community policing—a topic that deserves additional treatment later on.

Under community policing theory, crime control, emergency aid, and justice—as traditionally conceived—receive less attention, while nonemergency services receive greater attention. This reprioritizing has been justified on several grounds. First, the crime control, emergency, and justice functions constitute a small proportion of the total demand for police service, and thus, it is argued, should not be the hub of the police organizational structure and response system. Second, prior research (cited earlier) suggests that the police have not been very effective at these functions. Third, noncriminal, nonemergency problems represent the most frequent concern of neighborhood residents (Skogan, 1990a; Skogan & Hartnett, 1997).

The fourth, and most compelling, rationale for reordering the priority assigned to different police functions has to do with the nature of urban life and forces that contribute to neighborhood decline. The community policing model does not call for different policing *goals* (e.g., reducing crime is still a major police goal), but rather, it suggests that alternative *means* of achieving these goals should be given more attention (e.g., indirect strategies involving other police functions). The problem of neighborhood disorder will be used to illustrate how the community policing model is fundamentally different from previous models of policing. It is hoped that this example will also help to further elaborate and clarify the theory so that policymakers and critics can more easily distinguish this approach from its predecessors. For practitioners who are unsure whether community policing is anything more than cosmetic change ("old wine in new bottles"), the theory and research behind this approach are especially important.

Police researchers, policy analysts, and administrators have, in my opinion, underestimated the importance of social and physical disorders in their efforts to develop effective strategies for controlling crime and improving urban neighborhoods. When community residents are asked about the biggest problems in their neighborhood, they consistently mention various types of physical and social disorders that are low on the list of police priorities. In Skogan's (1990a) analysis of 40 neighborhoods, for example, the biggest *physical disorder problem* was vandalism (including graffiti), followed by litter and trash, garbage handling, and unkempt vacant lots. In some neighborhoods, abandoned buildings were the biggest concern to local residents. In the realm of *social problems,* public drinking was the biggest concern, followed by loitering youth, and drug use. (More recent data from Chicago neighborhoods suggest that street-level drug transactions are also a major concern of neighborhood residents; Skogan & Hartnett, 1997.)

The ranking of problems can vary significantly by neighborhood, but the pattern is consistent—disorders are the most frequently mentioned set of "big problems" facing urban residents.

As Skogan (1990a) notes, historically, dealing with disorder was a central function of the police as they walked the beat and listened to the concerns of local residents and business owners. Yet with the rise of serious crime, the centralization of the police bureaucracy, and the push for greater efficiency in handling a growing number of calls, disorder and other neighborhood problems were given less and less attention by the police.

The question here is this: Why should disorder and related community concerns be given a higher priority under this new model of policing? This question is especially important today, as a conservative backlash against "soft" policing gains momentum in the United States. In the context of a growing debate about "soft" versus "hard" policing, the answer to this question is fairly simple: There is a growing evidence to suggest that soft and hard problems are highly related; that the failure to attend to soft problems will only exacerbate serious crime; and that an indirect attack on crime through order maintenance may be a more effective, efficient, and just means of policing in urban areas.

Both advocates and critics of community policing should have a solid understanding of the theory behind this form of policing before they become too opinionated in either direction. A good place to start is by examining the forces that contribute to neighborhood crime. The concept of neighborhood disorder is at the heart of current thinking about the relationship between crime, community, and policing, and suggests how a community's capacity for self-regulation can be undermined (see Bursik & Grasmick, 1993; Lewis & Salem, 1986; Skogan, 1990a; Wilson & Kelling, 1982). The failure of a community and its police to respond decisively to the early signs of disorder is analogous to the failure of a patient and his or her doctor to detect and treat cancer in the early stages—the problem will spread uncontrollably. Disorder, although not easily defined, is something that "locals" will "know when they see or hear it" (i.e., various behaviors and physical conditions that violate the social norms of the local community). Research suggests that disorder is extremely important because it sends a clear signal to residents and others who use the local environment that the social order has broken down. Shattered windows, abandoned buildings, graffiti, litter on the streets, loud music, unsupervised kids hanging out—the message is clear to everyone—people are either unable or unwilling to intervene in defense of their neighborhood and their neighbors. The message to potential offenders is clear—because the social order has broken down in this area, no one is going to intervene if you decide to tag a grocery store, break a window in an apartment, mug an elderly women, or even shoot someone. The message to potential victims is clear—this is an unsafe area and one where you are likely to be victimized by crime. Indeed, research indicates that the higher the level of disorder in a neighborhood, the higher the level of fear of victimization (Hope & Hough, 1988;

Skogan, 1990a). A large-scale field study using qualitative data also supports the hypothesis that disorder stimulates fear of crime (Lewis & Salem, 1986).[3]

Fear of crime generates its own set of problems. Fear causes residents and nonresidents alike to use the local environment less frequently and to withdraw behind locked doors (Lavrakas et al., 1980; Skogan & Maxfield, 1981). This avoidance of public areas reduces a neighborhood's capacity to regulate social behavior, thus providing additional opportunities for potential offenders to engage in antisocial and criminal conduct without sanction. This absence of "guardianship" is a critical element in opportunity theories of crime (e.g., Cohen & Felson, 1979). In sum, there is reason to believe that disorder undermines a community's ability to exercise control over the behavior of those who use the area, and it increases the opportunities for criminal behavior.

The curious nature of disorder is that it feeds on itself, working to multiply and escalate urban problems. As Wilson and Kelling (1982) note, one broken window, if not repaired, will result in many broken windows. Furthermore, this process of decline can stimulate more serious criminal activity for the reasons stated earlier. Community research documents this relationship—the higher the level of neighborhood disorder, the higher the level of serious criminal activity (Skogan, 1990a). Clearly, crime and disorder are strongly correlated and both represent serious threats to the quality of urban life—contrary to conventional wisdom, disorder is not a "soft" problem that is unrelated to the "hard" problems that consume the thoughts of traditional enforcement officers. Hence, an indirect attack on crime (via disorder) may be an effective strategy of policing while not losing sight of the importance of crime.

Similar to disorder, the concept of "fear of crime" is another lightning rod for critics who argue that community policing is soft on crime. They claim that switching the focus of policing from fighting crime to maintaining order and reducing fear of crime is simply a "smoke and mirrors" tactic to make citizens feel good about themselves, the police department, and their neighborhood. These critics argue that such a "warm fuzzy" approach to policing will divert police attention away from the real job of arresting criminals. Again, this argument fails to appreciate the critical role of fear of crime in undermining urban neighborhoods and housing markets. As implied earlier, fear is one of the driving forces behind patterns of residential mobility and neighborhood decline (Skogan, 1986). Research by Taub, Taylor, and Dunham (1984) in eight Chicago neighborhoods shows that residents' perceptions of safety can influence their assessment of the housing market and their investment plans. For people considering a residential move, the issues are similar.

Every day, families in urban areas make decisions about whether a particular neighborhood is a good place to raise children, and safety concerns are at the top of their list.[4] When current or potential residents get nervous about the quality of life in a neighborhood, sociodemographic transition can be set in motion, and the neighborhood can be thrust into a cycle of decline (see Skogan, 1990a). The presence of graffiti, broken windows, and vacant lots not only arouses fear, but sends a clear message to move out or stay out of the area if possible.

In sum, disorder is the primary concern of neighborhood residents, and these problems can have a significant impact on residents' perceptions of, and reactions to, crime. These reactions, including the fear response, play a critical role in determining the residential stability of the neighborhood. In essence, disorder, if left unchecked, will undermine the social control processes by which communities maintain social order, stimulate fear of crime, exacerbate more serious crime, and destabilize the housing market. Collectively, these forces can lead to neighborhood decline and give rise to additional serious crime as part of a vicious cycle.

If disorder is a powerful contributor to urban crime, and if police have a renewed interest in pursuing *effective* anticrime strategies, then such incivilities should be given a higher priority on the problem-solving agenda. If police officers work with local residents to reduce the social and physical signs of disorder in their neighborhood, perhaps an area can be stabilized before it reaches the "tipping point."[5] In theory, a reduction in the signs of disorder will lead to a reduction in residents' fear. As a result, local residents should be more inclined to use the streets, interact with one another, develop social networks, and exercise greater informal control over what happens in their neighborhood. In the end, hopefully their desire to move away will subside and their pride in, and perceived ownership of, the area will increase.

How police go about reducing disorder and fear is another matter. The enforcement tactics used in the 1970s and 1980s were generally ineffective and judged to be unconstitutional. Rounding up groups of kids hanging out on street corners did not solve the problem. More creative and less aggressive policies will be needed. One of the greatest problems with traditional policing has been the overreliance on law enforcement as the primary tool of controlling crime and disorder. Whatever the problem, the first inclination of the police is to make an arrest, and this tendency is due to community pressure as much as pressure within the police organization. As a result, we now have a criminal justice system in the United States that is completely overwhelmed by the volume of cases, and that only serves as a revolving door for many criminal suspects. Consequently, the system has lost its ability to punish and deter potential offenders by using the threat of arrest.[6]

The community policing model gives police officers considerable latitude to help solve neighborhood problems. As Herman Goldstein (1993) notes, the community policing officer is expected to "exhaust a wide range of alternatives before resorting to arrest for minor offenses; to exercise broad discretion; and to depend more on resourcefulness, persuasion, and cajoling than on coercion, image, and bluff" (p. 8). Given the highly dysfunctional nature of the present criminal justice system, I would argue that the community policing officer should attempt to resolve problems outside of this bureaucracy, pursuing a new goal of *decreasing* (rather than *increasing*) the number of cases that have contact with the judicial system. When contact is unavoidable, the new goal should be to reduce the depth of penetration into the system by offering effective alternatives for young offenders.

This brings us to another distinguishing feature of the community policing model, namely, the focus on problem solving. If neighborhood problems are the source of community discontent and contribute to a cycle of urban decline, then effective policing will involve identifying the source and nature of these problems and working to develop effective solutions. In contrast, the traditional model—also known as "incident-driven policing" (Eck & Spelman, 1987a)—requires no thinking about persistent problems. Instead, the officer's responsibility ends when he or she responds to a citizen's complaint about a single incident.[7] Hence, the police are encouraged to drive around randomly in their beat until they are dispatched to an incident, but they are not required to look for, or address, patterns of incidents or "hot spots" that would suggest a persistent neighborhood problem.

A closer look at the problem-solving process highlights the most fundamental difference between the community policing and the traditional models. Problem solving is not done in isolation—it requires a high degree of community participation. This fact takes us to the heart of community policing theory.

COMMUNITY ENGAGEMENT AND PARTNERSHIPS

The role of the community is essential to community policing as conceived in theory, and constitutes the most distinguishing feature of this new approach. At the heart of this new model of policing is the empirically supported idea that the police cannot successfully fight crime alone, and must rely on resources in the community to address neighborhood problems effectively. Perhaps the biggest mistake in the history of modern policing was to give the police *full* responsibility and accountability for public safety. With the emergence of community policing, emphasis is now given to the "co-production" of public safety (Lavrakas, 1985; Murphy & Muir, 1984; Rosenbaum, 1988; Wilson & Kelling, 1982). In this framework, safety is viewed as a commodity that is produced by the joint efforts of the police and the community, working together in ways that were not envisioned or encouraged in the past.[8]

The rationale for this new orientation should be made clear to those who criticize the role of "community" in community policing. If we are interested in reducing crime, disorder, fear of crime, and other factors that lower the quality of urban life, we must be attentive to research findings (and personal experience) that remind us that crime-related outcomes are controlled by the social and economic forces in the community (see Bursik & Grasmick, 1993, for a review).

Jane Jacobs (1961) described this reality very clearly in her classic work, *The Death and Life of Great American Cities:*

> The first thing to understand is that the public peace—the sidewalk and the street peace—of cities is not kept primarily by the police, necessary as police are. It is kept primarily by an intricate, almost unconscious network of voluntary controls and standards among the people themselves, and enforced by the people themselves. (pp. 31-32).

This perspective is radically different from the one that is implied by the conventional crime-fighting model. In contrast to the widely accepted view that citizens are supplemental to the police ("eyes and ears" at best), the assumption here is that the police are supplemental to the community in fighting neighborhood problems. This is not to suggest that the police are irrelevant or unimportant. To the contrary, because our tax dollars for fighting crime at the street level have been invested almost exclusively in the police, it is incumbent upon the police to take a lead role and serve as a catalyst for community change. The challenge for police today and into the 21st century is to find creative ways to help communities help themselves.[9]

To prevent crime, we must first understand the forces behind crime at the neighborhood level. A growing body of research provides support for social disorganization theory, which is derived from the classic work of Clifford Shaw and Henry McKay (1942). According to this revived model, criminal activity is encouraged when a neighborhood is socially disorganized, meaning that it is unable to exercise effective informal social control over its residents and achieve common goals, such as reducing the threat of crime (see Bursik & Grasmick, 1993; Byrne & Sampson, 1986). Socially disorganized neighborhoods are unable to create and sustain local institutions. Because of population turnover and heterogeneity, residents are unlikely to develop primary relationships with each other and unlikely to work jointly to solve neighborhood problems.

Disadvantaged neighborhoods need outside intervention (on a large scale) if they are to have any hope for a better environment, but the options for citizen participation and empowerment within the neighborhood are numerous. Local residents can take many different actions to help prevent crime and disorder (DuBow, McCabe, & Kaplan, 1979; Lab, 1988; Lavrakas, 1985; Lewis & Salem, 1986; Rosenbaum, 1988). They can get involved in protecting themselves, their families, their property, and their neighborhood through individual or collective actions. Expanding the role of ordinary citizens in anticrime efforts has been recommended by several national commissions in the United States. Today, the community policing officer must take these ideas to the next level—to engage the community in experimental ways to solve neighborhood problems. Two key roles for the community are immediately apparent— community building and problem solving.

Community building. If communities suffer from social disorganization, then efforts can be made to strengthen social networks and bolster residents' attachment to the area. Getting residents to work together to achieve common, neighborhood goals is one way to stimulate social interaction and build social relationships. The involvement of local community residents in neighborhood anticrime or youth-oriented projects *may* strengthen informal social controls at the neighborhood level, and may contribute to the overall goal of creating *self-regulating* communities. By organizing local residents and encouraging more frequent social interaction, the hope is to create a social environment where people become more territorial about the neighborhood—that is, they increase their surveillance of suspicious behavior, provide greater supervision of local youths, and demonstrate a stronger willingness to intervene as needed to stop or deter antisocial behavior. The possibilities for involvement are limitless, although the outcomes remain uncertain. Continued experimentation is needed.

At this point, the talk about getting citizens involved in community policing has far exceeded the reality. For a variety of reasons, community participation in community policing has been limited in many cities (see Sadd & Grinc,

1994). In highly disorganized, highly disadvantaged neighborhoods, it may be too much to expect individual citizens or voluntary grassroots organizations to play a major role in stopping crime, drug activity, and disorder, except in narrowly defined geographic spaces. Therefore, I will appeal to a much broader definition of "community" and suggest that the primary task at hand is to mobilize *local institutions and agencies* that are invested in the neighborhood, such as churches, schools, and social service agencies (more about this topic below). In theory, the coordinated and persistent application of additional resources should help to empower local residents over time if the resources are used to reinforce independent, self-regulating behaviors.

There are unlimited roles for the police in the community-building process, but few of these roles resemble what was expected under the traditional model. Here we are talking about efforts to facilitate the creation of self-regulating and self-defended neighborhoods. The new community policing officer may pursue many different paths to achieve these goals, but the fundamental objectives are: (a) to seek community input and participation in defining local problems, (b) to work with the community to develop proposed solutions to these problems, and (c) to identify and mobilize the necessary resources—both inside and outside the community—to respond effectively to these problems. In this new role as facilitator, coordinator, and referral agent, the fundamental goal of the new community police officer is to strengthen the ability of local organizations, institutions, and individuals to build a physical and social environment that has fewer opportunities for antisocial and criminal behavior. This brings us to the second community function, and one where the progressive police agencies are making inroads, namely, problem solving through partnerships.

Problem Solving and Partnership Formation. As suggested above, one of the unique characteristics of the community policing model is its focus on problem solving, and this orientation has clear implications for community participation. As John Eck and I have observed, "Ideally, problem solving needs a high level of community engagement to identify problems, to develop an understanding of the particular circumstances that give rise to them, to craft enduring preventive remedies, and to evaluate the effectiveness of the remedies" (Eck & Rosenbaum, 1994, p. 9). Community policing officers know firsthand that community residents play a major role in solving neighborhood problems. We have witnessed how the new police role can involve seeking community input about local problems through door-to-door surveys, community meetings, the analysis of calls for service, and other data derived from citizen feedback.

The means by which identified problems are solved are often unique to the community policing model. Oftentimes, these remedies do *not* involve the application of criminal law. Solutions may be as simple as calling the sanitation department to report a persistent garbage problem or as complex as developing a long-term education and job training program to prevent youth violence in the neighborhood. In academia, we talk about a wide range of "situational crime prevention" measures that can be implemented to reduce opportunities for crime (Clarke, 1992), and "social crime prevention" measures that can be developed to attack the root causes of crime (Rosenbaum, 1988). In any event, the options are numerous and the appropriate choice will depend on how the problem is defined and what resources are available.

In addition to less reliance on criminal sanctions to solve problems, another critical and distinguishing feature of community policing is the development of partnerships with other institutions and agencies to mobilize additional resources. Today, the formation of "partnerships" and "coalitions" is a preferred strategy among social engineers seeking to "make a difference" in urban communities. From a police perspective, the creation and utilization of interagency partnerships represents a significant departure from the traditional police role. Not only does this co-production activity recognize the limitations of the police as a self-contained, self-reliant organization, but it underscores the importance of community resources as key elements in a comprehensive crime control plan.

The theory underlying partnerships is worth noting. The basic idea is that the problems being addressed are too complex and intractable for a single organization to solve. The process of accurately defining the problem and responding effectively requires the coordination and application of resources from multiple sources. Hence, partnerships are typically created for the purpose of developing and implementing comprehensive, coordinated strategies (see Cook & Roehl, 1993; Florin, Chavis, Wandersman, & Rich, 1992; Klitzner, 1993; Prestby & Wandersman, 1985).

In recent years, we have witnessed the formation of partnerships to combat violence and drug abuse, and this activity is part of a broader movement to develop communitywide strategies in response to a wide range of social problems. For example, promising evaluation results have been obtained from studying partnerships in the areas of health promotion (Shea & Basch, 1990) and drug abuse prevention (Johnson et al., 1990; Pentz et al., 1989), where parents, schools, the mass media, and other agents of change have teamed up to prevent the onset of these problems. With a grant from the National Institute of Justice, my colleagues and I recently evaluated the Community Responses to Drug Abuse Program in nine cities and found that police and community organizations can work effectively with other agencies at the level of both enforcement and youth-oriented prevention (Rosenbaum, Bennett, Lindsay, & Wilkinson, 1994). Two other projects—the Robert Wood Johnson Foundation's 15-site Fighting Back project (Klitzner, 1993), and the 250-site Community Partnership Program (Cook & Roehl, 1993) funded by the Center for Substance Abuse Prevention, represent major efforts to build coalitions to fight neighborhood drug abuse. More recently, the Justice Department has funded the Comprehensive Communities Program in 12 cities to support the development of multiagency partnerships to attack gangs and violence, with a focus on community policing.[10]

Coalitions or partnerships might include representatives from government agencies such as criminal justice, health, welfare, and social services; elected officials; private businesses; voluntary organizations; community/grassroots organizations; churches; and other groups that have a vested interest in the neighborhood. In theory, the more resources that can be applied, the better the chances of impacting the problem. Although larger coalitions seek to be all-inclusive, in reality, the number of agencies involved is often limited, and the program is often located in, and controlled by, one agency.

Partnerships can vary in size and type (e.g., grassroots vs. professional members), number of committees, ethnic diversity, number of staff, membership criteria, decision-making processes, and the group's approach/orientation to the target problem (Cook & Roehl, 1993). The dynamics among the members of the partnership can be especially important for determining the partnership's success. The levels of cooperation, conflict, and participation that exist among coalition members can be important for determining whether the problem is properly addressed or solved. Success is often linked to the presence of a key coordinating individual who has a vision, who believes in the importance of the initiative, is highly motivated to see it succeed, and has access to the resources and political influence needed to make it happen. A coalition must be able to achieve internal goals, such as planning, securing resources, recruiting all key organizations, maintaining stability, and keeping members satisfied about the group's progress. In the final analysis, holding partnership meetings is a desirable objective but the "bottom line" is whether the group can develop and implement a plan of action that will effectively address the target problem. This remains an empirical question in many cases.

In any event, the door is now open for police to play an important role by creating and/or facilitating partnerships to address neighborhood problems related to crime and disorder. As organizers, facilitators, coordinators, or service providers, under the full community policing model, police organizations are expected to "step up to bat" in a multiagency context. From command personnel to the officers on the street, partnerships can provide work for everyone. Who gets involved will depend on the size of the initiative and how easily the problem can be solved. When the problem is relatively small, a smaller partnership with fewer members will be sufficient. Under these conditions, line officers should be able to represent the police organization with limited involvement from top management. However, when the problem is characterized as large, visible, and perceptibly political, then the police organization (and the community) is best served by requiring the participation of management personnel.

Every neighborhood and every problem is unique, which means that the community policing officer will need considerable freedom to develop relationships with other agencies and make decisions about appropriate courses of action. This concept of empowering individual officers is both exciting and troublesome, depending on your perspective, but it is a central component of the new model. The exciting aspect is that individual police officers are expected to use their talents to think creatively about ways to solve neighborhood problems, unlike the current state of affairs in many agencies where officers are reluctant to do anything unusual for fear of punishment. Coincidentally, in addition to helping solve problems, this new approach to police work should yield happier employees. There is good evidence to indicate that police officers are more satisfied with their jobs under these arrangements (see Lurigio & Rosenbaum, 1994, for a review).

However, the idea of empowering police is troublesome to those who fear a return to the days of corruption and abuse of police powers. Obviously, in agencies where such problems are rampant, giving the beat officer more freedom could be very problematical. I am hoping that this concern will prove to be unwarranted. Most police organizations do not suffer from widespread corruption, and preventive measures can be instituted to prevent the spread of unethical conduct. The bigger concern should be whether beat officers have the training and skill level to function in this new capacity, and whether supervisors are prepared to supervise under these new arrangements.

EFFICIENCY OF COMMUNITY POLICING

During these times of fiscal austerity, the most important question facing many police administrators and city politicians is whether they can afford community policing and whether it is worth the investment. There are two related questions that should be addressed. First: What is the cost of community policing, and is it more or less expensive than traditional, reactive policing? Second: What are the benefits or gains associated with this new model of policing? Each of these questions is briefly addressed.

Regarding the cost question, I am unwilling to argue (as I know others have done in the past) that community policing is cheaper than traditional policing or that it will be cheaper in the near future when it becomes fully operational. In my judgment, cities can expect to spend *considerably more* on community policing in the next few years if police administrators continue to follow the current implementation plan. For the many organizations that simply want cosmetic changes, rather than substantive changes, cost should not be a major concern. But for those that are determined to introduce fundamental changes in the police organization and function, the present course of action is certain to bring added costs. To drive home this point, the question should be reversed. Specifically, how could it *not* cost more to (a) intensively retrain and restructure the entire police organization from top to bottom; (b) add *new* police roles and responsibilities; *and* (c) keep all of the existing police functions?

Who promised the taxpayer that real, substantive reform would be cheap? Cosmetic reform is cheap. Real reform is expensive, as it should be! For example, I'm not talking about a one-hour or one-day classroom training seminar, which I often see. Community policing is an entirely new way of thinking and behaving that will require months and even years of retooling in the classroom and in the field.

The biggest cost problem, however, is point (c) above, namely, the desire to add new police functions *without eliminating* or cutting back on current police responsibilities. If the community expects the police to attend community meetings, organize and maintain partnerships with other agencies, and so on, then beat officers cannot be expected to give the same response to all 911 calls. This is perhaps the most common and most serious implementation problem facing police organizations in large urban areas, namely, the failure to re-market police services to the public. Repeatedly, police organizations attempt to introduce new community policing activities on the present budget while continuing business as usual or making minor adjustments in the dispatching process. Unless existing activities are dropped or reduced in priority, cities should expect that additional police officers will be needed in the short run to achieve successful implementation. Fortunately, in the United States, police departments are able to add more police officers under the federally funded "COPS" (Community Oriented Policing Services) program. Unfortunately, local municipalities must be prepared to absorb the long-term cost of these additional resources once the COPS money has been phased out.

The debate about how many police officers are needed to fight crime is an old one, and the emergence of community policing has only reignited this discussion. Historically, the budget requests of police chiefs in the United States have been met by city government—every year, as the crime rate rose in the 1960s and 1970s, so did the municipal police budget (Jacob & Lineberry, 1982). Those budget days are now history, but police departments still face the issue of whether they need more police to implement community policing. During the transition period, when police organizations are in the process of converting from the traditional to the community policing model (and the length of this transition will depend on local circumstances), the argument can be made for increasing the size of the police force. This request for additional personnel assumes that police officers will take on new functions and responsibilities, yet will continue to operate within a traditional bureaucracy with few, if any, changes in the public's demand for service. There are several reasons, however, why community policing may *not* be more expensive than traditional policing when fully operational: (a) unnecessary layers of bureaucracy can be eliminated or scaled down as the organization becomes more decentralized; (b) decentralization will mean that officers on the street can handle many of the complaints that are currently fed through the 911 system; (c) the de-marketing of 911 and marketing of new procedures should reduce the demand for a dispatched car; and (d) by adopting a problem-oriented approach to policing, the volume of calls for service should decline as beat officers work with residents to resolve the underlying problems.

These are reasons why community policing may *someday* reach the point of not being *more* expensive than traditional enforcement policing. I believe, however, that this entire discussion of cost is misguided and reflects our inability as a society to engage in long-term planning or implement effective reform. The issue is not cost, but cost-effectiveness. The important question is this: Do we have any reason(s) to believe that community policing will yield more beneficial effects for society than reactive, enforcement-oriented policing? If so, we can then ask ourselves: Is it worth the investment—do the benefits outweigh the costs?

If community policing is more expensive, so be it. The real question is how much "bang for our buck" can we expect under this new model? If community policing is more expensive in absolute monetary terms, but yields a significantly greater impact on neighborhood problems in the long run, by all means, we should continue on the current path of reform.

The problem we face is the uncertainty about both costs and benefits. The potential costs are more tangible than the gains, but I have tried to suggest here that the gains could be substantial if community policing is exploited to the fullest extent. Let me continue this discussion of whether community policing is affordable by *briefly* summarizing what we know about the positive, short-term effects of these interventions, and then move into the realm of informed speculation regarding long-term benefits.

Short and Long-Term Effects. Controlled evaluations of community policing are few and far between (see Rosenbaum, 1994, for a collection of recent evaluations). In Canada, there have been only two widely publicized, quantitative evaluations—in Victoria (Walker & Walker, 1989) and in Edmonton (Hornick, Burrows, Phillips, & Leighton, 1991). The results of these evaluations can be viewed as encouraging, but not definitive. In Victoria, where mini-stations were introduced, official crime rates declined in five categories, but fear of crime did not change in the target areas (unfortunately, control groups were not used). In Edmonton, where foot patrols where introduced and measured in the context of a more controlled quasi-experimental design, two thirds of the target beats reported significant reductions in repeat calls, and citizens gave higher evaluations to foot patrol officers than to officers patrolling in cars. In the United States, Skogan's (1994b) reanalysis of 14 target neighborhoods in six cities (involving quasi-experimental pretest-posttest control group designs) provides the most systematic, rigorous look at the effects of community policing programs on residential neighborhoods. Across these 14 areas, Skogan found that 9 had experienced statistically significant improvements in residents' attitudes about the police, 7 experienced reductions in fear of crime, 6 showed declines in perceived neighborhood disorder, and 3 had experienced reductions in victimization rates. Recently, I conducted a comprehensive evaluation of community policing in Joliet, Illinois, and the results were mixed (Rosenbaum et al., 1994). After nearly 2 years, residents in the main target area reported significantly greater satisfaction with police contacts, but fear of crime and perceptions of neighborhood problems were unchanged. Residents reported a marginally significant drop in victimization experiences. The most positive findings came from our evaluation of intensive problem-solving activities along the main commercial strip in Joliet (Wilkinson, Rosenbaum, Bruni, & Yeh, 1994). Police records over a 4-year period showed *dramatic* declines in Part I crimes and disorders. The total number of reported incidents declined 68%—substantially greater than the citywide trends. Consistent declines were observed for violent crime, property crime, disorder, and other code violations.

Unfortunately, as critical methodologists have noted (Greene & Taylor, 1988; Lurigio & Rosenbaum, 1986), evaluations of community-based interventions often suffer from weak research designs and measures, thus making it difficult to draw any firm conclusions. Fortunately, the state of the art has improved in recent years. A series of stronger longitudinal evaluations funded by the National Institute of Justice is currently in progress and should yield more definitive findings.

In the literature on community and team policing, the benefits to police personnel are easier to document. Lurigio and Rosenbaum (1994) reviewed 12 studies that measured the effects of community-oriented programs and organizational changes on police officers. The results are generally encouraging, indicating positive effects in the areas of job satisfaction, perceived broadening of police functions, improved relations with co-workers and citizens, and greater expectations for citizen participation in crime prevention. Again, my own research shows fewer benefits for police officers, but more implementation time may be needed (Rosenbaum, Yeh, & Wilkinson, 1994).

In sum, early experiments with community policing show some promise for producing positive changes in police personnel, community residents, and (to a lesser extent) community crime rates. Despite these encouraging signs, some of the most basic questions remain unanswered: Are these effects long-lasting or short-lived? Do observed reductions in crime and disorder occur at the expense of other neighborhoods or other forms of crime where displacement is likely? Can community policing initiatives alter the nature or scope of social relations within high-crime neighborhoods? Can such programs strengthen local institutions or build lasting partnerships? Will the most innovative programs or reforms be institutionalized and sustained or will they be dropped with the next change of administration? Notwithstanding these uncertainties, community policing advocates can point to a fairly encouraging start, especially given the limited intensity of these early field tests.

A closer look at costs and benefits takes us beyond an assessment of immediate program effects into the realm of possible long-term gains from this reform movement. Unfortunately, there exist insufficient data on long-term outcomes, which forces us to think about these impacts from a rational and theoretical perspective. To this point, this chapter has tried to underscore some of the advantages of this new model from a *theoretical* (and to a lesser extent, *empirical*) standpoint. Let us revisit that discussion from an *economic* point of view, drawing attention to the potential cost savings that are inherent in this new approach as we look into the future.

The central purpose of cost-benefit and cost-effectiveness analyses is to determine whether the preferred program is one that "produces the most impact on the most targets for a given level of expenditure" (Rossi & Freeman, 1985, p. 325). Cost-effectiveness analyses compare monetary costs to some standard program outcome (e.g., percentage reduction in crime or fear of crime). Cost-benefit analyses compare monetary costs to monetary gains. In the final analysis, police officials and policymakers may be interested in a cost-benefit analysis, but the data are simply not available. Nevertheless, let us think in terms of monetary costs and gains for the moment.

At the core of this new model of policing is the idea that police organizations need to think differently about the resources (monetary costs?) that are needed, and are available, to combat crime. Eck and Rosenbaum (1994) characterized the problem this way: "Many of the assets needed to address problems are outside the boundaries of police organizations. These assets are the powers and resources of other government agencies, businesses, and the community itself" (p. 14).

The basic idea of police-community partnerships is to enhance our capacity to solve neighborhood problems. In theory, this is an excellent means of multiplying the resources available to the police without necessarily increasing the police budget. The multiplier effect of "community involvement" allows the police to maximize program effectiveness without a proportional increase in costs. When we begin to talk about "police efficiency" in the 21st century, we need to think in terms of identifying police organizations that have done a good job of mobilizing community resources to fight crime and disorder.

Turning from costs to benefits, I want to emphasize that utilizing *nonpolice* resources is more than a multiplication of assets, more than the provision of intensive, "high dosage" treatments, although this is certainly a welcome improvement. The community policing model, if fully implemented, should be not only *quantitatively* superior to the traditional model—but if the model is correct, it should be *qualitatively* different as well. In particular, the activation of local institutions and agencies, as well as other governmental agencies, reflects a commitment to pursue *preventive* strategies, as opposed to merely reactive approaches to neighborhood problems.

One of the most basic lessons that our society has yet to learn is that preventive programs yield larger benefit-cost ratios than reactive programs (in terms of national crime policy, the United States continues to move in the opposite direction, preferring after-the-fact punishment over all other strategies). The second lesson we have learned about prevention is equally clear:

The earlier we can intervene in the process of human development, the larger the program effects on crime and disorder, and the larger the monetary savings (see Schorr, 1988, for examples).

In economic terms, direct program benefits can be defined as "estimations of savings on direct costs" (Bootman, Rowland, & Wertheimer, 1979), and this includes the cost of prevention, enforcement, treatment, incarceration (including capital investments), and other tangible services. In 1992, for example, U.S. taxpayers spent approximately *93.7 billion dollars* to operate a totally reactive justice system (Maguire & Pastore, 1994). These massive costs do not include the costs of personal crime for Americans. Data from 1990 indicate that personal crime costs Americans an estimated *450 billion dollars* annually, including medical costs, lost earnings, pain and suffering, reduced quality of life, and public program costs related to victim assistance (Miller, Cohen, & Wiersema, 1996). The point is clear: To the extent that leveraging resources in the community will prevent even a small percentage of criminal and delinquent acts, taxpayers and potential victims can avoid paying the future costs associated with these transgressions. Given the possible economic savings, how can a society that has become increasingly self-interested with regard to taxation say "No" so quickly to prevention?

Admittedly, at this moment in time, there is a paucity of data to demonstrate the long-term crime prevention benefits of community-oriented policing initiatives (see Rosenbaum, 1988, 1994). There are many reasons for this shortage of compelling, conclusive data, including the fact that previous programs have been poorly funded, poorly implemented, and/or poorly evaluated, which makes it difficult to learn very much. The main reason, however, is that politicians are unwilling to wait 5 to 10 years for the results. Given this political reality, we are forced to move ahead using the best available data, our best theorizing about the possible program costs and benefits, and our own anecdotes.

CONCLUSIONS

By highlighting some distinguishing features of the community policing model, I have attempted to illustrate how this approach represents more than just a set of fancy slogans. I have tried to suggest that key components of the underlying theory are consistent with research on neighborhood disorder, fear of crime, community crime prevention, coalition building, and organizational reform. To be clear, this is not the same as rhetorically advocating community policing or stating that community policing has been shown to be a cost-effective response to crime and disorder. Although the available evidence is supportive of the model, many questions remain unanswered.

I hope that this delineation of key components of the theory and research behind community policing will help to debunk the common misconception that community policing will be "soft on crime." By promising to attack the social problems that contribute to crime, one could argue that community policing is "harder" on crime than traditional enforcement strategies. By the definition proposed here, to be tough on crime is to employ strategies that are *believed to be effective* in fighting crime (based on available theory and research), not strategies that are *known to be ineffective*. Given what we currently know about the causes of neighborhood crime, I have suggested that fighting fear of crime and local signs of disorder are promising, potentially effective means of attacking crime, and that creating police-community partnerships that lead to prevention strategies is another sensible strategy for being "hard" on crime.

My optimism about the future of community policing, however, should be tempered by widespread problems with program implementation. Whether these difficulties can be overcome remains to be seen and, in the final analysis, will determine the future of this reform movement. The internal and external obstacles to successful planning and implementation have been well documented through several process evaluations (see Rosenbaum, 1994). Problems within the organization that threaten to derail the reform process are numerous, and include inadequate training and supervision, top-down rule-driven bureaucracies that work to undermine officers' discretion, outdated performance evaluation systems that reward "bean counting" on enforcement activities, limited resources to carry out additional police functions, and, above all, employee resistance to change in general. In a nutshell, most police organizations are simply *not ready* for serious police reform, and even the most progressive administrators would prefer to develop special units or small programs within the department than to upset the status quo by introducing large-scale reform initiatives. "Organizational readiness," as I have defined it, implies that the agency "has in place the structure, policies, procedures, knowledge, and officer skills needed to deliver a new set of police services and a new approach to crime prevention and control" (Rosenbaum et al., 1994, p. 350). In the short history of community policing, one of the main lessons yet to be learned is that serious organizational changes are a fundamental prerequisite to *sustained* community policing. Anyone can start the process of change without much money or without much internal support from police personnel, but past experience reminds us that such reform efforts will not survive unless formal mechanisms are established to create a new work environment and, eventually, a new police culture. Most essential, the behavior of police officers (like that of all human beings) is shaped and controlled by rewards and punishments in their immediate environment. Thus, in the absence of a totally new system of performance evaluation—one that identifies and encourages community-oriented, problem-solving behaviors and discourages traditional responses—street-level police behavior will remain unchanged. Police chiefs and academics can talk about community policing until they are "blue in the face," but the day-to-day behavioral repertoire of the beat officer will remain unchanged.

Outside the organization, the problems with community participation are more serious than many experts suspect (Grinc, 1994). Public education through a professional marketing (and de-marketing) strategy will help to build a more functional relationship between the police and the community, but the problem of mobilizing local residents runs deeper. In the inner city, the new community policing officer must understand that a lack of citizen participation is due to feelings of hopelessness and despair, fear of gang/offender retaliation, and deep-seated distrust of and anger toward police officers, among other factors.

For these reasons, the future of community policing in disadvantaged neighborhoods should not be built entirely upon lofty assumptions about citizen mobilization and empowerment. Alternatively, in this context, the primary thrust of the community-oriented approach is best conceptualized in terms of *resource mobilization* and skills training rather than citizen mobilization. When neighborhoods reach a certain level of decline, community mobilization must go beyond traditional community organizing tactics to focus on the provision of needed services and opportunities for self-improvement. As I have noted in previous writings (Rosenbaum, 1987, 1988), past research has been unable to demonstrate that social order and residential cohesiveness can be "implanted" in neighborhoods characterized by high levels of social disorder and crime. This does not mean that this goal is impossible to achieve; only that it has yet to be documented. Along these lines, we must remember that economic instability is likely to have an adverse effect on residential transition, and, therefore, on efforts to build cohesive, self-regulating neighborhoods. In essence, police and other community-minded persons will be hard-pressed to find shortcuts to rebuilding inner-city communities where legitimate jobs and businesses are virtually nonexistent.

In this chapter, I have suggested that *prevention* is a unique and important characteristic of the community policing model. In the literature beyond policing, comprehensive community-based programs have shown considerable promise for arresting a wide range of social problems, especially when interventions are early and intensive. In the area of crime, the victims and perpetrators of violence are becoming younger each year, and this fact provides additional justification for police officers playing an active role in multiagency partnerships. Other agencies would benefit greatly from the police officer's firsthand knowledge of juvenile delinquency, juvenile justice, and various street-level youth problems.

In closing, the fundamental challenge behind current attempts to enhance police effectiveness is best articulated through an old (modified) parable: Once there was a young couple standing on the bank of a swift river, enjoying a sunny day, when they noticed a young boy swimming for his life and calling for help. They responded quickly and managed to rescue him, but before they could catch their breath, they noticed another young person calling for help from the middle of the river. They proceeded to rescue him as well, but the problem continued, as more kids were discovered in this treacherous river, struggling for survival. The couple quickly realized that they, alone, could not save all of these children, so they sought help from the citizens of the nearby town. Before long, dozens of helpers were pulling drowning children from the river. This crisis continued until everyone was approaching the point of exhaustion. Finally, one woman became angry. "That does it!" she said in a loud voice, and then took off running up the river bank. Her friends called out—"Where are you going? She turned and said—"I'm going up stream to find out who is throwing these kids in the water and put a stop to it!"

Whether or not she can "put a stop to it," and how much it will cost, is another story. But to stop her from venturing up stream to investigate the problem would be foolish.

NOTES

1. Interestingly enough, "community empowerment" began as a liberal concept to encourage citizens to demand their share of government resources, but in the 1980s and 1990s, conservatives found the empowerment concept very appealing as a cost-cutting strategy. With the latter interpretation, volunteerism was proposed as an alternative to many government-funded programs.

2. This is not the place to develop a complete theory of community policing, but I will attend to a few key areas that have been neglected or misunderstood in past discussions.

3. Taylor, Shumaker, and Gottfredson (1985) did *not* find a link between physical decay and fear after controlling for area, race, income, and home ownership. However, the bulk of extant data suggest a causal linkage, including studies with similar controls. Nevertheless, the disorder model has engendered serious criticism (e.g., Greene & Taylor, 1988), suggesting that additional work is needed on this topic.

4. *Money* magazine's annual survey of the best places to live in the United States illustrates, however unscientifically, the importance of crime in the housing market. Their 1994 readers' poll found that the desire for a low crime rate ranked first among 43 factors that people consider when choosing a place to live (September 1994 issue). Hence, crime rate was weighted heavily when ranking cities.

5. If we begin to think of crime as an epidemic (cf. Gladwell, 1996), and of neighborhoods in terms of reaching some critical threshold of crime-related problems, then perhaps we will better understand the process of rapid neighborhood decline or improvement. The tipping point, however, is likely to be different from one neighborhood to another.

6. To make matters worse, the emphasis on arrest has led to drug enforcement practices that are disproportionately focused on minority communities, thus producing differential increases in the Hispanic and African American prison populations.

7. To distinguish incidents from problems, Goldstein (1990) defines a problem as "a cluster of similar, related, or recurring incidents rather than a single incident; a substantive community concern; a unit of police business" (p. 66).

8. I should note that community policing was born in several major U.S. cities because minority communities expressed dissatisfaction with unresponsive and apparent inequitable treatment by the police. In these cases, the emergence of community policing can be viewed as an attempt by the police to build trust and establish better relations with inner-city neighborhoods.

9. Even the traditional, enforcement-oriented police agency is forced to recognize that there is little it can accomplish without the full cooperation of local residents who serve as witnesses and informants regarding crime incidents.

10. This demonstration program is being funded by the Bureau of Justice Assistance, with the evaluation supported by the National Institute of Justice. The research team includes George Kelling, Ann Marie Rocheleau, Jeff Roth, Wes Skogan, and Dennis Rosenbaum.

2

TAILOR-MADE POLICING

A Conceptual Investigation

Jean-Paul Brodeur

Reviewing the literature on the effectiveness and the efficiency of policing reveals at least two facts. First, there have been a great number of experiments aimed at reforming the police since 1945. Sherman, Milton, and Kelly (1973, p. xiii) traced the first experiment in team policing back to Aberdeen, Scotland, at the end of World War II; and in 1969, Germann published a paper titled "Community Policing: An Assessment." Since then, judging from the research literature, the pace of experiments, pilot projects, and organizational reforms has been relentless, each new wave of innovations having its own label and claiming to be the new paradigm for policing.

Second, despite the constant call for *more* evaluation research, there have been in fact numerous evaluation studies of policing. These studies range from groundbreaking assessments of traditional methods of policing (Greenwood,

AUTHOR'S NOTE: I would like to thank the Canadian Social Sciences and Humanities Research Council for its financial support of the research that provided the basis for this chapter and for all my other research efforts on policing. I also want to thank the federal ministry of the Solicitor General of Canada for its continuing support.

Petersilia, & Chaiken, 1977; Kelling, Pate, Dieckman, & Brown, 1974a; see Skolnick & Bayley, 1986, pp. 3-4; and Sherman, 1986, pp. 359-362, for reviews of these assessments), to evaluations of the new experiments in policing. The latter evaluation research varies widely in its methodological sophistication and in the aspects of policing that are taken into account (Bennett, 1983; Bloch & Anderson, 1974; Cohen & Chaiken, 1972; McElroy, Cosgrove, & Sadd, 1993; McIver & Parks, 1983; Spielberger, 1979; Spielberger, Ward, & Spaulding, 1979). Some studies embody a rigorous design and rely on experimental methods (Bennett, 1990a; Hornick, Burrows, Philips, & Leighton, 1993; McElroy et al., 1993; Skogan, 1990a, 1994b), whereas others rely more on an informed but largely intuitive grasp of a program's impact (Lambert, 1993; Skolnick & Bayley, 1986) or on random public opinion surveys and interviews with program participants (Murphy, 1993a). The results of evaluation research, whatever its degree of sophistication, have been reviewed periodically (Chacko & Nancoo, 1993; Greene & Mastrofski, 1988; Moore, 1992; Reiner, 1994a; Rosenbaum, 1994; Sherman, 1986; Skolnick & Bayley, 1988b; Weatheritt, 1986). The general impression made by this literature is that things are changing significantly in policing, or at least that there is a systematic endeavor to reform policing.

According to Eck and Spelman (1987b, p. 33), community policing results from the survival of three strategies that were part of a failed attempt to implement team policing, these three strategies being storefront police stations, foot patrol, and community crime watch, but there is more to the relationship between team policing and present developments in community and problem-oriented policing. In 1973, 4 years before Goldstein's *Policing a Free Society* (1977) and his subsequent articles on community and problem-oriented policing (Goldstein, 1979, 1987), Sherman et al. (1973) published seven case studies on police departments that were trying to implement team policing. If we compare the elements of team policing as described by Sherman et al. (1973, p. 7) with the elements of community policing that Skogan (1994b, p. 176, Table 9.1) and Hornick et al. (1993, p. 312, Table 1) used as the basis for their respective evaluations of community policing in U.S. and Canadian sites, we are compelled to agree largely with Eck and Spelman (1987b) that community policing is but a residue of team policing. We also experience a strong sense of déjà vu. For example, in describing Dayton, Ohio's program of team policing, Sherman et al. (1973) write that one of its primary goals was "to produce a *community-oriented* police structure that would be responsive to different neighborhood lifestyles" (p. 15; my emphasis). On the following page we also find that, "Preventive patrol was to be eliminated to enable members of the team to undertake *problem-oriented activities"* (p. 16; my emphasis).

Before all the hype about community and problem-oriented policing, team policing encompassed community and even problem-oriented policing as both a program and strategic innovations, to use a distinction formulated later by Sparrow, Moore, and Kennedy (1990, pp. 198-199). Nevertheless, Eck and Spelman (1987b, p. 33) express the consensual view, to the effect that team policing failed (also see Skogan, 1990a, p. 123). Taking the failure of team policing into account, it would seem that police departments have been trying to implement the same kind of reform since the 1970s with little or no success. One of the earliest assessments of community policing goes back to 1969 (Germann, 1969); other assessments were made in the early 1970s (Bloch & Specht, 1973; Schwartz & Clarren, 1975). They all associated community policing with team policing. Hence, with this perspective, it would seem that despite all efforts to reform the police, very little is happening except rechristening failed reforms with new names.

Adding a few more empirical evaluations of community or problem-oriented policing will not significantly change our perception that, on the one hand, everything is in turmoil and, on the other hand, that nothing really changes. Going back to the reform programs as they were originally formulated and undertaking a conceptual analysis of what they proposed will let us see more clearly where we are going. The aim of this analysis is essentially pragmatic: to unravel the different threads going through the reform of policing and to identify which of these threads—if any—holds the greatest promise. Like all conceptual analyses, this will focus on the analysis of texts, and more explicitly on the work of Herman Goldstein.

This chapter is divided into three parts. I first explore the origins of community and problem-oriented policing. Second, I argue that community and problem-oriented policing are not identical, and examine their relationship to each other. Finally, I examine problem-oriented policing against the background of evaluating its impact.

REFORMING THE POLICE:
A BRIEF SURVEY OF RECENT EFFORTS

The phrase "community-oriented policing" was already in use in the early 1970s. Most of the experiments described by Skolnick and Bayley (1986) were undertaken in the early 1970s as attempts to remedy the racial riots of the 1960s.

The reform movement that was to lead to community and problem-oriented policing started in the United Kingdom just after World War II. According to Sherman et al. (1973, pp. xii-xiv), the first experiments with team policing were conducted in Aberdeen, Scotland, and in Accrington, in the county of Coventry. These experiments embodied two different models of team policing: In Aberdeen, a team of 5 to 10 police officers was allocated to different parts of the city according to workload need; in Coventry, they experimented with Unit Beat Policing, that is, with a team of men that remained in a specific area and that fed information to a collator who was responsible for disseminating this information and for maximizing coordination, so that a larger area could be covered with fewer men. The important point about these early experiments with team policing is that they were undertaken not because of external pressure, but *internal pressure.* The Aberdeen experiment was intended to counteract the low morale, boredom, and loneliness of officers patrolling deserted streets alone. In Coventry, Unit beat policing was a way to remedy a shortage of manpower.

In the early 1960s, team policing was imported into the United States. The Aberdeen system was attempted by the Tucson, Arizona, police department, as well as other police forces in small cities, even though it had been abandoned in 1963 in England. The Unit Beat Policing system was expanded to other British forces and was also adopted by several U.S. forces under the name of "neighborhood team policing." According to Sherman et al. (1973, p. xiv), the police department in Richmond, California, tried to combine the Aberdeen and Coventry systems.

In 1967, the President's Commission on Law Enforcement and the Administration of Justice recommended that police departments try a team policing concept that envisioned patrol and investigative officers working together under a unified command, taking flexible assignments to deal with crime problems in a defined sector. Several departments followed the recommendations and experimented with team policing. Goldstein (1977, p. 63) describes the concept of team policing as implying that a group of officers is given permanent responsibility for all police services in one area. This decentralization of command resulted in the police officer responsible for a team in one area actually becoming the police chief for that area. Sherman et al. (1973) describe team policing experiments in seven U.S. cities: two small cities (Holyoke, Massachusetts, and Richmond, California), two middle-sized cities (Dayton, Ohio, and Syracuse, New York), two large cities (Detroit, Michigan, and Los Angeles, California) and one super-city (New York). The operational elements of team policing are defined by Sherman and colleagues (1973, p. 7) as (a) stable geographic assignment; (b) intra-team interaction; (c) formal team conferences; (d) police-community communication; (e) formal community conferences; (f) community participation in police work; and (g) systematic referrals to social agencies. The organizational supports included unity of supervision, lower-level flexibility, unified delivery of service, and combined patrol and investigative functions. The details of implementing team policing in these seven cities reveal that almost all of the tactics of community-oriented policing that are presently used—for example, foot patrol, storefront headquarters, home visits, community crime watch—were utilized then. Sherman and his colleagues (1973) give a negative assessment of team policing: "Team policing was conceived as a means to an end—a decentralized professional patrol style. In none of the cities studied has that end yet been achieved" (p. 107).

The researchers identified the main reasons for this partial success, and in some cases complete failure. The most important is that middle management in the departments, seeing team policing as a threat to their power, subverted, and in some cases, actively sabotaged the plans. It should be stressed that Sherman et al. (1973) tried to assess only whether team policing had actually been implemented. They did not evaluate its impact on the external problems that the police are mandated to solve.

At approximately the same time that team policing was being experimented with, several U.S. cities, such as Oakland, Philadelphia, and Seattle, developed the concept of Neighborhood Watch, also known as Block Watch, Apartment Watch, Home Watch, and Community Watch. The basic idea was to involve citizens in the protection of their own property by convincing them to organize and by assisting them with equipment, information, and expertise. Bennett (1990a) describes the development of this concept in the United States and its importation by the United Kingdom, where Neighborhood Watch programs have multiplied. Bennett (1990a, p. 18-22) identifies what he considers the principal elements of Neighborhood Watch, which are completed by structural and organizational elements. He also sees in the "new" community-oriented policing developed by Goldstein (1987), the conceptual and theoretical background of Neighborhood Watch. Bennett (1990a, p. 26) also views directed patrol, team policing, and citizen contact patrol as the new community-oriented policing in practice.

A review of these developments yields interesting insights. For example, team policing was initially used as a means to resolve internal police problems, such as low officer morale and lack of manpower. More significantly, there exists a great deal of uncertainty in the conceptualization of police reform, which is reflected in the confusion of police administrators when they have to decide which orientation they are going to implement. An example of the magnitude of the misunderstandings is provided by comparing Bennett (1990a) and Eck and Spelman (1987b) on the relationship between team and community policing. Taking an operational perspective, Eck and Spelman (pp. 32-34) view community policing as consisting of little more than the implementation of three residual strategies that were all that remained of the failed and ambitious team policing project, namely, foot patrol, storefronts, and community crime watch. It must be recognized that evaluations of community policing rarely go beyond assessing the impact of these strategies and some of their variants (Skogan, 1994b, 1995). In contrast, Bennett adopts a conceptual perspective and sees in team policing one among many implementations of the community policing concept. Both Eck and Spelman (1987b, p. 34) and Bennett (1990a, p. 172), however, agree that Community Crime Watch has little, if any, impact on crime rates; in the best of cases it makes communities feel safer and increases communication between the community and the police, giving the latter a better image and its members increased job satisfaction. This limited impact of community crime programs on crime rates and even on community feelings of security is verified by most evaluation research conducted in different sites where community policing was implemented (Hornick, Burrows, Philips, & Leighton, 1993; Kennedy, 1993; Murphy, 1993a, 1993b; Rizkalla, Archambault, & Cartier, 1991; Sadd & Grinc, 1994; Skogan, 1994b; Walker, Walker, & McDavid, 1993). An additional result noted by Hornick et al. (1993) in Edmonton is that community policing accounted for a significant decrease in calls for service.

The results of evaluation research are largely inconclusive and, as Pawson and Tilley (1994, p. 1) have stressed, it is even difficult to interpret the convoluted language in which the research is cast. As police reformers are notoriously impatient for results and are quick to trade the latest panacea for a new scheme, there have been questions, particularly since the publication of Goldstein (1990), on whether problem-oriented policing actually coincided (as generally claimed) with community policing and on whether problem-oriented policing might provide community policing with what community policing presently lacks and so produce more substantive results.

With regard to the relationship between community and problem-oriented policing, there are three competing positions. First, there is what we might call the *differentialist* position. It is represented by Eck and Spelman (1987b, p. 33) and Goldstein (1990, p. 24), and is usually based on operational grounds. We have already described the position of Eck and Spelman, who argue that community policing is a residue of team policing and has little impact on substantial community problems. Although problem-oriented policing relies on and supports community policing, the two are not synonymous (Eck & Spelman, 1987b, p. 46). Goldstein (1990, p. 24) distinguishes two patterns in the wide range of programs to engage the community. According to one pattern, there should be an ambitious but somewhat amorphous effort to develop new relationships with all or with large segments of the community. Goldstein appears skeptical about this approach and actually raises several fundamental questions about its viability. The second pattern is to involve those affected by a specific problem in its solution (Goldstein, 1990, pp. 24-25). This approach appears more fruitful to Goldstein; the role of the community is limited to what it can contribute to the solution of a particular problem and the overall approach is more adequately described as problem-oriented policing than as community policing. Goldstein (1990, pp. 70-71) underlines other limitations to the role played by the community in, for instance, identifying the problems that must be given priority.

The second position is *integrative and conventionalist* and it was developed by Goldstein himself in an article published in 1987. Despite a first flurry of criticism directed against community policing both in the United States and in the United Kingdom by Holdaway (1984), Manning (1984), Mastrofski (1983), Short (1983), and Weatheritt (1983), Goldstein (1987) proposes that community policing "could provide an umbrella under which a more integrated strategy for improving the quality of policing could be constructed" (p. 8). He also asserts that "the recurring themes in the newest [community policing projects] are so synonymous with the values inherent with the policing of a free society, one could argue that the label itself (community policing) is redundant" (Goldstein, p. 8). Hence, Goldstein does not seem to be strongly committed to this quasi-redundant umbrella; this is why I characterized his position as conventionalist. John Eck, in his paper with Dennis Rosenbaum, also appears to have relinquished his former differentialist position in favor of the integrative/conventionalist approach (Eck & Rosenbaum, 1994).

The third position is wholly pragmatic: Regardless of theoretical considerations, a police force actually proceeds to integrate community and problem-oriented policing. This is what the NYPD did in its CPOP project, which was evaluated by McElroy et al. (1993). Sparrow (1988) also proceeded to amalgamate community and problem-oriented policing.

Goldstein's endorsement of community policing as an umbrella under which might come all efforts directed to the improvement of the quality of policing is *conditional*. He endorsed community policing only to the extent that it become a different way of thinking about the police instead of merely providing another label for public relations. I now propose to examine whether this condition was in fact met by community policing and whether it was possible in principle for community policing to respect Goldstein's condition.

PROBLEM-ORIENTED POLICING
AND COMMUNITY POLICING

In this section I will try to describe community and problem-oriented policing from the latter's perspective. There does not seem to be any reluctance on the part of the advocates of community-oriented policing to integrate problem-oriented policing. The proposals made in Goldstein (1987) were generally favorably received, and most definitions of community policing (e.g., Normandeau & Leighton, 1990; Skogan, 1990a, 1994b) begin by acknowledging the need to expand the police mandate in the way suggested by Goldstein. Some of the proponents of problem-oriented policing, however, are not equally enthusiastic about all the features of community policing.

Goldstein (1987, pp. 8-10) identifies the common characteristics of community policing as using increased visibility to deter crime and reduce fear of crime, practicing crime prevention through informing and organizing community involvement in crime watch initiatives, and responding to the full range of problems that the public expects the police to handle. Community policing implies that officers will have more freedom to contact citizens; the most ambitious programs aim at developing a reservoir of respect and support that could increase the capacity of police officers to solve problems without resorting to the criminal justice process. Goldstein sees this as community policing's ultimate potential and a reactivation of the original British notion of policing by consent.

Policing by consent is obviously not a new concept. The real test for community policing is to see whether it is a policing strategy that is relevant to the problems that cities currently face in the context of multiracial and multiethnic diversity and whether it can solve or alleviate the problems of the 1980s both efficiently and effectively. Hence, Goldstein (1987, p. 10) enumerates the basic requirements that community policing must meet to be able to confront the present challenges. The last and foremost of these is precisely that the police be able to focus on substantive problems, which is actually just another way of saying that community policing should become problem-oriented policing (Goldstein, 1987, p. 15).

Problem-oriented policing was defined by Goldstein in two books (Goldstein, 1977, 1990) and two very influential articles (Goldstein, 1979, 1987). On a practical level, it was also developed by Eck et al. (1987) and by McElroy et al. (1993). Goldstein (1990) is a lucid, detailed, and very clear exposition of problem-oriented policing, which will not be repeated or elaborated upon here. I will focus on themes that can be contrasted with community-oriented policing.

Goldstein was early concerned with the exercise of police discretion (Goldstein, 1963, 1967a, 1967b) and with the improvement of police performance (Goldstein, 1967c, 1969). He coauthored a small book on criminal justice in the United States (McIntyre, Goldstein, & Skoler, 1974); his contribution is the chapter on policing (pp. 5-12). Although the chapter is brief, he nevertheless delineates two themes that recur in all of his subsequent work. The first theme is the discovery of the diversity of police work and of the large amount of police activity devoted to tasks other than the handling of serious criminal activity (McIntyre et al., 1974, p. 5; this part of police activity is estimated to take as much as 80% of a police officer's shift). It should be remembered that Egon Bittner, who discovered the variety of problems that the police are called upon to solve, acknowledged his debt to Herman Goldstein "in all matters concerning the police" (Bittner, 1990b, p. 264). Goldstein's second theme is the police officer's discretionary power to arrest someone as a means of solving a problem that is not of a criminal nature. In other words, police may arrest a person for a minor violation in order to send that person to a therapeutic facility (McIntyre et al., 1974, p. 6). In this context, *law enforcement is only a means to solve a substantial* problem that is unrelated to the perpetration of a crime. This idea—that law enforcement is one means to solve the great variety of problems with which the police are confronted—recurs throughout Goldstein's work.

Goldstein (1977) elaborates on these themes in *Policing a Free Society,* although he does not yet use the phrase *problem-oriented policing.* For example, he notes once more that arrest is used by police for purposes other than to arraign a person who has committed a criminal offense (p. 23). Community-based policing is briefly discussed in the context of Cincinnati's team policing project (pp. 63-64), yet the foundation for these new styles is already being laid in this book. First, Goldstein (1977) realizes the significance of the amount of time that police spend on noncriminal matters, and he views this challenge to the stereotype of the police function as having "tremendous significance." This leads him to develop a conceptual framework for viewing the police, one in which the police is seen as an agency of municipal government that houses a variety of functions (Goldstein, 1977, p. 33). Goldstein then proceeds to derive the main implications of this absolutely basic insight.

The first implication is that such an agency by definition pursues a large variety of objectives, which must be distinguished from the methods available to the police for attaining these objectives. From this distinction follows one of Goldstein's key insights, that law enforcement is not an end in itself, but a method to reach a policing goal (Goldstein, 1977, p. 32). In later work, Goldstein coins the expression "the 'means over ends' syndrome" to chastise a general police tendency to neglect the end product of policing in favor of internal organizational reform (Goldstein, 1979, p. 238). The original manifestation of this syndrome remains: viewing law enforcement as the end product of policing.

The second implication is that it is necessary for the police to resort to alternatives to the criminal justice process in order to fulfill its multiple objectives. "It is ironic," writes Goldstein (1977), "that there is so inverse a relationship between the diverse array of tasks the police are expected to perform and the extremely limited methods available to them for getting the job done" (p. 71). Not only must the presently available informal alternatives be reassessed, but new ones must be found, if necessary by expanding the powers of the police. It should be insisted upon that the search for alternatives is one of the main features of Goldstein's thought and of what was to become "problem-oriented policing." A long chapter in his book *Problem-Oriented Policing* (Goldstein, 1990, pp. 102-147) is precisely a discussion of the search for alternatives. As I shall try to show, this is the feature of problem-oriented policing that is the most difficult to implement. It has far from realized its full potential.

The third implication is a direct consequence of the second. Not only do police need to develop alternatives to fulfill their many objectives, but these measures must be tailored to their needs (Goldstein, 1977, p. 81). This is another theme that becomes the subject of further development as problem-oriented policing takes shape. The chapter devoted to this in Goldstein (1990) is titled "The Search for Alternatives: Developing Tailor-Made Responses" (chap. 8).

Without implying that everything that would be associated with problem-oriented policing was already implicitly contained in Goldstein (1977), it can be said that in his subsequent work he coined striking phrases, such as the "means over ends" syndrome, that captured his previous insights. Goldstein's breakthrough article is underpinned by an opposition between internal process and external output (Goldstein, 1979, pp. 238, 242). Internal processes are generally administrative, and their goal is the amelioration of the organization itself. External output refers to the quality of the services provided to the community. Goldstein (1979) likens the situation in police forces to that of a private industry "that studies the speed of its assembly line, the productivity of its employees, and the nature of its public relations program, but does not examine the quality of its product" (p. 243). In order to reestablish the proper balance in favor of external output, Goldstein develops his well-known themes of the importance of the end product over the means (see Goldstein, 1979, pp. 238-241; Goldstein, 1990, p. 3) and of the need to focus on substantive problems (Goldstein, 1987, p. 15).

There is, however, at least one significant new development in Goldstein's work after 1979. On the whole, Goldstein (1977) is concerned with finding answers to the problems that confront police; that is, with finding alternatives to the criminal justice system. Goldstein (1979, 1987, 1990) devotes considerable effort to developing the process whereby problems are identified, analyzed, and given a fitting response. One concept plays a central part in this development: specificity. Goldstein (1979, pp. 244-245) explicitly cautions us against using categorical headings like "crime," "disorder," "delinquency," or even "violence," in defining problems. He shows, for instance, that even a relatively precise label such as arson may in fact refer indiscriminately to very different problems, including vandalism, psychopathy, the destruction of criminal evidence, economic crime, and criminal intimidation (Goldstein, 1979, p. 245). It follows from these remarks that problems must be "disaggregated" and that using the categories of criminal offenses as they are defined in criminal codes may not be the best way to identify specific problems (Goldstein, 1990, pp. 38-40). Eck and Spelman (1987b, pp. 35-36) make an important distinction in this regard between crime control policing, which uses crime analysis units, and problem-oriented policing. Crime analysis relies on police records to determine patterns followed by offenders. The identification of such patterns may lead police to perform their traditional operations, such as investigations and individual arrests, more efficiently. This prompts Eck and Spelman (p. 36) to criticize the reliance on crime analysis units as prejudging what the established response will be without having understood what the specific problem is.

This emphasis on specificity may eventually drive an actual wedge between community policing and problem-oriented policing. First, problem-oriented policing seems to stress the role of the police rather than the role of community. Whether in granting the community freedom to select alternatives for solving problems (Goldstein, 1987, p. 21), in determining the role of the police in policy-making decisions (Goldstein, 1987, p. 24), or in relying on police input to define problems (Goldstein, 1987, p. 16; 1990, p. 70) and selecting which should be given priority (Goldstein, 1990, p. 77), Goldstein generally appears to reserve a greater role for the police than for the community. For example, "however clear members of a community may be in setting out their problems, the police cannot agree in advance that they will focus on the community's choices" (Goldstein, 1990, p. 71); again, "police officers on the beat are in the best position to identify problems from the bottom up" (Goldstein, 1990, p. 73).

Nevertheless, there is an element of community policing that may be much more fundamentally dissonant with problem-oriented policing. Goldstein (1979, p. 237) refers to a police spokesperson's assessment of the use of officers as decoys for apprehending offenders in high-crime areas. According to this spokesperson, a major value of the program was its positive impact on the police image within the community. Goldstein notes rather wryly that "the effect on robbery was much less clear," thus implying that this police department was one more victim of the means over ends syndrome (Goldstein, 1979, p. 237). We have already seen that Goldstein (1990, p. 26) made a distinction between two patterns of police-community engagement. In one case, the police try to engage on a permanent basis the whole of the community, whereas in the other case, only the relevant part of the community is provisionally mobilized to assist in the solution of one specific problem. Goldstein is critical of the broader effort to engage the community, and not only because it is amorphous. This broad effort is suspected of being just an effort to reduce tensions between the police and the community and to generate more positive community attitudes toward the police. The measure of police success may then be viewed as the number of meetings with the community and in the participation of community members in these meetings. The cardinal risk of this broadly based strategy of community policing is that of falling prey to the means over ends syndrome: "The first pattern—setting out in a general manner to engage the total community—is reminiscent of past police reforms. It risks perpetuating the imbalance of means over end" (Goldstein, 1990, p. 26).

Judging from present evaluation research, community policing not only risks manifesting the means over ends syndrome, in certain respects it has become the victim of this syndrome, at least as it was defined by Goldstein (1979, p. 237). In one of the more systematic attempts to evaluate the impact of community-oriented policing,[1] Wesley Skogan (1994b) concludes "that it is apparent that these programs had the most consistent effect on *attitudes* toward the quality of police service" (p. 176, my emphasis). Indeed, significant positive changes in attitudes toward the police were the most consistent results of evaluative research into 14 project areas (9 of the 14 areas experienced these changes). I don't dispute that improving the image of the police is beneficial with respect to increasing the quality of its end product, particularly in policing minorities that have been previously antagonized by the police, as well as in the field of crowd control. Improving features of the organization is bound to translate, even if very indirectly, into an improvement of the end product of policing. Yet judging from the *theory* of problem-oriented policing, merely bringing about positive changes in the image of the police is an example of the means over ends syndrome, against which this theory was initially developed.

With this in mind, I address the problem of evaluating the impacts of community policing and problem-oriented policing.

EVALUATING PROBLEM-ORIENTED POLICING

Although the need for evaluating the results of problem-oriented policing is acknowledged—how could it not be by a policing strategy that claims to focus on the end product of policing?—such an evaluation appears to be shrouded in difficulties. Goldstein (1979, p. 243) enumerates 11 questions that must be answered in order to develop the process of problem-oriented policing. How to measure the effectiveness of the response to a problem that has been identified and analyzed is only one of these questions, and no indications are given on how to answer it. Actually, Goldstein (1979, p. 256) is more interested in using evaluation research to demonstrate the inadequacy of traditional policing responses than in showing the effectiveness of alternative responses.

Similarly, the measurement of productivity is barely mentioned in Goldstein (1987, p. 13). Actually, Goldstein (1987) admits that "the effect of some of the changes being advocated may simply not be subject to evaluation" (p. 26). In this article, Goldstein goes on to quote Skolnick and Bayley (1986) to the effect that the burden of proof of the effectiveness of policing strategies should be on those who want to maintain the traditional strategies (Goldstein, 1987, p. 27).

Goldstein (1990) is equally laconic on questions related to evaluating the effectiveness of problem-oriented policing. His 1990 book has separate chapters on identifying problems, analyzing problems, and searching for alternatives in developing responses to problems. Yet there is no chapter on assessing the response; this is dealt with in one page at the end of the chapter on the basic elements of problem-oriented policing and in three more pages at the end of the chapter on the search for alternatives (Goldstein, 1990, pp. 49, 145-147, respectively). Addressing the specific issue of measuring the performance of individual officers engaged in problem solving, Goldstein (1990) raises more difficulties than he answers:

> We have not yet figured out how to measure the effectiveness of an officer in handling problems on his or her beat. The old adage "one knows one when one sees one," seems to describe aptly the officer who is good at problem solving, but translating that criterion into language and factors that can be used by supervisory and command officers is difficult. (p. 164)

It indeed appears very difficult. Goldstein refers in this regard to Newport News (Virginia) police department supervisors who motivated their subordinates to incorporate problem-solving policing into their work by emphasizing these efforts in performance reviews (Goldstein, 1990, p. 164). In their study of problem-oriented policing in Newport News, Eck, Spelman, and their colleagues (1987) surveyed the opinion of 70% (148) of the officers involved in problem-solving policing. They were asked (a) if their efforts at problem solving had been successful; (b) if the time spent on problem solving had been worthwhile; whether (c) other officers, (d) private citizens, and (e) other agencies were cooperative; (f) whether supervisors had given them enough encouragement; and (g) *whether they had received the recognition they deserved for their efforts.* The officers had a choice between a positive, a negative, and a neutral answer. For the first six questions, the proportion of officers who answered positively varied between 54% and 60%, and the proportion of negative answers fluctuated between 6% and 11% (the rest of the answers were neutral). For the last question, however, the proportion of positive answers fell to 33% and the negative answers rose to 23% (Eck et al. 1987, p. 98, Table 12). So despite the efforts of the Newport News supervisors, it does not seem that officers involved in problem-oriented policing believed that they were adequately rewarded.

Finally, in one of the latest and most systematic efforts to evaluate community/problem-oriented policing, McElroy et al. (1993, chap. 4) evaluated the performance of New York Community Police Officers (CPOs) as problem solvers on many dimensions (e.g., problem identification and analysis, strategy development and implementation, the capacity to involve the community). However, because of measurement problems, which the authors discuss at length, "it is important to note that impacts on the problems were not considered as part of the officer's performance evaluations" (p. 71; see also p. 64).

It seems clear that the evaluation of problem-oriented policing raises serious difficulties at both the theoretical and the practical levels. We can ask ourselves whether there is something built into the concept of problem-solving policing that causes its proponents to acknowledge that measuring its effectiveness is very difficult. This admission is confirmed by the problems that were met by those who tried to evaluate the impact of problem-oriented policing.

We may begin by stressing that the proponents of problem-solving policing distinguish it from merely adding programs or tactics to the prevalent forms of policing. Problem-solving policing is defined as a *department-wide strategy* by Eck et al. (1987, see Summary, p. xv). For Goldstein (1990), it is "a whole new way of thinking about policing that has implications for every aspect of the police organization, its personnel and its operations" (p. 3). Sparrow, Moore, and Kennedy (1990, pp. 197-201) view community and problem-oriented policing as a strategic innovation that changes a police department as a whole and implies a "paradigm shift" encompassing all dimensions and features of policing. Department-wide strategies, whole new ways of thinking, and paradigm shifts are difficult to recognize, let alone to evaluate empirically. More significantly, however, Sparrow et al. (1990) argue that neither community nor problem-oriented policing should be seen as a definitive answer. Rather, such strategies "initiate the conditions under which the police *may continue to be adaptive and innovative,*" and they "set the stage for continued innovation at all levels" (p. 201, emphasis in text). Hence it would seem as difficult as it is futile to measure with precision the extent to which the new strategy has been implemented. Such a measurement implies freezing a paradigm that is characterized by its open-endedness.

Nevertheless, if we are to remain faithful to problem-oriented policing's focus on the external product of policing, what ought to be measured above everything else is the success of responses to problems previously identified and analyzed. Hence, it might be interesting to examine how both the problem and the response to it are conceived by the theory of problem-solving policing. Eck et al. (1987, p. 41) define a policing problem as a group of incidents occurring in a community that are similar in one or more ways and that are of concern to the police and the public. This definition is generally accepted. For example, Goldstein (1979, p. 242; 1987, p. 16; 1990, p. 66) proposes almost identical definitions.

There are features of problems, some of which have already been identified, that deserve further consideration. The first and most fundamental feature of a problem is that it is external to a policing organization (Goldstein, 1979, p. 242). This feature is relatively unproblematic because it is descriptive. The second important feature of a problem—its specificity—is essentially normative. The specificity of a problem is not something that is immediately apparent to the police; it must be discovered through a process of identification, analysis, and disaggregation that, as we saw, must disentangle the problem from the legal and police operation categories that mask its specificity. Yet, in their initial descriptive sense, the problems that face the police are characterized precisely by the fact that *as a category* they are nonspecific and represent a very mixed bunch of problematic situations. Indeed, problem-oriented policing is contrasted with traditional policing as a new strategy precisely because it goes beyond crime fighting and law enforcement to confront a variety of problems that are so heterogeneous that no common adjective has been found that applies to all of them (Goldstein, 1979, p. 242; 1990, pp. 66-67). In contrast, crime fighting and law enforcement are internally defined and are (relatively) specific. Hence a problem may be worked out as specific *only after* having been recognized as a policing problem. However, how problems come to be recognized is a fuzzy process that may vary from one police agency to another (Eck et al., 1987, p. 41).

A related trait of problems that came to be more explicitly identified by Goldstein in his later work is that they involve a cluster of interests that may not be compatible in all cases. Thus, Goldstein (1990, pp. 40-41) enumerates at least 13 different stakes in the resolution of a problem of prostitution. Needless to say, these stakes are grounded in different dimensions of a problem that exist at various levels of social reality. Hence, Eck et al. (1987, Summary, p. xv) refer to the *underlying* circumstances of a problem in their definition of problem-solving policing. It would then seem that there is an element of specificity in a problem that tends to limit its scope and make its solution easier, and an element of multiplicity that makes the scope of the problem broader, more complex, and much more difficult to resolve. I dub the element of specificity a "shrink" element and the element of multiplicity a "sprawl" element. These elements are not truly conflicting, but they are divergent.

There is a whole body of untapped literature, beginning with the groundbreaking work of Spector and Kitsuse (1987), that addresses this "sprawl" element in problems that require police intervention. This literature, which falls under the forbidding label of symbolic interactionism, is extremely relevant for problem-oriented policing.

There is a final feature of problems that is as important as the others. The police must deal with certain problems because no other means has been found to resolve them (Goldstein, 1979, p. 243). These problems are residual and are passed on to the police because of its crucial position as the final instance of control. Yet being the final instance does not necessarily mean being the definitive instance. Goldstein stresses how limited the capacity of the police is to solve problems, despite its image of omnipotence (Goldstein, 1990, p. 179). Consequently, due both to their nature and to the limits of police intervention, a significant number of the problems that police face are untractable and cannot be solved absolutely (Goldstein, 1990, pp. 17, 36).

How does the work of the proponents of problem-solving policing help us envision responses to these problems? The responses are determined by the problems themselves, and by the capacity of the police to solve them, as well as by the divergent features of the problems.

First, the police may intervene in such a way that the incidents generating the problem cease (Eck et al., 1987, Summary, p. xvii). This kind of problem, which admits of a definitive solution, is characterized by what I call the shrink element and is resolved by a tailor-made response (Goldstein, 1990, pp. 43-44 and chap. 8). However, in all the cases involving the "sprawl" element, problems will not be solved decisively. Either the incidents will decrease in number and/or seriousness or the police will find better suited responses (Eck et al., 1987, Summary, p. 17). In the worst of cases, police will refer the problem to another agency altogether.

Second, the more sprawling a problem is, the more intense will be the search for an alternative response, since the capacity of the police to resolve it is limited (Goldstein, 1977, chap. 4; 1990, chap. 8).

Finally, the police response will ultimately be conceived as facilitation rather than intervention, "the police role [being] more akin to that of facilitators, enabling and encouraging the community to maintain its norms governing behavior, rather than the agency that assumes total responsibility for doing so" (Goldstein, 1990, p. 179). This managerial conception of a police response is somewhat at odds with the more authoritarian notion of increasing police powers, which is also voiced by Goldstein (1990, p. 128).

How do we now answer our original question? Is there anything built into the original concept of problem-solving policing that accounts for the difficulty of evaluating its effectiveness? The answer is to a large extent positive.

There is no need to speculate; the theory of problem-oriented policing provides the answers.

From Goldstein's first coauthored work (McIntyre et al., 1974, p. 6) to his later book (Goldstein, 1990, pp. 49, 147), it is always clear that the standard measures of police performance such as clearance rates, the number of arrests and convictions, and heroic deeds in fighting crime are not satisfactory. These standards measure only law enforcing performance, which is only a means of policing and not its substantial aim. Furthermore, crime prevention cannot be evaluated from statistics recording police reaction.

What would adequate measures be? The answer is both predictable and disappointing. It is predictable in that it is consistent with the main tenets of the theory: Problem-solving policing essentially looks for tailor-made responses. Consequently, evaluation of police responses also have to be tailor-made (Goldstein, 1990). The difficulty with this answer is that it is formulated as a program for which there is not even a sketch.

Actually, the swing from a shrink to a sprawl element that is exemplified in both the definition of problems and the characterization of the responses is also evident in the theory of evaluation. The basic dilemma in respect to evaluation is lucidly formulated in Goldstein (1990):

> When a *specific response is related to a specific problem*—especially when the problem is finite—the effectiveness of the response is often obvious. Judging effectiveness for other types of problems may be so complicated that not even an elaborate, controlled experiment—in which attempts are made to isolate what the police do from other influences—could produce meaningful results. (p. 145; emphasis in text)

In other words, evaluation is either unneeded or unfeasible. That it is not feasible in the case of sprawling problems is not unexpected. Since these problems involve the collaboration of agencies other than the police, which is cast in the role of a facilitator that does not bear full responsibility for the response, it is overwhelmingly difficult to imagine an evaluation research design that could encompass this multiagency approach. Furthermore, it might prove impossible to perform an evaluation that takes into account all of the interests at stake. In the case of specific problems in terms of behavior, territory, persons, and time (Goldstein, 1990, pp. 67-68), the impact of the response may indeed be obvious.

There have been efforts to generate new measures of evaluation. For instance, in 1983, Mastrofski conducted research in which the patrol officer's knowledge of his or her own beat was used as a measure of performance. The measure was actually rather weak: All an officer had to do to be considered knowledgeable was to name one or more citizen groups operating in the area in different capacities (e.g., as part of a Neighborhood Watch; Mastrofski, 1983, p. 55). Only 38.5% of the 888 respondents could identify at least one citizen organization. The results were either predictable or puzzling. In a discriminant analysis, for instance, the visibility of citizen organizations in each neighborhood turned out to be the control variable with the highest explanatory power for a patrolman's knowledge of at least one organization. This result was predictable enough. However, the research also showed, somewhat surprisingly, that the availability of unassigned time to patrol officers was inversely correlated with their knowledge of the neighborhood. In other words, "giving officers large amounts of undirected discretionary time is less conducive to developing beat awareness than keeping officers busy answering calls for service" (Mastrofski, 1983, p. 58). What is unexpected in this result is that incident-driven reactive policing is generally contrasted with community and problem-oriented policing. For example, Sparrow et al.'s (1990) book is precisely titled *Beyond 911*. Mastrofski actually showed that the key operation for incident-driven policing—answering calls—appears to be the best means to know a neighborhood.

CONCLUSIONS

I have discussed several difficulties of assessing community and problem-oriented policing. Before drawing conclusions that may be too pessimistic, it might be timely to remember Goldstein's (1987) assessment of what stage we are in in trying to reform the police: "On a scale of one to ten, I would estimate that we have yet to reach one in development of our thinking and, most important, in the validation of some of our assumptions" (p. 26).

Three things have been demonstrated in this chapter. First, there has been a continuous movement to reform policing since the end of World War II. This movement has generated a wealth of concepts, such as unit beat policing, team policing, citizen contact patrol, Neighborhood Watch, and several variants of community policing and problem-oriented policing, not to mention other trends in intensive policing, saturation patrol, and riot control and the attendant militarization of the police. The problem with these concepts is that they are almost synonymous in certain respects and antithetical in certain others. Is community policing just a tactical residue of the aborted project to implement team policing or is it the proper umbrella under which all these new initiatives should take place? The proliferation of new concepts, strategies, and tactics is bound to generate confusion in police forces. As a result of this confusion, needed police innovations may be diluted into the general assertion that the true meaning of all this movement is really "a new way of thinking about policing." I fear that such a dilution would be tantamount to putting all of the blueprints for reform on the shelf, to resting content with thinking in the right way and so postponing action indefinitely. In order to avoid shelving a needed reform, we need to recognize that there is no predetermined use of these new concepts and that it is futile to strive for orthodoxy in reform. It is incumbent on police departments to use this wealth of reform material as a tool-kit to develop a policing model that is tailor-made to answer the particular needs of an environment (urban, regional, or rural).

Second, it seems to me that we should not follow the example set by Goldstein in his article of 1987, but rather follow his 1990 book. Goldstein (1987) puts problem-oriented policing under the umbrella of community-oriented policing. As a public relations strategy, community policing is a label with more appeal than problem-oriented policing. However, problem-oriented policing has a much wider application than community policing: (a) It is not, for example, tied to the existence of a community, which is something more than just the population in a particular area. (b) Nor is problem-oriented policing addressed to a particular group of police persons, in contrast to community policing, which is mainly carried out by uniformed patrol officers. There is an immediate sense in the notion of applying problem-oriented policing to criminal investigation, whereas the implementation of community-oriented police is not immediately obvious in CID. (c) In addition, there is a genuine risk that community-oriented policing will perpetuate the means over ends syndrome.

Last, the difficulties of measuring the effectiveness of problem-oriented policing with regard to its end product are quite real and should not be underestimated. If they are to be solved, it will be through a trial-and-error process that will require a persistent commitment in time. Police departments will have to withstand public pressure and resist undertaking an endless string of superficial experiments, which tend to cancel each other out and are merely a change in the organization's makeup.

The most difficult problem with respect to evaluation is overcoming the obstacle to measurement that is posed by one of the fundamental tenets of problem-oriented policing. Problem-oriented policing is in great part defined by its emphasis on the search for alternatives to the criminal justice system as we now know it. This recognition of the need for networking and for integrating the operations of the public police with other police agencies and with nonpolice agencies is gaining ground. In this regard, the British Independent Committee Into the Role and Responsibility of the Police recently proposed that the nature of the relationship between the public services and other forms of policing be developed and more precisely defined and regulated in order to foster better complementary action (Morgan & Newburn, 1994). Yet the more we increase the role of partners in an undertaking, the more complex the research design for measuring their joint performance is likely to be. I do not see, at the present time, any way to avoid this complexity while keeping problem-oriented policing's commitment to the search for alternatives alive.

POSTSCRIPT

After completing the first draft of this chapter, I sent a copy of it—with the other chapters of this book—to Professor Herman Goldstein. He was kind enough to reply in a June 1995 letter. This was more than a year and a half before he gave a lengthy interview to *Law Enforcement News* (LEN, Vol. XXIII, No. 461, February 14, 1997, pp. 8-11). In his June 1995 letter, Professor Goldstein stated that he found himself "in full agreement with my analysis." He agreed in particular with two of my points. First, that he had not devoted adequate attention to the problems of evaluation in his 1990 book on problem-oriented policing. Second, that he had "erred in the talk (and published article) [he] gave at New York University Law School in accepting community policing as the umbrella under which we could place problem-oriented policing." He goes on to add, "Since then, community policing has become such a meaningless and almost corrupt term, I wish I would have insisted on the subtle distinctions, and contributed to sharpening them."

Professor Goldstein goes a long way in spelling out the differences between community and problem-oriented policing in the interview he gave to *LEN* in February 1997, where he stresses that he sees "a major difference between the two concepts." Community policing, as he sees it, "is designed to place emphasis on one great need in policing, which is to engage the community." Problem-oriented policing "places the major emphasis on the need to reconceptualize what the police are doing more generally, to focus attention on the wide range of specific problems that police confront and to try to encourage a more analytical approach to those problems." These two quotes define the two major differences between community policing and problem-oriented policing. The first is in the *scope* of the reforms entailed by each: community policing emphasizes *one* great need in policing—to engage the community; problem-oriented policing stresses the need to reconceptualize the *general* police function. The second difference may be even more important for the future of policing. In his emphasis on a more analytical approach to the problems confronting the police, Herman Goldstein calls our attention to the fact that problem-oriented policing depends on information, knowledge, and expertise. That the collection, processing, analysis, and dissemination of information will be at the core of policing in the future has been recognized by police practitioners who herald their Compstat strategy and by researchers such as Albert Reiss (1992) and Peter Manning (1992a). Expert policing may point the way to the future.

NOTE

1. This example is cited by Pawson and Tilley (1994, p. 1) at the beginning of their paper, "What Works in Evaluation Research."

PART II

ISSUES IN PERFORMANCE ASSESSMENT

3

PROCESS OR PRODUCT?

Problems of Assessing
Individual Police Performance

Robert Reiner

There is a gaping hole at the heart of debates about policing. What is *good* police performance, and how can it be assessed? Throughout the now voluminous academic research literature on the police that has burgeoned in Britain, North America, and elsewhere in the past 30 years, this has seldom been raised as an issue, let alone resolved. Almost 20 years later, Herman Goldstein's (1979) rather caustic comments remain apposite, for police researchers as much as managers: "The situation is somewhat analogous to a private industry that studies the speed of its assembly line, the productivity of its employees, and the nature of its public relations programme, but does not examine the quality of the product being produced" (p. 243).

AUTHOR'S NOTE: The final draft of this chapter was written shortly before the recent British election, which brought Prime Minister Tony Blair and the Labour Party to power. However, the analysis in this chapter still holds, as the present Labour government has not significantly changed its predecessor's policies with respect to policing, during its first year in power.

In the United Kingdom the former Conservative Government stepped into this breach, driven partly by its long-standing drive to secure "value for money" in all public services. This was intensified recently by the political predicament it found itself in vis-à-vis "law and order," with soaring crime rates and Labour unprecedentedly capturing public confidence on this issue with its new realist policy of "tough on crime, tough on the causes of crime." Yet the way the Government-appointed Sheehy Committee rushed in where others have feared to tread exposes the pitfalls of a crude, mechanistic approach to the question of assessing police performance. Similar pressures of coping with rising crime rates during a period of cutbacks in public expenditure have led to similar concerns with value-for-money and cost-effectiveness in most other jurisdictions in recent years, not least Canada and the United States.

This chapter will explore why the issue of assessing individual police performance has been side-stepped by most researchers in all countries where there exists a tradition of research on the police. Is there anything about policing that renders it especially recalcitrant to definition, let alone measurement, of good performance? Can there be a more satisfactory approach than the Procrustean one exemplified by the Sheehy Committee, which recently examined the issue for the British Government? If so, what would be its lineaments? This chapter necessarily has the character of an a priori exploration into largely virgin territory rather than a report of clear conclusions and settled results. Nevertheless, it will attempt an analysis of a problem that lies at the heart of constructing satisfactory systems of police management and accountability. This is a vital policy and academic problem for police policy-makers, managers, and researchers in all countries.

The chapter will consider the following particular questions: (a) Why has police research largely skirted around the issue of *good* individual police work, and how it can be assessed? (b) the implications of the mainstream body of Anglo-American research on policing for the definition and assessment of good police work; (c) the implications of conceptions of the goals of policing for criteria and methods of assessment; (d) a discussion of some of the existing attempts to assess the attainment of the diverse goals of policing; (e) a case study of the recent Sheehy Committee approach in England, as an object-lesson in how *not* to go about the business of individual police performance assessment; and (f) some tentative conclusions about how the task can be approached.

POLICE RESEARCH AND PERFORMANCE
ASSESSMENT: EXPLAINING AN ABSENCE

Why has police research for the most part ignored the question of how individual police performance can be assessed for its quality? The answer lies in examining the various problematics that have animated police research in the past. Some years ago I suggested that in Britain, at any rate, the development of research on policing went through a number of distinct stages (Reiner, 1989, 1992a, 1992c). Similar phases can be discerned in police research in North America (Reiner, 1994a; Rumbaut & Bittner, 1979). The earliest, the "celebratory" stage prevalent up to the mid-1960s, was concerned with identifying the qualities of what was assumed to be a successful British style of policing, achieving effective and legitimate peacekeeping. While concerned with "good" policing rather than bad, it was directed at describing and explaining it, not raising the reflexive issue of how it was to be assessed.

During the 1970s and 1980s there were two succeeding phases of increasingly critical analyses of policing, which I called the "controversy" and "conflict" stages, respectively. The first was associated with the birth of systematic empirical research on policing, and did much to advance understanding of police organization, culture, and the exercise of discretion. In policy terms it was above all concerned with the analysis of police deviation from the rule of law, and how this could be regulated. The "conflict" stage was characterized by a more structuralist and radical analysis identifying the roots of police practice not in the culture or micro-interactions of the rank-and-file police world but in the place of the police in the state apparatus. Police malpractice was better understood as "organizational" rather than individual deviance, as an influential Canadian collection of essays argued (Shearing, 1981). The focal concern in this perspective was the construction of adequate channels for democratic accountability of the police organization.

Until relatively recently, most academic research and theorization about policing has been within one of these two critical problematics. The question of assessing police performance is central to their concerns, but in an oblique way. They are dominated by the issue of police malpractice and the barriers to its regulation. The central issues are the autonomy of the police organization as a whole from effective democratic policy-setting, and the largely unfettered practical discretion operated by the rank and file because of the inevitable low visibility shrouding everyday police work. It was these anxieties that animated police research in Britain and North America during its formative years (Reiner, 1994a, pp. 707-715).

The mainstream of Anglo-American empirical research on the police, concerned above all with the problem of police malpractice, conceived of the issue of individual performance assessment primarily in negative terms. It was directed at identifying the barriers to monitoring of police deviance, and how these could be eliminated. In practical terms this meant systems for safeguarding suspects against the improper exercise of police powers, and of effective complaints and legal mechanisms for rectifying grievances, which remains an issue in all jurisdictions (Goldsmith, 1991). Defining and assessing *good* individual police performance was outside the field of concern.

In recent years this has changed, with the rise of new "managerialist" approaches in government and the police service, and the conversion of much (but by no means all) of British and North American radical criminology to a new "realism" (MacLean & Milanovic, 1991; Young, 1994). Both managerialists and new left realists are concerned with achieving the delivery of effective police services, and not only with regulating malpractice. However, from the point of view of constructing adequate means of assessing individual performance, managerialists and left realists alike dodge the thorniest problems. Each adopts a very restricted conception of the police role, concentrating almost entirely on the crime control function. The former British Conservative Government made this explicit in its 1993 white paper on *Police Reform:* "The main job of the police is to catch criminals" (Home Office, 1993b, p. 4, para. 2.2). This objective underpins the whole structure of its current policing policies, as we will see below. For their part, the left realists have specifically espoused a "minimalist" conception of the police role, focused exclusively on law enforcement (Kinsey, Lea, & Young, 1986, chap. 9).

This new-found enthusiasm, at different parts of the political spectrum, for accentuating the positive in policing rather than just eliminating the negative has concentrated on questions of crime control. The problems of finding adequate indices of force or individual performance in crime investigation are thorny enough (Audit Commission, 1993). They pale into insignificance, however, when compared with the problems of assessing peacekeeping or service work. Yet most research, as well as—until the British government's recent change of tack—most policymakers, have concurred in seeing peacekeeping as the paramount police role.

The traditional view of the British police model, influentially rehearsed not many years ago by Lord Scarman (1981), saw its virtue as lying precisely in the prioritization of peacekeeping—"the maintenance of public tranquillity"—above strict law enforcement. This conception of policing, usually flying under the banner of "community policing," has become increasingly influential as an ideal around the world, but especially in North America (Skolnick & Bayley, 1988a). However, it raises the most acute problems for specifying, let alone measuring, "good" performance.

Thus we see that the question of defining and assessing the performance of individual officers has not been an issue for almost all approaches to research and policy that have been influential in recent times. These have either been concerned primarily with rendering the police accountable with respect to wrongdoing, or have focused primarily on crime control only. With some notable exceptions (Bayley & Bittner, 1984, and Muir, 1977, which will be considered below), the assessment of the quality of individual performance in the most common types of police work remains a lacuna in research.

POLICE RESEARCH AND PERFORMANCE ASSESSMENT: THE MAINSTREAM

The picture of routine police work built up by the mainstream research literature over the years has implications that the core activities of the police (notably routine patrol) are particularly recalcitrant to efforts to define or assess its quality precisely. In this it is congruent with the rank-and-file police culture that has been the focus of much of its analysis.

From its inception, research on the everyday activities of police officers, especially the patrol officers who are the majority of personnel (cf. Tarling, 1988), has stressed the special difficulties facing attempts to define, assess, and regulate police work (see the summaries in Reiner, 1992a, chaps. 3 & 4, and Reiner, 1994a). They include the diffuse functions the police are called upon to perform, the high discretion inevitably afforded the streetlevel operatives, the low visibility of decisions to organizational (nominal) supervisors, the unpredictable danger encountered that militates against after-the-event second-guessing of split-second choices, and the inherently conflict-ridden character of most of police interventions making a consensus on the "right" outcome or manner of handling any interaction a matter of perspective. These findings have been repeated in research in Britain, North America, and elsewhere, suggesting it is not a parochial and contingent phenomenon but bound up with the exigencies of policed contemporary urban societies.

These qualities of police work create a traditional culture within the organization that is fiercely protective of autonomy and discretion. Assessment of "good" work is something that can really only be done by the seasoned professional, with experience of the difficult, ambiguous, unpredictable, messy, often intractable, nature of many of the problems tackled.

Three interrelated and fundamental problems face evaluation of police performance, as suggested by the Anglo-American research literature. First, the circumstances of routine police work create substantial practical problems for any post hoc assessments of encounters. This arises from the necessarily dispersed nature of patrol work and indeed many aspects of crime investigation. The low visibility of everyday policing creates an inevitably wide practical discretion whether or not this is regarded as legitimate or desirable. This bedevils attempts to regulate policing, whether these are concerned to control potential malpractice through complaints systems and the like, or to ensure effective crime control or service delivery. Thus the first problem is the practical one of establishing what happened in incidents with no objective record without having been there.

Low visibility would not matter so much if most police work had clearly definable, visible, and measurable outcomes or products. However, many of the disputed but crucial aspects of police work, for good or bad, concern issues of process not product, *how* the task was done rather than what discernible outcome (if any) there is. Crime control work does lend itself more readily to assessment, because successful investigation has a clear end product—the detection of an offender, and prevention activities should produce a discernible drop in offending. The difficulties of measuring either end product are legion and will be discussed later. However, they pale into insignificance compared to the problems of assessing the quality of service or peacekeeping work. The only conceivable end product is a counterfactual: the avoidance of disorder that would have occurred but for the police intervention. Assessments of quality must rest on evaluations of the *process,* the way an encounter is handled, rather than its product or outcome.

How can the quality of a process be ascertained after the event? The ideal would be a continuously running videotape recording all encounters from all possible vantage points. Short of this we are forced to rely on partial records (audiotape, paper forms), or the accounts of participants or witnesses, which are themselves partial in the double sense of being both incomplete and biased from a particular perspective.

In interpreting such accounts to arrive at an assessment of police performance in an encounter, we run up against the third distinguishing characteristic of routine police work that makes its evaluation peculiarly problematic. In all private enterprise organizations and most public services there is one party whose viewpoint is uniquely privileged: the recipient of the product or service—the customer or client. They are the intended beneficiary of the activity and their assessment of the quality of service is the bottom line. Policing is unique in the nature of the prime service it offers: peacekeeping, the regulation of conflict by a variety of means but with the ultimate resource of legitimate force (Stephens & Becker, 1994). As the popular U.K. TV police series *The Bill* recently put it in an episode title: "Force is part of the service." Policing is largely about conflict, so there is inevitably a multiplicity of viewpoints with none being inherently privileged. Deciding which account to believe is to take a partisan stance in a controversy. Policing the police, like policing itself, is an exercise of power rather than objective reason. The relativism of the Bob Dylan line, "You're right from your side and I'm right from mine," applies to most policing situations. Thus the most intractable problem confronting the construction of systems for police performance assessment is the inescapably political character of most police work, rendering the criteria for evaluation essentially contested concepts. The police, in short, are "streetcorner politicians" (Muir, 1977).

THE CONTESTED GOALS OF POLICING

Police performance can be assessed only in relation to particular goals and criteria of success. Deciding what the objectives and priorities of the police should be, however, is (as the previous section concluded) inevitably a contested, political matter. This suggests that there cannot be any definitive, once-and-for-all-time statement of the goals of policing. Ultimately specifying these has to be the prerogative of democratic processes of governance, and has to alter to reflect shifting balances of public opinion as registered by elections.

Yet in the British tradition of policing (which has been the dominant influence in the United States, Canada, Australia, and most other common-law countries) there has over the past couple of centuries been a fair degree of consensus about the basic objectives of policing. Often labeled "policing by consent," a number of authoritative statements from official commissions of inquiry and the like have echoed the fundamental approach articulated first in 1829 for the new Metropolitan Police in London by Sir Robert Peel and the first two Commissioners, Rowan and Mayne (I have traced the conditions of emergence of this tradition in detail in Reiner, 1992c, chaps. 1 & 2). Until the last couple of years (when the previous British government attempted to substitute a much narrower conception of the police mission) there has been no significant dissent among policymakers (although the rank-and-file police culture has always espoused a different idea of what is "real" police work).

This traditional conception of the purposes of policing has been neatly summed up in the 1991 Statement of Common Purposes and Values issued by the Association of Chief Police Officers (ACPO) in conjunction with the other staff associations. This unprecedented attempt by the police staff associations to develop an explicit mission statement was a reaction to a perceived loss of popular support and legitimacy for the police over a number of years. It amounted to a "Back to the Future" approach, reinvoking in modern terms the principles attributed to the tradition Peelian British police model. This was also the approach taken a decade earlier by Lord Scarman in his report on the Brixton disorders (Scarman, 1981), which became the politically correct orthodoxy for the Home Office and the police elite in the 1980s (Reiner, 1991, chap. 6).

The 1991 "Police Service Statement of Common Purposes and Values (England and Wales)"—there is a separate but similar text for Scotland—is the most explicit official rendering from within the police of their own conception of their mission. It reads in full:

> The purpose of the Police Service is to uphold the law fairly and firmly: to prevent crime; to pursue and bring to justice those who break the law; to keep the Queen's Peace; to protect, help and reassure the community: and to be seen to do all this with integrity, common sense and sound judgement.
>
> We must be compassionate, courteous and patient, acting without fear or favour or prejudice to the rights of others. We need to be professional, calm and restrained in the face of violence and apply only that force which is necessary to accomplish our lawful duty.
>
> We must strive to reduce the fears of the public and, so far as we can, to reflect their priorities in the action we take. We must respond to well-founded criticism with a willingness to change.

The Statement of Common Purposes and Values is a rearticulation of the traditional British police idea in which a single organization is responsible for a range of functions—crime prevention, law enforcement, peacekeeping, and order maintenance—and a diffuse service role "to protect, help and reassure the community." In a comparative perspective, the British police have been unique in combining this omnibus mandate in a single organization. Over the past century, however, a complex bureaucratic structure of internal specialization has developed, with particular units and departments concentrating on aspects of the overall task.

MEASURING GOAL ATTAINMENT

The degree of difficulty in assessing individual police performance varies according to different tasks and specialisms. Crime prevention activity is of three basic kinds. The original Peelian conception was that the police would prevent crime by regular uniform patrol deterring would-be offenders by their actual or expected intervention—a scarecrow function. This cannot be evaluated at the individual level as the role is basically just to provide a visible presence. In recent years this scarecrow concept has been augmented by two further, more proactive, styles of prevention (in addition to the detective role, which is intended to prevent crimes through actual or potential apprehension of offenders; cf. Bottoms, 1990; Pease, 1994). The main contemporary conceptions of crime prevention are: target hardening and other forms of situational crime prevention; and community crime prevention. Situational crime prevention efforts by the police tend to be located in specialist departments. The officers in these offer expert advice on hardening potential targets of crime by recommending forms of security equipment and so on. Community crime prevention projects initiated by or involving the police are normally aspects of a broader community policing style. They involve a variety of activities to provide facilities for potential offenders (especially young people) to engage in legitimate activities, to enlist citizen cooperation in such projects as Neighborhood Watch or volunteer patrols, or various types of multiagency cooperation such as police-schools liaison schemes. Assessments of such activities at an organizational level are possible by rigorous before-and-after testing of the impact of such schemes, attempting to hold constant other significant variables as much as is possible. Evaluating individual performance by output measures cannot be done meaningfully since it is likely that any one officer's effect on any indicators of crime will be minimal. Thus individual crime prevention performance measures are usually of an input kind: How many homes have been advised by a specialist crime prevention officer? How many Neighborhood Watch schemes has a community constable initiated? Tangential as these are, they are probably the most that can be achieved.

The area of individual performance where the most work has been done to develop means of measurement is crime detection. The politically most significant index of police work remains the clear-up rate, although the pitfalls that vitiate it to a point of virtual meaninglessness have long been known to policymakers, police, and researchers alike. Yet in England, at any rate, the regular publication by the Home Office of the clear-up rates for each police force area remains a source of pride to those who appear relatively successful, while the losers resort to plausible but politically rather ineffective arguments about the inadequacies of the figures.

The problems of the clear-up rate are evident. The numerator, crimes deemed to have been "cleared up," is vague and subject to considerable massaging of the figures by police, as crimes can be claimed to have been cleared up on evidence falling far short of what is necessary for prosecution, let alone conviction. The denominator, the number of crimes "known to the police," is subject to all the well-known problems of official crime statistics as measures of offending (Maguire, 1994). The ratio between the two can vary for reasons other than shifts in the quality of police investigative work. The most obvious is that if recorded crime rates increase relative to police numbers and resources (as they have for the past four decades), then the clear-up rate necessarily falls, ceteris paribus, even if police efficiency is stable or improving.

Apart from technical limitations, the clear-up rate is highly vulnerable to police massaging to achieve apparent improvements, either by tactics to accumulate meaningless clear-ups such as prison visits to convicted offenders in order to bargain favors for confessions, by "cuffing" crimes reported to the police in order to keep the denominator of recorded crime low, or by concentrating on crimes that are 100% self-clearing such as vice offenses where offenders are detected simultaneously with the discovery of the offense. In recent years, a series of scandals about police massaging of figures has surfaced in the United Kingdom. The most notorious occurred in Kent, where it was revealed that detectives would engage in corrupt practices such as sitting in cafes noting the license numbers of passing cars, record them as reported stolen, and then some time later claim they had been recovered, while the unsuspecting owners remained blissfully unaware of their supposed victimization. Research has shown that such tactics are just the revealed tip of a subterranean tradition of playing the numbers game (Young, 1991, chap. 5).

During the later 1980s, much attention was given to the development of more adequate performance measures for police work, above all by Her Majesty's Inspectorate of Constabulary (HMI; Weatheritt, 1986, 1993b) and the Audit Commission (Audit Commission, 1990, 1993). While trying to develop indicators of noncrime work as well, most attention was given to improving upon simple clear-up rates as indices of investigative performance. The Audit Commission pointed to the desirability of relating clear-ups to the number of police rather than the crime rate, as well as tightening the criteria for counting clear-ups and assessing the degree of skill required for various types of crime cleared up. Despite the development of more sophisticated matrices of performance indicators for assessing police work for the regular reviews by HMI and other internal purposes, the clear-up rate remained the most significant politically.

In the early 1990s a number of reforming chief constables attempted to clean up the way their forces processed their crime figures, most prominently

Paul Condon when he was in Kent prior to his elevation to the Commissionership of the Metropolitan Police. While acquiring reputations for professionalism, which did not hurt their careers, such chiefs paid the price of an apparent decline in clear-up rates. In the past couple of years, the government's package of reforms aiming at a more "business-like" police force have restored to preeminence the numbers game in its most simple-minded form, with proposals to develop league tables with crime, clear-up rates, and response times as the key variables.[1]

Given the sanctions contained in the new employment conditions recommended by Sheehy, police officers at all levels will have to concentrate their minds and activities on doing well on these figures, or suffer financially and perhaps even lose their jobs. We will be back to the numbers game with a vengeance. Recent crime figures indicate this may already have started to happen. The officially recorded crime rate showed an all-time record drop of 6%, duly celebrated by Ministers as a triumph for their get-tough law-and-order policies. However, the British Crime Survey showed a continuing rise in victimization. The main explanation of the discrepancy was that the proportion of offenses reported to the police by victims had declined, but so had the proportion of reports that were recorded by the police. A plausible hypothesis is that the increased salience of declining crime levels and improved clear-up rates to individual officers as well as the police organization as a whole has led to a revival of "cuffing" to boost the figures purporting to measure performance.

With regard to crime work, far more sophisticated measures than crude crime and clear-up rates have developed, even if current government policy involves a renaissance of the simplest figures. The same cannot be said of noncrime work, however, in particular peacekeeping. Although the Audit Commission and HMI are acutely aware of the need to measure the full range of police work, and have done much to develop indices of performance across the range of activities (Weatheritt, 1993b), these still have two crucial limitations. First, all the effort to date has been on developing indices of force rather than of individual performance. Second, even in these terms most of the indicators are of forms of input, not the quality of the process or outcome of police activity. For example, as measures of response to public calls, the indicators used by HMI include the proportion of calls responded to within given target times and the number of accidents en route. The only outcome measures are based on surveys of public satisfaction. Given the problem mentioned above—that most police encounters involve someone being policed against expressed satisfaction of people—calling the police is only a partial indication of the quality of policing.

The few examples in the observational literature on police patrol work that do attempt to tackle this problem indicate the daunting complexity of defining, yet alone evaluating, good quality peacekeeping. A neglected work, but the first to attempt an analysis of the characteristics of good policing was William Ker Muir, Jr.'s, *Police: Streetcorner Politicians* (Muir, 1977). This was based on closely detailed observation of 28 patrol officers in a U.S. city. Muir sees the essence of police work as the use or potential use of coercive power to maintain the peace in a variety of situations of interpersonal conflict (although Bittner's work is not explicitly referred to by Muir, his conception of policing has clear affinities to the perspective developed in Bittner, 1974, which has been very influential in the research literature). The quality of an officer's handling of encounters is attributed to how he copes with the "paradoxes of coercive power."

The good cop, argues Muir, has to develop two virtues. "Intellectually, he has to grasp the nature of human suffering. Morally, he has to resolve the contradiction of achieving just ends with coercive means" (Muir, 1977, pp. 3-4). The cop's intellectual vision may become "cynical," defined as having a dualistic vision of people as "us" versus "them," and being fault-finding and individualistic. The good cop, however, is one who is able to develop a "tragic" vision, seeing all mankind as of one unitary substance and potential moral value; regarding action as complexly produced by chance, will, and circumstance; and recognizing the important but fragile nature of human interdependence. Moral understanding may be "integrated," that is, able to accommodate the exercise of coercion within an overall moral code; or "conflictual," where it creates guilt because it is not related to basic moral principles. Combining both dimensions produces a fourfold typology of police officers: the "avoider" (cynical perspective + conflictual morality) who tends to shirk duties; the "reciprocator" (tragic perspective + conflicted morality) who hesitates to use coercive power even when it is appropriate; the "enforcer" (cynical perspective + integrated morality) who acts in the heat of conflicts with violence and without understanding the need for appropriate restraint; and the "professional" (tragic perspective + integrated morality) who is the "good" cop, able to handle coercive force when it is essential and unavoidable, but also able to exercise discretion suitably adjusted to a sensitive, compassionate, and wise assessment of characters and circumstances. This officer is capable of deploying violence where necessary in a principled way, but is adept at verbal and other skills that enable solutions to be achieved without coercive force whenever possible. Muir's analysis is subtle and insightfully illustrated by detailed interpretations of observed incidents. It underlines the complexity of assessing individual peacekeeping performance. Far from being measurable by some unambiguous indicators, the argument implies that the "good" cop can be identified only by a searching viva in moral philosophy!

The study that most explicitly attempts to analyze head on the necessary ingredients for specifying and identifying the quality of patrol work in a more practical way is by Bayley and Bittner (1984). Bayley and Bittner argue convincingly that "only by developing canons for better/worse, proper/improper, more/less useful patrol action can policing become truly professional" (p. 56). Yet their detailed analysis of the complex ingredients of decision making in a couple of routine and commonly occurring police interventions (domestic disputes and proactive traffic stops) illustrates the formidable obstacles to formulating adequate measures of skill. The steps undertaken by a patrol officer dealing with an incident can be divided into three broad stages, Bayley and Bittner argue: contact, processing, and exit (p. 56).

Better or worse ways of dealing with each can be discerned, and each in turn is analyzable in terms of a set of decision points. Bayley and Bittner (1984) claim that at

> contact in domestic disputes, police may choose from at least nine different courses of action. As one would expect, these serve by and large to establish immediate control over events, to shift the axis of interaction from the disputants to the officers. The possible courses of action are: to listen passively to disputant(s), verbally restrain disputant(s), threaten physical restraint, apply physical restraint, request separation of disputants, impose separation on disputants, physically force separation, divert attention of disputants, or question to elicit the nature of the problem. (p. 45)

In processing the encounter, patrol officers face at least 11 other detailed tactical choices that are elaborated by Bayley and Bittner, and another 11 or more alternative options can be discerned in the way officers handle the exit from such disputes (p. 45; a vivid illustrative analysis of the subtle process of dealing with one such case is found in Chatterton, 1983). An almost equally formidable list of tactical choices is discerned in their analysis of traffic stops: 10 at contact, 7 at processing, and 11 at exit. Experienced patrol officers will argue fiercely about the best way of handling these situations, and while they might shelter behind the mantra that "experience" teaches what works best, there is really minimal basis for such claims. However, this applies a fortiori to the imposition of rules and procedures from above or from outside the organization that are not grounded in the disciplined testing and rigorous evaluation of recipe knowledge.

What Bayley and Bittner's analysis of the complexity of routine patrol discretionary decision making illustrates is that we are only in the infancy of being able to identify the elements of police work in detail. This is nonetheless the essential prerequisite for developing adequate specifications and assessments of the quality of individual police work. The hazards of proceeding without such a knowledge base are illustrated by the recent British experience of the Sheehy Committee, which will be discussed in the next section.

THE SHEEHY INQUIRY INTO POLICE RESPONSIBILITIES AND REWARDS: A CAUTIONARY CASE-STUDY

Throughout the 1980s and early 1990s, two contradictory pressures formed the former Conservative government's policing policies, and their shifting weight accounts for the twists and turns in this. Commitment to a tough stance on "law and order" was an important ingredient of Mrs. Thatcher's electoral victory in 1989, and this included as its centerpiece the strengthening of police resources, numbers, and powers. This was always in tension with the government's overall concern to limit and tightly regulate public expenditure. The general policies intended to achieve "value for money" in public services were applied to the police in principle as early as Home Office Circular 114 of 1983 on *Manpower, Effectiveness and Efficiency in the Police Service* (Reiner, 1992a, pp. 241-242, 258-259). The tough "law and order" approach prevailed over the economizing drive until the late 1980s.

The continuing rapid rise of recorded crime rates coupled with the expenditure demands of expanding police strength prompted a U-turn after the mid-1980s, with an espousal of more pragmatic policies centered around a variety of notions of crime prevention, encompassing both target hardening and community policing (Reiner & Cross, 1991). When this in turn failed to stem the apparently inexorable rise of crime rates, a new tack has developed since the early 1990s, under the two most recent Home Secretaries, Kenneth Clarke and Michael Howard. This is essentially a synthesis of tough "law and order" policies under the slogan "punishment works," with a package of police reforms.

The aim of the "reform" package is to streamline the police function by concentrating it on catching criminals as the overriding priority, and delivering this efficiently by running the organization on "business-like" lines

(Reiner, 1994a, pp. 751-755; Reiner & Spencer, 1993). The elements are contained in a variety of sources: the Sheehy Committee *Inquiry Into Police Responsibilities and Rewards* (Sheehy, 1993); the white paper, *Police Reform* (Home Office, 1993b); the *Police and Magistrates' Courts Act 1994,* which includes many of these proposals (albeit in attenuated form because of a savage mauling in both Houses of Parliament but especially by a number of former Conservative Home Secretaries); and an ongoing internal Home Office *Review of Core and Ancillary Tasks* (see Reiner, 1994b, for details).[2]

A central plank of the program is to try to enhance the performance not only of police organizations as a whole but of individual officers (of all ranks and specialisms) by introducing market disciplines and private enterprise management principles. The Sheehy Inquiry was the part of the package concentrated on this. The Inquiry was set up in July 1992 and reported in June 1993. Its terms of reference were to review the rank structure, remuneration, and conditions of service of the police, and to recommend changes

> to ensure:
> — rank structures and conditions of service, which reflect the current roles and responsibilities of police officers;
> — enough flexibility in the distribution of rewards to ensure that responsibilities and performance may be properly recognised in changing circumstances;
> — remuneration set and maintained at a level adequate to ensure the recruitment, retention and motivation of officers of the right quality. (Sheehy, 1993, p. 1)

The essence of the recommendations that resulted was to accomplish the efficient delivery of police work by subjecting it to market disciplines. All officers were to be placed on fixed-term contracts, and regular pay increases on an incremental scale were to be replaced by a system of performance-related pay (PRP). This aroused a storm of protest, above all from the police staff associations. The campaign by the Police Federation (the rank-and-file quasi-union) was the most vocal and high profile. Its centerpiece was a highly publicized mass rally at Wembley Stadium, which was addressed by representatives of ACPO, local government associations, and the Opposition parties. The protests by chief officers (individually and through ACPO) and superintendents were slightly more muted, but nonetheless unprecedented as a public condemnation of Conservative policies by senior police spokespersons.

The campaign gained much public and political support, and the beleaguered Home Secretary Michael Howard has attempted to emphasize the extent to which he has departed from the strict Sheehy package. Its essence remains largely intact, however, and the police are undoubtedly being sub-jected to a reorganization of conditions of service that can be called "ghost of Sheehy." Fixed-term appointments are being introduced for all senior ranks, and a system of PRP is being thrashed out at the Police Negotiating Board. Thus the pay of all officers, and the job security of senior officers, will depend on achieving precisely defined objectives as measured by a battery of indica-tors, largely emanating from the Home Office.

The heart of the Sheehy proposals was an elaborately constructed scheme for assessing individual police performance for the purpose of determining appropriate levels of PRP. These are set out in detail in Chapter 6 and Appendix XIX of the Report. In essence, each officer would be subject to annual appraisal leading to placement in a ranked grid in terms of five performance categories ranging from "outstanding" to "unsatisfactory" (Sheehy, 1993, p. 58). Pay levels would depend upon this performance mea-sure, together with the results of grading: the scope of the role performed by the individual; the degree of difficulty of the "policing circumstances" worked in (e.g., inner-city vs. rural location, etc.); and the particular experience and skills relevant to the role that the individual had acquired (Sheehy, 1993, p. 43). There was much controversy about the problems of assessing each of these elements in any objective way, but the performance assessment compo-nent was widely regarded as the most problematic.

The Sheehy recommended scheme illustrates the problems of individual police performance assessment almost by a reductio ad absurdum. There is a complex structure of apparent objectivity and scientism. An elaborate grid has to be completed by assessors, with the individual's agreed objectives specified as well as their attainment in terms of nationally and/or locally specified indicators of the "principal accountabilities" (the "main enduring tasks" associated with each role in the organization). It is accepted that the summary of the individual's competence overall cannot be a simple mechanical scoring of the individually measured items but must be produced by the line manager in "narrative form" (Sheehy, 1993, p. 57). Nonetheless, the objective of the exercise is to produce an unambiguous single overall performance rating (p. 57) that will determine the individual's level of pay.

What the presentation almost covers over is the inescapably subjective element in evaluating the quality of work in the core function of policing, peacekeeping patrol work, for reasons elaborated in the preceding section of this chapter. In the end, however, this is implicitly conceded by the Sheehy Report itself. Thus Para.6.39 states that line managers should "not be con-strained by any predefined weighting. In a very results orientated role, performance in terms of objectives and principal accountabilities might carry a heavier weighting than in a role where the way things are done is more important" (Sheehy, 1993, p. 57). In other words, while there may be a relatively clear and measurable end product for some parts of the police organization (e.g., traffic, much internal administration, and, perhaps most important, crime investigation), for much police work (notably peacekeeping) it is the *process* not the *product* that is crucial. This would seem to drive a coach-and-horses through any rigid scheme of individual performance assessment such as Sheehy proposed.

The lesson of this cautionary tale is twofold. The introduction of any such scheme to enhance individual and/or group accountability will be likely to encounter the understandable opposition of occupational interest groups and this requires delicate political handling. However, this will be fatally incapacitated to the extent that the scheme does not acknowledge fully the complexities and ambiguities of most routine police work, as demonstrated by the observational research literature discussed earlier. As stated earlier, the portrait of police work and culture painted by North American researchers is broadly analogous to the British data. The lessons of this negative object lesson provided by the previous British government's reforms ought to be heeded in the United States and Canada as well, where similar political and fiscal pressures might tempt policymakers down similar paths.

CONCLUSIONS

Assessment of individual police performance is not only desirable as the atomic basis of democratic accountability, but is inevitable. De facto, it is continuously going on, formally when management makes personnel decisions about commendations, complaints, discipline, selection, and promotion; and informally in the culture of the rank-and-file police themselves and the approval or censure accorded colleagues and their actions.

What the preceding arguments have underlined is the complex character of such judgments, and the largely subjective and systematic basis on which they are made. While some aspects of police work may lend themselves to relatively precise assessment in terms of an end product, the most common police activities can be evaluated only in terms of the quality of the process involved. Because they are largely about conflict regulation, there will inescapably be competing viewpoints about the criteria for evaluation. Thus assessment can never be on a precisely calibrated scale, such as Sheehy attempted. Such efforts can only be counterproductive, arousing rank-and-file opposition and to the extent they are backed up by inescapable sanctions, diverting energies into manipulating the figures rather than doing effective work. Even in relation to work with an end product like crime detection, assessment requires some estimation of the difficulty of particular tasks, the "value added" by the officer's skill and effort, not just whether there was a "result."

Thus evaluation of police work involves inescapable value and qualitative judgments. It cannot be sensibly aimed at constructing a continuous calibrated scale such as would be required for finely tuned PRP schemes such as Sheehy's. At best all that could be reasonably aspired to are allocations of individuals into very rough and crude categories: Outstanding achievements and/or potential, broadly satisfactory, totally unacceptable. Yet for most practical purposes this is all that is needed: in order to make the crucial and unavoidable management decisions about who must be sanctioned negatively or positively, who must be fired or otherwise disciplined, who merits selection for particular tasks or promotion.

The way forward requires some moves by police policymakers and managers and by police researchers. The former will have to abandon the private enterprise chimera of precise payment by performance. The latter will have to take forward the pioneering work of Muir and of Bayley and Bittner in the United States, and others elsewhere, and develop the understandings of what precisely is entailed in good police performance.

NOTES

1. The popular comedian Ben Elton did a sketch that vividly punctured the pretensions of league tables for police performance (league tables rank soccer and other sports teams in order of performance): "If I get mugged in Kilburn High Road [an inner-city London area]," he mused, "can I ring up Devon and Cornwall and say 'I hear your detection rate is ace, please come and help me!' Who are these league tables going to help? Only the villains! I can see them reading them every week and saying 'Look Reg: Sussex's clear-up rate has gone down this week. Start up the motor we're off to Brighton!' "

2. The Police Foundation in conjunction with the Policy Studies Institute has also set up an *Independent Committee on Police Roles and Responsibilities* to provide an independent voice in the debate (cf. Newburn & Morgan, 1994).

4

EVALUATING SERVICE DELIVERY OF POLICE AGENCIES

Suggestions for Focus and Strategy

Jerome E. McElroy

In July of 1984, the New York City Police Department (NYPD) introduced an experimental program in one of its 75 precincts. The Community Patrol Officer Program, or CPOP as it came to be known, represented the Department's initial effort to introduce the principles of community policing into its regular patrol operations. It was intended that the department would make decisions about the future of the program after assessing the feasibility of implementing it over the course of a year. In fact, the Commissioner decided to expand it to the other precincts after the pilot had been operating for only 3 months. The expansion began in January 1985 and was completed in September 1988.

Staff from the Vera Institute of Justice, including this author, designed the program under a consultant agreement with the Department, and designed and implemented, over the next few years, a rather comprehensive study of the program's operations and its effects in six precincts.[1] This chapter summarily describes the evaluation that was conducted, and culls from the experience some lessons that may be useful to others attempting similar studies in other agencies.

The approach taken to evaluating police service delivery must vary with the type of service being studied. Obviously, the approach used to describe and assess the effectiveness of an agency's performance in responding to service calls would be quite different from that used to study the agency's investigative activities. Thus, I will begin with a brief description of the program we undertook to study.

THE CPOP PROGRAM

CPOP was New York's version of community-oriented, problem-solving policing, which was then understood to be a strategy for focusing, organizing, delivering, and assessing police services. As such, it aimed to: correct problems of street crime, drug dealing, and disorder at the neighborhood level; reduce mutual ignorance, mutual suspicion, and mutual perceptions of unresponsiveness between the police and citizenry on the neighborhood level; reduce the sense of fear and insecurity that people experience in the city's neighborhoods; and assist communities to use their own resources in efforts to control local problems of crime and disorder.

The program sought to pursue these goals through creating the Community Patrol Officer role to be performed by a single police officer (the CPO) assigned continuously to a portion of the precinct, referred to as a "beat," and charged with establishing working relationships with residents, merchants, and local organizations, to initiate a local problem-solving process with them intended to correct, or alleviate, the major crime and disorder problems with which they were concerned. The CPO was to function as:

- a *Planner,* assisting the community to carry out a process of problem identification, analysis, and the development of corrective strategies
- a *Problem Solver,* facilitating the implementation of corrective strategies that, ideally, would use several types of resources including the officer himself or herself, other police resources, other public and private service agencies, and citizens and organizations working in the neighborhood
- a *Community Organizer,* identifying and motivating existing resources to become involved in the problem-solving process, and stimulating organizing efforts when existing organizational resources are insufficient
- an *Information Exchange Link,* providing the Department with information about neighborhood problems, fears, sensitivities, resources, and proposals for improving the quality of local life, while providing the citizenry with timely information

about their problems, the pertinent activities and limitations of the police, and about other public and private resources that might be brought to bear on neighborhood needs

A CPOP unit was established in each precinct consisting of 8 to 10 officers, each assigned to a specific beat, and all working under the direction of a CPOP sergeant. In turn, the sergeant was responsible directly to the commanding officer of the precinct. Although members of the unit sometimes worked together in addressing a neighborhood problem, when that was not the case, each officer was expected to move about his or her beat alone and on foot.

In its design, the CPO's role was dramatically different from that of the conventional patrol officer, whose typical tour was consumed by riding, with a partner, to respond to calls anywhere in the precinct, at the direction of a central dispatcher. In fact, to assure that CPOs would have the time and flexibility to perform their role, they were taken off the "911 queue," given handheld radios, and instructed to monitor dispatches and respond, usually as backup, when they had the time to do so.

The sergeant was expected to provide both procedural and substantive guidance to the officers in implementing the problem-solving process, and to represent their interests and concerns within the precinct. This included working with other units in the precinct and with the precinct commander to elicit their involvement in carrying out the problem-solving strategies developed by the CPOs.

Eighty hours of training were provided to the CPOs before a unit began operation. They were expected to maintain "Beat Books" describing various features of their beats and containing monthly work plans that identified the principal crime and order problems on which they concentrated, and the corrective strategies they attempted to implement. These work plans were to serve as a problem-solving tool for the officer and a supervisory tool for the sergeant, who was expected to approve all work plans and to review progress each month.

THE GOALS AND METHODS OF THE RESEARCH

The research was guided by both practical and theoretical interests. The department hoped it would provide information that would enable the program managers to improve CPOP operations even before the research was completed. The research staff hoped that it would also shed some light on some of the questions that police scholars had raised concerning community-oriented and problem-solving policing. The principal research questions included:

1. Can regular police officers implement all four dimensions of the CPO role? What are the major obstacles to implementation, and how do the officers adjust to them?
2. How do they react to the role in terms of their job satisfaction and their image of themselves as police officers; what features of the role do they like or dislike especially?
3. How do CPOs attempt to establish relationships with the community and involve community representatives in the problem-solving process? How effective are they at this aspect of the role?
4. How well do the officers implement the problem-solving process? Are particular aspects of that process more difficult for the officers to master than others, and, if so, why?
5. What kinds of neighborhood problems are identified using this process? What kinds of strategies are developed by the CPOs, and what strategies appear most effective in dealing with particular problems?
6. What sort of challenges to conventional models of supervision are posed by the community-oriented, problem-solving aspects of the CPO role? How are these challenges met, if at all?
7. What is the impact of CPOP, if any, on the volume of calls-for-service, and on robbery and burglary complaints?
8. What is the nature of community reaction to the program?

To address these questions, the staff developed a comprehensive research strategy that focused detailed attention on 6 of the 37 precincts in which the CPO program was operating at that time. Together, the research precincts offered a notable degree of racial, ethnic, and socioeconomic heterogeneity, and they appeared to have reasonably well-functioning CPOP units at the time of the selection.

A full-time field researcher was assigned to each research precinct for 6 months to observe the activities of each of the unit members, as well as the problematic conditions in the community, the strategy implementation efforts of the officers (and the effects of those efforts on the targeted problems), and the interactions between the CPOs and other police personnel in the precinct.

Structured interviews with each of the officers were conducted at the beginning and at the end of the data collection period. The initial interviews focused on the officer's experiences in the department prior to joining CPOP; the reasons for deciding to join the program; his or her knowledge of and expectations about the program prior to joining; the officer's perceptions of and attitudes toward the community prior to becoming a CPO; the features of the program that the officer liked and those he or she disliked especially; those aspects of the role with which the officer had most difficulty, and why he or she believed them to be difficult; and what the officer wanted to be doing and the rank he or she hoped to hold in the department 5 years in the future.

At the end of the 6-month data collection period, another structured interview was conducted with each CPO. This interview sought some similar perceptual and attitudinal data in the hopes of determining whether any measurable change had occurred over that period. This Time 2 interview also solicited information regarding how the officer distributed his or her time across a number of tasks associated with the role; whether the role was preferred to that of the regular RMP officer and why; whether the officer thought that the program produced benefits for the community and/or for the department; and the steps the officer would like to see taken to improve the program.

The field researchers were instructed to identify three to five crime or quality-of-life problems that each CPO considered as priority concerns in his or her beat. For that purpose, the field researchers reviewed the officer's beat book and then asked the officer directly to designate such problems. A structured data collection instrument, called the "Problem Process Record" (PPR), was completed by the field researcher on the priority problems that each officer identified and worked on within his or her beat over the course of the 6-month data collection period. The PPR called for the collection of information about the nature of the problem identified and the process by which it was identified; the nature of the analytic process that the officer carried out with respect to the problem, and the major findings that it produced; the nature of the strategy that the officer designed to correct the problem and the extent to which representatives of the community were involved in design and implementation; the extent to which the components of the strategy were implemented and what, if anything, the officer did when others were failing to carry out their responsibilities within the strategy; and the apparent impact of the strategy on the problem identified.

The research staff attempted to use five indicators of impact on the problem: the officer's assessment of impact; the sergeant's assessment; the researcher's assessment; the assessments provided by a small sample of residents and merchants who lived and/or operated in immediate proximity to the problem; and statistical or archival data where pertinent.

Using the PPRs as data sources, a scale was constructed for assessing the problem-solving performance of each of the officers on each of the problems with which he or she dealt. The scale uses subscales for different dimensions of the task: problem identification and analysis, strategy development, strategy implementation, and community involvement.

While we expected to encounter notable individual successes and failures, the research sought to describe the median performance level that might be expected when hundreds of CPOs were called on to perform the problem-solving role. This required a focus on elements of the problem-solving performance that were performed well and those that were performed poorly, in order to suggest modifications that could produce generally higher levels of performance.

Nor was it our intention to describe and assess various strategies for addressing particular problems. That would have required considerably more time and resources than we had available, as well as a considerably larger pool of problems to study. Of course, we recognized the value of such "resource manuals" for the officer in the beat, and we recommended that the department expend the effort required to produce them in the future.

In-depth interviews were conducted with the sergeants and the commanding officers toward the end of the research period in each precinct. The sergeants were also asked to assess the overall performance of their officers on a questionnaire that the research staff had prepared for that purpose.

The uniqueness of the CPO role in the NYPD presented a real challenge to supervisors and command staff. The freedom of movement, the opportunity to work tours that were not part of a standard chart, the unobstructed access to residents and merchants in the community, the lack of preconceived definitions of the problems the officer should address or the strategies and tactics that should be employed, the expanded discretion available to the officer, and the detachment from the central dispatching system were all features of the CPO role with which supervisors had no prior experience. Although it was clear that most conventional supervisory techniques were not applicable, the skills and techniques that were appropriate were not at all clear. Therefore, a good deal of the field researcher's time was devoted to observing the sergeants and discussing with them the challenges posed by the new role and the supervisory tactics they adopted in response. In addition, in-depth interviews about these and other matters were conducted with the sergeants and the precinct commanders at the end of the research period in each precinct.

Expanding contact between the police and the community, increasing police responsiveness to the major concerns of the community, and undertaking collaborative efforts to address community problems were prominent reasons for starting the CPOP program. In addition to describing the efforts made by the police to achieve these objectives, it was necessary to document perceptions and assessments held by community residents. For that purpose, the research team conducted a series of interviews with leaders in each precinct designed to determine: what they perceived to be the purposes and methods of CPOP; the extent of their awareness of the program's operations; the nature of the conventional street crime and quality-of-life problems in the community; what they perceived to be the police response to these problems before and after the advent of the program; and their perceptions of the effects of the program on these problems and on the general state of police/ community relations in the precinct.

Statistical information was collected on calls for services, robberies, and burglaries in the research precincts before and after the beginning of the CPOP program to determine whether there were any significant changes in these data corresponding to the presence of the program in the precincts.

Data describing some of the demographic characteristics of patrol officers in the department were collected from the personnel division to determine how and to what extent the officers in the research sample differed from their patrol colleagues in general. Data concerning civilian complaints made against the sample members were collected from the Civilian Complaint Review Board (CCRB), and data about corruption complaints against the officers were collected from the Internal Affairs Division.

Finally, members of the research staff, especially the research director, had frequent opportunities to interact with CPOs, supervising sergeants, and precinct commanders from many other precincts in which the program operated. These contacts, though largely informal, provided another source of information on the program. In some cases, they provided insights into program-related concerns that never appeared in the research precincts. In other instances, the contacts in the non-research precincts were helpful in estimating whether patterns observed in the research precincts were generally true elsewhere.

LESSONS LEARNED FOR FUTURE RESEARCH

While the findings from this research would be the appropriate matter for other forums, it is the evaluation experience itself, and the lessons taken from it, that are the focus of this chapter. There are five points that we would like to share in the hope of provoking a dialogue that might produce benefits for both researchers and practitioners.

Limitations of Traditional Approaches to Evaluation. CPOP was a vehicle for introducing the principles of community-oriented, problem-solving policing into the NYPD. It was composed of a series of best guesses as to how that might be done and what the effects of doing it might be. The CPO role was complex and unpredictable, making it virtually impossible to control for other factors that might affect police officer performance, community attitudes, the state of community problems, and the levels of street crime and calls for service. Even before-and-after comparisons were precluded by the timing of the research and the department's political and budgetary need to expand the program rapidly to all precincts. In the study of this multidimensional initiative for system reform, the experimental designs understandably prized by evaluation researchers were neither feasible nor appropriate.

This appears to be generally true for most community policing initiatives that are attempting anything more ambitious than attacking a well-defined problem with a specific, well-defined tactic that can surely be implemented by police officers. Typically, community policing initiatives are strategic as well as tactical, call for activities with which the actors have little or no prior experience, aim to create a whole series of changes in police behavior and in the community as prerequisites to achieving meaningful reductions in crime and fear, and, at least implicitly, envision a long path to those achievements.

All of this suggests that both researchers and program managers should abandon images of evaluation as a process aimed at providing a "bottom-line" assessment of a program's worth. Rather, what is needed is a program research strategy that will help the agencies to identify the whole range of assumptions that is embodied in their program (e.g., assumptions that the police can do collaborative problem solving, and that community residents will welcome and join in the effort), and to collect data needed by the managers to test and reflect on those assumptions. Research of this sort will also help to define the path that leads to the agency's goals, and to identify realistic interim markers that can indicate progress along the path. Such research must also focus carefully on what is actually done in the field to implement the initiative, and explain how and why it deviates from the program design. That information will enable managers to direct resources at the obstacles to implementation, or to revise the program design to make its implementation more feasible, or both.

This need for less traditional approaches to program evaluation is being recognized by others. During the Montreal Conference at which part of this chapter was presented, Clifford Shearing suggested that, despite its breadth, the concept of community policing unnecessarily limits concern with public safety and security to the public police. In Shearing's view, security is produced by local communities using all of their resources, formal and informal, public and private. He is translating this conception into social control strategies for local communities, and in discussing an appropriate approach to evaluating such an effort, he says,

> [It is not clear] whether we want evaluation in a kind of either/or: has this thing worked or failed. I think what I want to try and build is a process of reflection where people can see what they're doing all the time, as a sort of information feedback process—so building a reflective process to allow problem-solving.[2]

The Aspen Institute in New York is currently involved in an effort to develop evaluation models appropriate to studying their Comprehensive Community Initiatives, which resemble community policing system change efforts in their goals, their untested tactics, and their complex structures.[3]

The Annie E. Casey Foundation, in Baltimore, Maryland, is supporting several system change initiatives concerned with the delivery of services to children and families, and they are evolving rather interesting approaches to studying and assessing them.[4]

Those interested in studying the delivery of police services, especially delivery mechanisms that require or produce broader system change, may learn much from the work of both organizations.

The Pressing Need for Data Describing What Police Officers Actually Do. In the past, evaluations of social programs often concentrated their resources on measuring outcomes, and assumed that the intervention described in the program design was actually implemented. In other instances, programs with similar goals (e.g., reducing poverty) were grouped together for evaluating outcome, without first determining whether they were comparable operationally. This mistake can have disastrous consequences in a field as operationally diverse as community policing. We now know that there is typically a gap (often a very large gap) between the program design on paper and the program design as it is implemented in the field. Thus, knowing the details of operations is essential both to understanding what the actual intervention is, and to assessing its feasibility. Our experience in studying CPOP suggests that meeting this challenge is a good deal more difficult that it sounds.

The core of the CPO role was the implementation of the problem-solving process at the neighborhood level. To determine how and how well it was being implemented required the construction of a database describing: problems identified by the CPOs; the extent to which CPOs analyzed the dimensions of the problem; the strategies they proposed for alleviating the problem; the nature of the resources that the strategies sought to deploy; the extent to which the strategy was carried out; the efforts of the CPO to review implementation and effects and modify the strategy, if necessary; and the extent to which the CPO involved community residents and organizations throughout the process.

When the research strategy was designed, we assumed that all of that information could be taken from the officers' beat books, since the program encouraged them to use those books for that purpose. It was quickly apparent that most of the officers did not understand this to be the principal purpose of the beat book, disdained and largely ignored the requirement to maintain the beat book, and generally avoided writing anything other than the briefest notations regarding problems or the actions they took with respect to them. At the same time, our field researchers assured us that the typical officer was identifying problems, knew a fair amount about them, and was applying some effort to correct them. Therefore, we had to create a form, the Problem Process Record, for the field researchers to complete by examining the beat book for whatever information it contained; by talking with the CPO to elicit his or her knowledge, goals, and strategy for correcting the problem, as well as his or her perceptions regarding implementation of the strategy; and by recording the researcher's own observations concerning strategy implementation. It was the database created by this arduous process, on over 100 problems in approximately 60 beats, that enabled us to describe how the CPOs actually carried out the problem-solving activities that were at the center of their role.

The research called for more than simple description in this regard, however; judgments had to be made about how well the process was carried out—about what aspects of the process proved most difficult to the officers and why. To do that, we had to create a normative model of "good problem solving"[5] against which a team of "judges" from the research staff could measure actual performance of each of the officers on each of the problems. The model took the form of a series of scales that assessed the adequacy of problem identification and analysis, strategy development, strategy implementation, and community involvement in the process. There were no standardized scales available for this purpose at the time.

In any case, documenting actual practice in the field will be a difficult and demanding task for researchers and agency managers unless and until police managers and researchers develop a feasible means for doing it routinely. At the present time, such routine systems do exist for recording arrests and responses to service calls, although even these systems usually lack some of the detail one would need for assessing the quality of response. Recently, staff at the Vera Institute of Justice developed a computerized system, called an Electronic Beat Book, for documenting the problem-solving process used at the beat level. Although it was developed with specific reference to the operation in New York, others may want to consider its utility for their purpose.[6]

Measuring the Effects of Problem-Solving Strategies. In his provocative chapter titled "Community Policing and Police Organization Structure" (Chapter 9, this volume), Stephen D. Mastrofski distinguishes between the "technical and institutional" dimensions of the police environment, and claims that police organizations suffer from a weak "technical core" of knowledge about what works to alleviate specific problems under specific circumstances. In these terms, he sees community policing as essentially an effort at institutional reforms thought necessary as prerequisites for advancing the technology of controlling crime and disorder. While recognizing value in many of the institutional reforms promoted by community policing, Mastrofski argues for a strong focus on what officers actually do and how that affects the problems to which they respond. During the Montreal Conference, he said, "It's not that these structures don't matter, but they can't matter too much until we have a better handle on what works out there."[7]

Our emphasis on the importance of describing what police officers actually do is perfectly consistent with Mastrofski's call for research that enhances the technical core of policing. But our experience indicates just how demanding such research is. We agree, as well, on the importance of developing knowledge about what strategies work under what conditions, but our experience again underscores the difficulty involved in assessing the effects of problem-solving strategies, especially at the neighborhood level.

This is a particularly vexing problem in the context of a program as decentralized as CPOP. The problems cannot be anticipated in advance of the CPO's efforts in the beat; the priorities vary from one beat to another, as do the contexts in which the problems arise; the problem-solving strategies, which are supposed to be developed in response to the peculiarities of context, may also vary even though they may be addressing similar problems; for some problems, such as conventional street crimes, data describing their extent and characteristics are routinely collected, but for others, including most quality-of-life problems, this is not the case.

In the study of CPOP, we tried to use several indicators of impact for each problem. The strategy did not always work. Although the officer's assessment was not always positive, by itself it was suspect. Interestingly, the sergeant's assessments never challenged those of the officer, and were sometimes even more positive. Indeed, we concluded that the sergeant's assessment was the least useful of the five indicators. The field researcher's assessment seemed to be the most objective and informed, when it was available. On several occasions, however, the researcher had not had sufficient opportunity to observe the state of the problem and was reluctant to offer any assessment; in other cases (e.g., inside drug-trafficking locations), because of concern for the researcher's safety, he or she was not permitted to get close enough to make observations. Community residents and merchants directly affected by the problem offered apparently reliable assessments, except when they refused to say anything because of fear for their own safety. This was frequently the case when the problem involved drug trafficking. Finally, statistical data were useful when they were available.

Candidly, we were unsatisfied with our efforts to measure the impact of problem-solving strategies. To meet this challenge it may be necessary for police agencies to focus serially on major problems and the actions taken to correct them. This would require the agencies to make a long-term commitment to research and development using a wide variety of methods to assess impacts. In any case, there is a need for much more literature describing how others have addressed the methodological, logistical, and inferential problems posed by this challenge.

Measuring the Effects of Community Policing on Conventional Street Crime. We found a modest, short-term effect on robberies, and no significant effect on burglaries or the volume of calls for service. However, we were not satisfied with our measures for several reasons.

The principal difficulty has to do with the units of analysis. The underlying assumption of the program was that when this style of community policing was implemented effectively, it would produce reactions in the community (e.g., wider adoption of collective self-defense techniques, provision of more useful information to the police regarding problem locations and persons, greater use of informal means of social control) that would, in turn, deter or lessen various forms of street crime. But the quality of community policing may vary considerably from one beat to another, so that one ought not to expect these effects in beats where community policing is ineffectively implemented. This suggests that testing the effects on crime levels requires the compilation of both performance data and crime statistics by neighborhood. Department information systems may not lend themselves to that level of analysis, however. Even when they do, the actual number of selected offenses occurring in specific neighborhoods, within quarterly, or even annual, time periods, is often too small to permit reliable analysis.

In the CPOP study, these concerns led us to compare precinct level statistics for those precincts in which the program was operating with those in which it had not begun at the time of the research. However, we had no way of controlling for the quality of implementation in the precincts with the program, nor had we any way of controlling for exogenous factors that may have independently effected both the crime levels and the scheduling of CPOP implementation in the precincts. Moreover, the program assumes that it will take time before implementation reaches a reasonable level of effectiveness and before its intermediate effects are manifest in the community. Thus, neither the database nor the time period needed for an adequate test of CPOP's effects on the volume and forms of street crime were available at the time of the research.

Measuring the Community's Perceptions of the Program and Its Effects. Obviously, any research on a community policing initiative will make some effort to measure community perceptions. We suggest that the data collection strategy used should vary with the kinds of information sought, the purpose for which it is needed, and the resources available for collecting it.

The CPOP research was principally concerned with how the program was being implemented in the neighborhoods. The perceptions of community residents and merchants were needed, but we chose to collect those data through a series of interviews with community leaders, rather than through a random survey of community residents. People who were involved with various community groups were likely to have a broader perspective on community problems and to have knowledge of the nature and quality of local police operations. Prior experience with random surveys of community residents had revealed that only a relatively small proportion of the sample possessed any specific knowledge of changes in police operations. Thus, the focus on leaders was substantively appropriate at this point in the development of the CPOP program (see Vincent F. Sacco's interesting chapter on the ambiguities of community surveys in this arena in Chapter 7, this volume).

Once the initiative has been established and stabilized, researchers and program managers would wish to monitor changes in the levels of fear and discontent, as well as the perceived seriousness of previously identified problems and the public's assessment of the quality of police services. For such purposes, repeated panel or random surveys are more appropriate, as well as being considerably more expensive.

Cost considerations can be especially important in relation to the chosen geographical unit of analysis; that is, the city, the precinct, or the beat. The need for more local and specific information requires samples drawn from smaller geographical units. Generalizing from a random sample of 250 residents may provide valid and reliable information about a precinct, but offer no reliable insights into specific neighborhoods within the precinct. To be usable for both purposes, a precinct-wide sample would have to be considerably larger and a good deal more expensive.

Although these are important considerations for a special research project, they are even more important for a department or a city that wishes to establish a continuing process of monitoring community perceptions as part of a performance measurement system. It would be valuable, therefore, to compare the yield from a survey that is large enough to provide reliable information on the neighborhood level with that from the use of focus groups in the same neighborhoods. If the utility of the information is comparable, the focus group strategy would be considerably less expensive for a department to use repeatedly.

Community policing remains a promising corporate strategy for changing the services, accountability systems, and internal organizational forms of police agencies. It should be studied extensively over the next decade, especially in the United States and Canada. Our experience suggests that such research should be designed: to examine the very broad range of assumptions that are explicit and implicit in these initiatives; to produce a much more detailed understanding of how police officers carry out these community policing roles in the streets, and the effects of their actions on the problems they address; and to understand a good deal more about the community's expectations of the police and its willingness to collaborate in producing higher levels of security and order at the neighborhood level. Finally, we stress the need for a more intensive dialogue among researchers and police managers on the strategies, designs, instruments, and analytical tools being used in conducting such research.

NOTES

1. Substantial portions of the language used here to describe the program and the research strategy have been taken from the report of the research; see McElroy, Cosgrove, and Sadd (1993).

2. Clifford Shearing's remarks at the Workshop on Evaluating Police Service Delivery, International Centre for Comparative Criminology, Montreal, Canada, November 2-4, 1994; see "Transcript of Discussions," p. 173.

3. The Aspen Institute, "Round-table on Comprehensive Community Initiatives for Children and Families: The Evaluation Steering Committee," 345 East 46th Street, New York, NY 10017, 1994.

4. Douglas Nelson, "Reforming Systems, Reforming Evaluation"; speech given at evaluation conference sponsored by the Annie E. Casey Foundation of Baltimore, Maryland, September 28, 1994.

5. There are several models of the problem-solving process in policing. The CPOP program developed one of its own, which is described in McElroy et al. (1993). This was shaped appreciably by Goldstein (1990) and Eck and Spelman (1989).

6. Inquiries can be directed to Sarah Lyon at the Vera Institute of Justice, 377 Broadway, New York, NY 10013; (212) 334-1300.

7. Stephen Mastrofski's remarks at the Workshop on Evaluating Police Service Delivery, International Centre for Comparative Criminology, Montreal, Canada, November 2-4, 1994—see "Transcript of Discussions," p. 139.

5

COMMUNITY PARTICIPATION AND COMMUNITY POLICING

Wesley G. Skogan

This chapter examines the role of the public in community policing. Every definition of community policing shares the idea that the police and the community must work together to define and develop solutions to problems (Sadd & Grinc, 1994). One rationale for public involvement is the belief that police alone can neither create nor maintain safe communities. They can help by setting in motion voluntary local efforts to prevent disorder and crime; in this role, they are adjuncts to community crime prevention efforts such as Neighborhood Watch, target hardening, and youth and eco-

AUTHOR'S NOTE: This research was supported in part by grant No. 91-DB-CX-0017 awarded by the Bureau of Justice Assistance and by award No. 93-IJ-CX-KO14 from the National Institute of Justice, Office of Justice Programs, U.S. Department of Justice, Office of Justice Programs, U.S. Department of Justice. Points of view or opinions contained within this document are those of the author and do not necessarily represent the official position or policies of the U.S. Department of Justice.

nomic development programs. A common justification for diverting resources from responding to 911 calls is that community policing will ultimately prevent problems from occurring in the first place, and that many that still do will be dealt with locally without police assistance, or by agencies other than the police (Trojanowicz, 1986).

Community involvement is also frequently justified by pointing to the growing customer orientation of public service agencies. It is argued that by opening themselves to citizen input the police will become more knowledgeable about, and responsive to, the varying concerns of different communities. Police already knew that even the conventional crimes that are reported vary from place to place in mix as well as by frequency, and that many of the tactics developed downtown in response to media or political pressures do not make sense in particular areas. However, "one size fits all" is too frequently the way policies are tried on in police departments. Another strand of this argument is that police have "over-professionalized" themselves and their mission, and as a result systematically overlook many pressing community concerns because they lie outside of their narrowly defined mandate (Skogan, 1990a). Because these concerns (which can range from public drinking to building abandonment) frequently have deleterious consequences for the communities involved, expanding the scope of the police mandate by making them more "market driven" helps the state be more effective at its most fundamental task, maintaining order.

Yet in an environment dominated by skepticism about the ability of police departments actually to implement serious community policing efforts, it is easy to underestimate how difficult it can be to build effective community commitment as well. In a recent evaluation of community policing programs in eight cities, the Vera Institute found that all of them experienced great difficulty in establishing a solid relationship between the programs and neighborhood residents (Grinc, 1994; Sadd & Grinc, 1994). Efforts to do so floundered in part on decades of built-up hostility between residents of poor or minority communities and the police. Distrust and fear of the police were rampant in many of the neighborhoods where community policing was instituted. Residents' fear of retaliation from drug dealers further stifled participation in public events. The evaluators concluded that the assumption that residents *want* closer contact with the police, and want to work with them, is "untested."

It is also uncertain that rank and file officers involved in these programs are any more enthusiastic, especially at the outset. This chapter reports on the findings of an evaluation of community policing in Chicago, and surveys there of officers who were involved in the program found that they were particularly resistant to letting citizens "set their agenda." For example, 72% of them were pessimistic about "unreasonable demands on police by community groups" under the new policing strategy (Skogan, 1996). Many police in Chicago were initially skeptical about whether citizens would participate in the program, fearing that "loudmouths" and "gimmie-guys" would dominate public proceedings and use the program to advance their own personal and political agendas. Behind the scenes, they were nervous about how they would be greeted and treated at public meetings. At the outset, police often defined the public's appropriate role in community policing in the most narrow and traditional terms, as their "eyes and ears."

Another difficulty is that programs that rely on citizen initiative and self-help can be regressive rather than progressive in their impact. Often it is home-owning, long-term residents of a community who learn about and participate more readily in voluntary programs. An evaluation of community policing in Houston (Skogan, 1990a) found strong evidence for this. In several experimental districts, community policing efforts were much more visible among whites than among African Americans or Hispanics, and they were more likely to become involved. Analysis of the impact of the program indicated that its positive effects were confined to whites, while the lives of other residents of the heterogeneous program areas were unaffected. There seemed to be two reasons for this. First, better-organized home-owning whites were poised to take advantage of the resources that the program brought to their neighborhoods. Second, the management of the program allowed officers to pick and choose their target populations. They naturally focused their efforts in places where they felt most welcome and where their initial efforts seemed to be most effective because people got involved.

It is also clearly possible to conduct "problem-solving policing" without widespread citizen participation, or even much public input. Several of the examples of problem solving documented in Newport News involved police analyses of calls-for-service and crime incident data, and data from other public agencies. The department's operating Task Force and Problem Analysis Advisory Committee were both made up just of police officers (Eck & Spelman, 1987a). Newport News developed the "SARA" process for problem identification and problem solving for its own, internal consumption.

Murphy (1993b) argues that the Canadian approach to community policing has been particularly conservative in this regard. He notes, "the community is viewed as a resource, a support group and an information source rather than as an authoritative body" (pp. 20-21). In Canada, community policing remains police-managed and seldom involves civilians in policy or accountability issues. For example, Edmonton relies on foot constables to gather community input through their day-to-day contact with area residents and merchants (Hornick, Burrows, Philips, & Leighton, 1993). In Victoria, the principal role for civilians was to serve as staff volunteers in a storefront police office (Walker, Walker, & McDavid, 1993). Leighton (1993) describes the formation of "community consultative committees" in several cities, and indicates they are still finding a role for themselves in advising police operations. In contrast, Chicago's community policing effort provides a structured avenue for citizen participation in problem identification and priority setting, and creates a channel through which community residents can demand some measure of accountability for police performance in their area.

THE CHICAGO EVALUATION

This chapter examines the role of citizen participation in a new community policing program. It focuses on two roughly comparable police districts, and contrasts what happened there over the course of the program to parallel changes in matched comparison areas. The latter represented "what would have happened" if there had been no program. The data are drawn from an ongoing evaluation of the adoption of community policing by the City of Chicago (Skogan & Hartnett, 1997). While the new model of policing that was crafted by the Chicago Police Department is multifaceted, at its core lies the (anticipated) formation of police-community partnerships focused on problem identification and problem solving at the neighborhood level. The agency's mission statement notes, "the Department and the rest of the community must establish new ways of actually working together. New methods must be put in place to jointly identify problems, propose solutions, and implement changes. The Department's ultimate goal should be community empowerment" (Chicago Police Department, 1993, p. 16). Behind the lines, the agency seems driven by two concerns: to increase the effectiveness of the patrol force by targeting issues of public concern, and healing the yawning breach that has opened between the police and racial and ethnic minorities in the community. The first 14 months of the program provided a laboratory for examining the role of the public in community policing. While it is too soon to determine if the public has indeed been "empowered" by the program, there is now some evidence concerning patterns of program awareness and participation in several experimental police districts.

The Program

Beginning in May 1993, Chicago's community policing program (dubbed CAPS, for Chicago's Alternative Policing Strategy) was tested in five police districts. In those areas, patrol officers were divided on a rotating basis into beat teams and rapid response units. Tasks were assigned so that beat team members would have sufficient free time to attend meetings and work with community members. An average of 45 extra officers (an increment of about 12%) were assigned to each district, so that commanders had the personnel they needed to attend to both beat and rapid response needs. Other units were decentralized, so that local commanders had control over various plainclothes tactical units and youth officers and could integrate their efforts with plans being developed at the grassroots level. The department launched a training effort to ensure that officers and their immediate supervisors understood the new roles and responsibilities that they were being called upon to adopt. In recognition that problem-solving policing needs the support of a wide range of agencies, an effort was made to rationalize the delivery of city services by linking them to service requests generated via beat teams.

Beat Meetings

One of the most visible components of the department's new structure was beat meetings. Beats are the smallest geographical unit of police organization in Chicago; the city's 25 Police Districts are divided into 279 beats. At the median, beats in the 5 experimental districts covered 48 city blocks and included about 9,000 people and 3,000 households. Before community policing, officers were not regularly assigned to work in small areas; the bulk of police work in the districts was done by pairs of officers responding to 911 calls, driving anywhere in (and sometimes out of) their assigned district. It is likely that most officers did not know where the boundaries of the beats lay. The city's new model of policing, on the other hand, is turf based. Teams of beat officers are assigned to their job for at least a year. The experimental districts were staffed and 911 dispatching was controlled to allow these officers to stay on their beat about 70% of the time, handling selected classes of routine calls as well as doing less traditional work.

Beat meetings are regular gatherings of small groups of residents and police officers. The meetings are open to the public, and for the period considered here, most beats met once a month. In each of the two prototype police districts that will be examined below there were approximately 135 beat meetings—one per beat, per month—during the evaluation period. These gatherings were held in church basements, meeting rooms in park buildings, and school rooms throughout the districts. Beat meetings were to be the forum for identifying and prioritizing local problems and developing plans to tackle them. The vision driving the program calls for the formation of "partnerships" between the police and the public in identifying, prioritizing, and solving those problems. The program calls for police to become proactive problem seekers, along with their civilian partners. They are to work together to prevent crime, rather than just continuing to respond to an endless stream of seemingly disconnected incidents (Goldstein, 1990).

To this end, police and residents are supposed to meet one another at the beat meetings, so that civilians will know who is working in their area and police will learn who the "good people" are in their area. To facilitate this, officers who serve on beat teams from all three working shifts are assigned to be present at each meeting, along with a sergeant who supervises activities on the beat, gang and tactical unit officers, and other officers from the Neighborhood Relations unit. In the experimental area with the best recordkeeping, meeting logs compiled by the officers who attended indicate that an average of seven officers attended each meeting. At least one representative of a city service agency was also usually present, and someone representing a local community organization made a statement at about one half of the meetings.

Beat meetings are also supposed to lead to the exchange of information between police and the public. Over time, we observed that police increasingly brought with them district and crime maps, lists of offenses and arrests, and other information. For their part, residents were rarely reticent to bring up specific problems or problem areas. Beat meetings are intended to break barriers of distrust between residents and the police. Officers initially objected to working with people who came to meetings because they perceived that they would be somehow "unrepresentative" of the community. We observed that over time some of the initial fears that police brought to them—that the meetings would be dominated by "loud mouths," and that the officers present would be "put on the hot seat" as charges against the police were hurled around the room—were not founded. What they encountered were, by and large, reasonable and concerned people who applauded when they stood to be introduced. Officers also seemed to overcome their initial fear they would not be good public speakers, for speeches were rarely called for. No one seemed put off by blunt, practical talk.

In both experimental areas there were extensive efforts to advertise beat meetings, and to turn out residents in large numbers. Community newspapers

TABLE 5.1 Organizational Efforts Surrounding CAPS Meetings

Organizational Activity	Morgan Park (%)	Rogers Park (%)
Holding general, public meetings related to CAPS	53	56
Distributing newsletters or flyers related to CAPS	64	64
Encouraging people to attend CAPS-related meetings	87	81
Sending representatives to CAPS-related meetings	89	88
Number of organizations	(45)	(59)

printed beat meeting schedules. Activists posted announcements and shoved flyers into people's mail boxes. In a related study, we identified 250 neighborhood organizations active in the five test districts and interviewed two informants each about their organization's activities. Ninety organizations were studied in the two prototype districts examined here: 59 of them were active in Rogers Park, and 45 in Morgan Park. Table 5.1 indicates the percentage of those organizations that were involved in each of a checklist of efforts to mobilize their communities around CAPS. Encouraging people to attend beat meetings and sending representatives to the meetings was nearly ubiquitous. A large majority of these groups was involved in advertising CAPS-related activities. A majority even held their own public meetings about the program, and, as will be detailed below, community groups played an important role in hosting and running them as well.

While it hard to judge what a "good" attendance figure would be, police department logs for Morgan Park indicate that an average of 35 people attended each beat meeting in that district. This figure agrees with an areawide survey conducted 14 months after the program began. The survey asked respondents who had attended a meeting how many people typically came; their average estimate was similar, 31 in Morgan Park, and 30 in Rogers Park. A plot of the over-time data on beat meeting attendance in Morgan Park indicates that it was seasonal, low in January and February.

Data and Research Design

To gauge public opinion on the eve of the new program, survey interviews were conducted with residents of the prototype districts and the matched neighborhoods that serve as comparison areas for the evaluation. The interviews were conducted by telephone, using a combination of listed directory and randomly generated telephone numbers. The first round of interviews was completed before the program began. In June 1994, respondents in two of the prototype districts and their comparison areas were reinterviewed in order to assess changes in levels of program awareness and contact during the first 14 months of the program. Residents of the remaining prototype and comparison areas were reinterviewed later.

The two prototype areas were both diverse. Morgan Park (District 22) residents were 60% African American, and 80% were home owners. Nine percent of households there fell below the poverty line, and 62% of residents had lived in the community more than 10 years. Rogers Park (District 24) residents were 58% white, 17% African American, and 14% Hispanic. About 16% of households were below the poverty line, and only 24% of residents had lived there more than a decade.

Opportunities for Participation

Potentially, one of the most important aspects of CAPS is that it created new opportunities for participation in anticrime efforts that were relatively uniform across the city. This is quite unlike the distribution of autonomously created and independently active groups. Research on the social and geographic distribution of opportunities to participate in organized group activity indicates that they are least common where they appear to be most needed—in low-income, heterogeneous, deteriorated, high turnover areas. Ironically, community organizations focusing on crime issues are more common in better-off neighborhoods, while poorer areas characterized by high levels of fear, fatalism, mutual distrust, and despair are less well served.

This is important because individuals participate within a neighborhood context that defines the alternatives open to them. With the exception of those few entrepreneurs who create new organizations, people can participate only by affiliating with active groups. Who participates and in what capacity thus turns on what opportunities for participation are available—which varies from place to place. By creating relatively uniform opportunities for participation, CAPS went one step down the road toward mobilizing wider participation among all segments of the community.

The first question is, then, Did the program indeed create new opportunities for citizen participation? If there was little awareness of the new program or knowledge of how to participate, the impact of all of the effort surrounding the inauguration of beat meetings in the prototype districts would be severely muted. To examine this, respondents were asked two questions in sequence that probed their awareness of neighborhood opportunities to participate:

During the past year, have you heard about efforts to get community meetings started up in your neighborhood?

During the past year, have there actually been any community meetings held here in your neighborhood to try to deal with crime problems?

These questions gave respondents two opportunities to recall instances of organizational efforts in their community. We did not ask specifically about "beat meetings" because that term was unlikely to be recognized by people who did not attend any meetings, nor by anyone in the survey conducted before the program began. Responses to these two questions were combined to identify the extent of awareness of organizing efforts in the program and comparison areas. Changes in levels of program awareness in the prototype and comparison areas between 1993 and 1994 provide evidence about the impact of the program.

Figure 5.1 illustrates the extent of this impact. In both prototype areas, awareness of organized activity increased during the 14 months between the surveys, and both changes were statistically significant. Awareness of opportunities to participate actually declined in the Morgan Park comparison area, and they did not change significantly in the Rogers Park control area. Parallel citywide surveys were conducted at the same two points in time, and they also indicated that awareness of opportunities to participate did not change for city residents as a whole.

Although the changes presented in Figure 5.1 were statistically significant, the magnitude of the program versus comparison group differences depicted there probably were muted by the sheer level of preexisting organized activism in Chicago. It is a highly neighborhood-oriented city with strong local political organizations, decentralized municipal services, and a long tradition of achieving community goals through turf-based organizing. As a result, even before the program began, levels of awareness of opportunities for participation were already very high. This imposed a "ceiling" on potential program effects against which even the most effective program must bump.

WHO GOT THE MESSAGE?

Not surprisingly, awareness of opportunities to participate in community policing was not evenly distributed in the population. In fact, it very much resembled the findings of past research on the distribution of opportunities to participate. By the time of our second survey, stable, family-oriented people

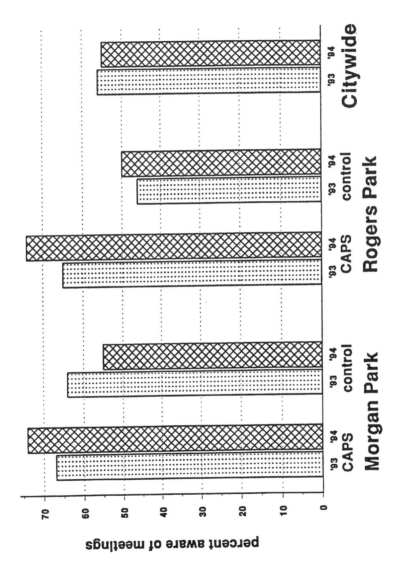

Figure 5.1. Opportunities for Participation

97

with investments in the community were more likely to have gotten the message. While patterns of awareness varied a bit by area, program awareness in the prototypes was more extensive among higher income, more highly educated people, middle-aged married couples, home owners, and whites. Awareness was higher in households that were heavily networked with others in the community. Compared to those who had not heard about community organizing efforts in their area, those who had were already (measured at Wave I) more concerned about crime, physical decay, and disruption in the schools serving their neighborhood. People with past victimization experience also were more likely to have heard about organizing efforts. The impact of many of these factors on program awareness is illustrated in Figure 5.2.

Patterns of Participation

The next question is: Who took advantage of these new opportunities to participate? Two issues are involved in that question. The first is *levels* of participation. Did more people participate following the onset of community policing, taking advantage of the regular, visible opportunities for participation that it created? The second, and perhaps more important, issue is that of the *distribution* of participation. Inevitably, relatively few residents will ever be directly involved in community policing, even to the level of just attending a public meeting. In my view, the important questions this raises are: Are the processes of public involvement broadly inclusive? Are all of the interests and issues facing the community being represented? In particular, we are interested in whether participation followed familiar patterns, encouraging yet higher levels of activism among better off people who already dominate organized community life. Or, was participation in some fashion redistributive; that is, did community policing bring in "new blood" that along important dimensions represented new and less enfranchised elements of the community? We have already seen that awareness of the opportunities to participate that Chicago's program provided were more distributive than redistributive, calling for a close look at the data concerning this issue.

The issue of levels of participation is addressed in Figure 5.3. It illustrates the results of before-and-after surveys of residents of the prototype and comparison areas. If respondents indicated that they had heard of organized group efforts in their neighborhood, they were asked, *Were you able to attend any of the meetings?* Figure 5.3 classifies each respondent as a participant or nonparticipant (those who had never heard of meetings were also classified as nonparticipants), and charts the percentage of respondents in each evaluation area that fell in the former category.

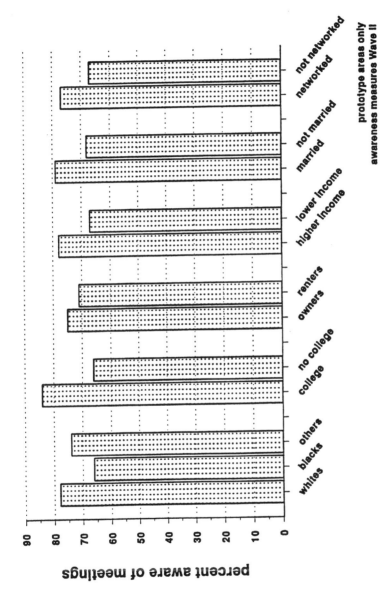

Figure 5.2. Demographics of Program Awareness

99

None of the before-after differences in levels of participation depicted in Figure 5.3 are statistically significant. In Morgan Park, participation rose an insignificant one percentage point, and in Rogers park it stood rock-steady. The slight declines in participation in the two comparison areas were not significant, in light of the sample sizes involved. More elaborate analyses that pooled program and comparison areas and controlled for the effects of individual-level demographic factors such as sex, age, and length of residence before looking for effects attributable to the program did not change this picture at all.

It was still possible, however, that extensive outreach and organizing efforts in the prototype areas changed the *character* of participation. The experimental districts may not have had to rely so heavily on "self-starters," given the broad opportunities for participation created by the program and the extensive effort that went into generating participation in beat meetings. Unlike many past efforts at local organizing, the structure imposed by the program ensured that meetings were held on a regular basis in every beat, not just in places that had the resources to sponsor them, or where initial organizing efforts were well received. As Table 5.1 above indicated, considerable effort was also put into generating participation in beat meetings, by many organizations in each of these relatively small areas. In Morgan Park, a large and powerful community organization representing white home owners in one part of the district extended their franchise to cover the entire district, and put their considerable resources and political influence into generating participation in meetings all over the area. Another powerful organization serving the southern end of Rogers Park hired a professional community organizer to generate attendance and nurture the program in their service area. The most intensive organizational efforts in Rogers Park were in its higher crime beats, which are diverse and feisty neighborhoods.

In both Morgan Park and Rogers Park, our evaluation indeed found some evidence that both program awareness and actual participation was mildly redistributive in character. That is, new elements in the community were mobilized as a result of CAPS.

To examine this it was necessary to distinguish between two groups of activists: those who at Wave II were involved in organized community efforts for the first time ("new blood") and those who had been involved in community affairs before the onset of Chicago's program and continued to be aware and active after it came to their district ("retreads"). At the time they were reinterviewed, about 68% of residents in Morgan Park and Rogers Park who were aware of opportunities to participate in their area were retreads, while

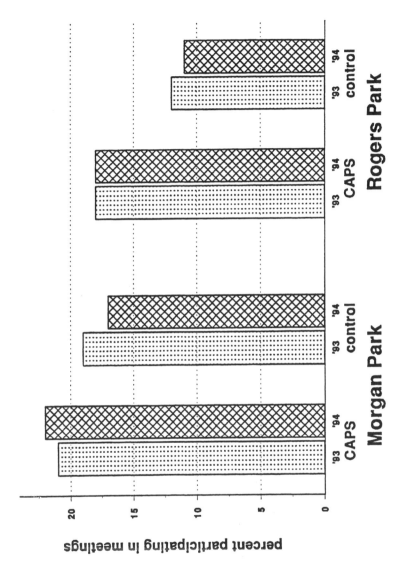

Figure 5.3. Participation in Community Meetings

the remaining third were newly informed. Among participants, those in Morgan Park split about 50-50, while about 70% of participants from Rogers Park were experienced activists and 30% were new to the scene.

Retreads and newly informed or involved area residents differed on several important dimensions. The first of these is illustrated in Figure 5.4. It depicts the percentage of retreads and new blood in June 1994 who were either black, Hispanic, or of another race ("percent nonwhite"). It compares respondents drawn from the prototype and comparison areas, to examine the potential impact of CAPS on the breadth of community mobilization. All prototype and comparison-area respondents are grouped together because of the smaller sample sizes involved in this detailed analysis, but the trends described here were at work in each experimental and control area. As Figure 5.4 suggests, differences in the racial composition of the two groups were large (and statistically significant) in the prototype areas, and small (and insignificant) in the comparison areas.

The same pattern can be observed for other key demographic factors, some of which are detailed in Table 5.2. Relative to events in the comparison areas, it appears that beat meetings expanded involvement for women, nonwhites, and those nearer the bottom of the educational ladder (here presented as the percentage that did not go to college, a significant general predictor of awareness and participation). One important factor that did not appear to change as a result of this apparent expansion in the participation base for the program was home ownership. In the prototypes, slightly *more* new participants than old were home owners.

Did new participants differ in significant ways in terms of the kinds of *concerns* they brought to the meetings? The survey included questions measuring three different views of the police. One set of 10 questions tapped respondents' views of the quality of police service; 3 others asked about police aggressiveness on the street and their use of excessive force; and 2 judged respondents' optimism about the future of policing in Chicago. None of these attitudes varied significantly with participation status. Similarly, new participants were neither more nor less fearful of crime, nor more nor less concerned about crime or neighborhood decay. In terms of their views of the neighborhood, they closely resembled those who were already involved in anticrime efforts. Both groups differed more from nonparticipants; those who were not involved perceived less crime and neighborhood decay, and were less positive about the future of policing in Chicago, than participants of any stripe.

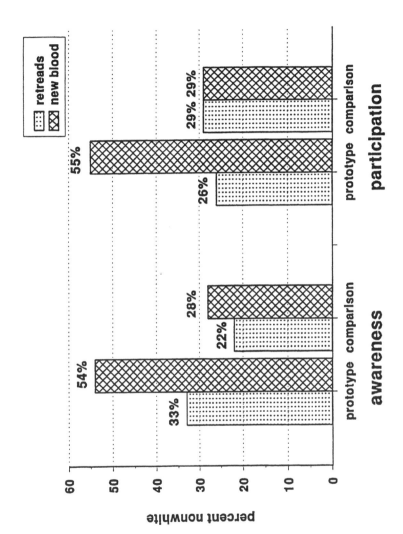

Figure 5.4. New Versus Recycled Activists; Percentage Nonwhite

TABLE 5.2 Demographics of Awareness and Participation by New and
Continuing Status

Demographics of New and Continuing Involvements	Awareness		Participation	
	Proto	Control	Proto	Control
Percentage Nonwhite				
Retreads	33	22	26	29
New blood	54	28	55	29
(significance)	(.01)	(.46)	(.01)	(.99)
Percentage Noncollege				
Retreads	48	69	48	67
New blood	53	44	70	52
(significance)	(.58)	(.01)	(.05)	(.36)
Percentage Own Home				
Retreads	76	78	69	81
New blood	64	51	81	76
(significance)	(.06)	(.01)	(.21)	(.72)
Percentage Female				
Retreads	62	67	48	62
New blood	54	56	76	76
(significance)	(.29)	(.24)	(.01)	(.33)
Number of Cases				
Retreads	229	121	42	21
New blood	61	39	33	21

Effectiveness of Participation

Has anything come of beat meetings? In our report on the first year of the program (Skogan et al., 1994), we were fairly critical of the beat meeting process. In important ways what happened there did not fit a community policing model. Meetings that we observed were frequently run by community relations specialists and did not actively involve beat officers. They frequently sat mute in the back, unless called upon. Too often the exchange between residents and the police was one-sided; the former would bring up a long list of specific complaints, and the latter said they would "check on it." Everyone involved still had a narrow, crime-related view of what kinds of problems were suitable for discussion at the meetings, and they all took a traditional, enforcement-oriented view of what appropriate solutions for these problems might look like.

However, our survey respondents took a much more sanguine view of the meetings. If they indicated they had attended a meeting, they were asked a series of questions about what typically happened there (we asked them to typify meetings because they went to an average of 3.8 meetings apiece). Their responses were similar enough across the two districts to combine them. They reported that someone from the community or a community organizer had conducted two thirds of the meetings, and that the police had run only 21% on their own. Seventy percent thought that the meeting itself had been arranged by a community group, 17% thought that police had jointly sponsored the meeting with a group, and only 10% thought police organized the meeting on their own. Fully 86% of those who went to a meeting indicated that they had learned something at the meeting, and 71% reported that action was taken or something happened in their neighborhood as a result of the meeting. When asked how useful these meetings were "for finding solutions to neighborhood problems," 38% said they were very useful, 53% somewhat useful, and only 9% not useful. Half thought the meetings were very useful "for improving the community's relationship with the police," and another 42% thought they were somewhat useful in this regard.

Other Vehicles for Participation

It is important to note that beat meetings are not the only vehicle for public participation in community policing. Another is the civilian advisory committees that have been established in each district. The committees typically involve between 15 and 20 civilians. They are named by the District Commander, and include area residents, local merchants, religious leaders, and representatives of civic associations. We observed all of the advisory committee meetings in the five experimental districts, and can report only that their efforts were highly variable. Participation ranged from highly inclusive to closed and exclusionary. Some committees had close links with beat-level activists, while others were fairly disconnected from events at that level. Some committees focused on broad social issues important to the community but probably beyond the range of the police, while others lavished attention on internal activities like writing extensive bylaws. Some viewed themselves as a support group for their District Commander, while others were viewed by Commanders as contending with them for control of operational policies in the district. No single model of how these committees should function emerged early from this stew.

Community members were also involved at the citywide level, agitating on behalf of the program and pressuring its administrators to hew closely to their commitment to keep the public informed and involved. To date, citywide organizations have been concerned about police performance measures; their accountability to the public; the extent to which beat teams have actually been freed from responding to 911 calls, and the extent to which they have been able to stay on their beats as planned; and the openness of beat officers to information sharing and cooperation in problem solving. These pressure groups are convinced that the program cannot work unless the community "comes to the table" as a powerful, informed, and competent partner, rather than as a supplicant (Friedman, 1994). To make some progress on this front, one of them organized a series of beat-level training sessions to prepare neighborhood residents to be more effective problem-solving partners.

CONCLUSION

Chicago's new community policing program provided an opportunity to examine a fledgling effort to involve the public in joint police-citizen efforts at preventing crime and responding to neighborhood decay. Structural changes were made in police task organization to facilitate this new model of policing, and the program was linked to the improved management of a broad range of city services. The principal mechanism for coordinating this effort with the public is beat-level public meetings that are to provide police and citizens an opportunity to identify, prioritize, and discuss solutions to a broad range of neighborhood problems.

This chapter examined some aspects of the effort. It found that awareness of the opportunities for participation that the program provided were widespread, and significantly higher in the prototype districts than in the evaluation's comparison areas. Levels of organized participation were not significantly higher in the program areas than in the comparison areas. However, there was some evidence that both awareness and participation were more widely distributed within the prototype areas, perhaps as a result of the uniform nature of the opportunities for participation created by regular and widely publicized beat meetings and extensive efforts by groups and organizations to stimulate participation in the meetings.

POLICE AND PUBLIC
INVOLVEMENT IN THE DELIVERY
OF COMMUNITY POLICING

Trevor Bennett

The police and the public each plays a role in the delivery of police service. The police are involved in the delivery of policing during routine reactive policing (e.g., at the point of contact with the public following a crime report or other call for service) and during proactive policing (e.g., at the point of contact with the public as part of the component parts of community policing such as community consultation or crime prevention). The public is involved in the delivery of policing during routine reactive policing (e.g., in their reporting of crimes or incidents to the police) and in the contributions that they make during proactive policing (e.g., in their involvement in the component parts of community policing).

The main aim of this chapter is to evaluate what is known in the research literature about the effectiveness of both the police and the public in the delivery of police service. The evaluation will include an assessment of both reactive and proactive policing of the kind that involves contact between the police and the public. It will focus on general uniform policing rather than on the work of the traffic and criminal investigation departments (although a review of the service delivery of these departments could also be conducted). The review of research will be selective rather than exhaustive and will focus in particular on research conducted in Britain.

RECENT DEVELOPMENTS IN THE
ROLE OF THE POLICE IN BRITAIN

Policing in Britain is currently in a process of reform both in terms of reactive policing (including developments in "quality of police service") and in terms of proactive policing (including developments in community policing and problem-solving policing).

Quality of Police Service

The delivery of police service during routine encounters with the public is a central element of police reform in Britain known as the "quality-of-service" initiative. As part of this initiative, and as part of the general move toward "managerialism" within most public sector services, the police are encouraged to think of the public as "customers" of the police service and to pay attention to their wishes and concerns. The quality-of-service initiative was in part a product of government policy that has found expression in various government circulars and documents, including two government white papers. The police, however, have also been keen to embrace the idea of "quality of service" as a means of maintaining public support and public confidence.

Police support for the idea of improved police service can be found in two important police documents: the *Operational Police Review* (The Joint Consultative Committee, 1990) and the ACPO's *Strategic Policy Document* (ACPO, 1990). As part of this process, all police forces in Britain now conduct regular public attitude surveys to determine how well they are performing in the delivery of police service to the public (Fyfe, 1994)

Community Policing

Community policing in Britain is viewed largely as it is viewed in other countries, as primarily a philosophy of policing that can find practical expression through a number of different organizational structures and operational strategies (Trojanowicz & Bucqueroux, 1990). It is possible to identify changes in British policing by looking at each of the three main elements of community policing: (a) policing philosophy, (b) organizational structures, and (c) operational strategies.

Current policing philosophy can be observed indirectly through police force annual reports. In Britain, police annual reports typically include many references to community policing and typically offer many statements of support for the principles of a community-oriented policing philosophy. Current policing philosophy can also be found in the two police reports referred to above (ACPO, 1990; The Joint Consultative Committee, 1990) that, through their "statement of common purposes and values," emphasize the commitment of the police service to the core functions of policing, including a willingness to reflect the priorities of the public in the actions that they take.

The main organizational reform in policing in Britain over the past few years has been a move toward decentralization. The main method of doing this has been the adoption by forces of some version of sector policing (also known as zone policing, neighborhood policing, and geographic policing). Sector policing typically involves subdividing the old police divisions into three or four sectors to provide smaller administrative units and allocating an inspector or higher ranking officer to take "geographic responsibility" for all policing needs in the area.

There are a large number of policing strategies that aim to deliver community policing at the operational level, including: police shops, police clinic, foot patrols, community consultation, and community crime prevention. The most widespread and longest lasting operational strategy for implementing community policing at ground level in Britain is the use of community constables (also known as area beat officers, home beat officers, and resident beat officers). Community constables comprise dedicated police officers (usually foot patrol officers) who are allocated to particular areas (usually single beats) on a permanent or semi-permanent basis, with the specific task of providing a full police service to the local community of that area. The aim of these officers varies both across and within forces. However, there is some agreement in the literature that the work of community constables involves making contact with, and speaking to, members of the local community; getting to know their area; and generating good police-public relations. Community constables (in their present form) have been a feature of British policing since the end of the 1960s. Nevertheless, they are still regarded as the main vanguard of community policing and are widely used by forces to implement whatever component of community policing is currently in fashion (e.g., community beat officers are used to set up Neighborhood Watch schemes and to provide a lead in sector policing).

Problem-Solving Policing

One of the key elements of the reform process concerns the role of the police in crime prevention. In the introduction to a recent government white paper on police reform, it was argued that "fighting crime should be the priority for police officers" and it was noted that local communities should share and support this priority (HMSO, 1993b, p. 1). The white paper also identified crime prevention as one of the five main aims of the police service (along with order maintenance, detection, reassurance, and value for money).

The main strategies for crime prevention identified in the white paper that involve the police were contained in a section on partnerships between the police and the public. In this section, police involvement in crime prevention was seen as including: the use of special constables (public volunteers), Neighborhood Watch schemes, advice to individuals and businesses on security, crime prevention panels, encouraging the public to participate as informants and witnesses, and involving the public in crime prevention, both individually and through local partnerships.

A much fuller elaboration of the methods by which the police might prevent and detect crime in the future is outlined in two Audit Commission reports, the first (HMSO, 1993a) dealing with crime management and the second (HMSO, 1996) dealing with the effective use of patrols. One of the themes that runs through these two reports (and that has been given strong government support) is that the future direction of operational policing should be in the direction of targeted policing and problem solving. The first report, titled *Helping With Enquiries: Tackling Crime Effectively"* (HMSO, 1993a), proposed a more proactive approach to crime management and encouraged forces to redirect resources into proactive work with particular reference to targeting prolific and serious offenders. The report concluded that greater emphasis on crime prevention through developing partnerships with the public and other groups and proactive and targeted investigation could result in crime reduction and improvement in clear-up rates.

RECENT DEVELOPMENTS IN THE ROLE
OF THE PUBLIC IN POLICING IN BRITAIN

The public has always played a role in routine policing through its crime reporting and through other demands for police service. As such, the public plays an important role in defining the nature of police work. The public has also played a role for some time in the implementation of community policing programs as a result of its involvement in community consultation arrangements and community crime prevention and other kinds of collaboration with the police in the prevention of crime.

The most recent development in public involvement in policing includes the rapid expansion of Neighborhood Watch (NW) schemes. Recent figures suggest that there are more than 100,000 NW schemes in England and Wales (Mayhew, Maung, & Mirrlees-Black, 1993). Another recent development in Britain has been government promotion of the recruitment of special constables to work alongside the police in local areas. A further proposal made by the government in 1993 to develop street patrols has experienced much less support from the public ("Watch Schemes," 1993). Some concern has been expressed over the principle of citizens patrolling their own residential areas in order to discover crimes in action or to observe suspicious behavior (Travis, 1994a). In response to public opinion, the Home Secretary changed the terminology of his policy from "patrolling" the streets to "walking with a purpose" in order to take some of the formality out of the concept (Travis, 1994b).

The public has also taken on a greater role in policing its areas through the recent widespread expansion of private street patrols (patrols hired by local residents to protect their areas) and community security patrols run by local authorities for the same purpose. It has recently been estimated that private policing in Britain (including private patrols and private security guards) now exceeds public policing in terms of numbers of personnel (Johnston, 1996a).

EVALUATION OF POLICE DELIVERY
OF ROUTINE POLICING

The most common method of measuring the effectiveness of routine policing is through national or local public attitude surveys of public satisfaction. The main national public attitude survey in Britain is the British Crime Survey, which is conducted approximately every 2 years and covers a national representative sample of more than 10,000 respondents. The main methods of measuring public satisfaction are (a) asking all respondents how good a job they think the police are doing; and (b) asking people who have come into contact with the police how satisfied they were with the outcome.

The last four British Crime Survey reports have shown that general public confidence in the police has declined successively over the past 10 years. The reports show that the proportion of the public who felt that the police were doing a "very good job" declined from 43% in 1982 to 24% in 1992 (Skogan, 1994a). This reduction was supported by evidence from other surveys. A survey conducted by the Royal Commission on the Police in 1962 showed that 83% of people interviewed said that they had a "great respect" for the police (HMSO, 1962). A similar survey conducted in 1993 by MORI revealed that 46% of respondents reported that they had "great respect" for the police ("Crime Wave," 1993).

The reasons for the decline in public satisfaction with the police are not entirely clear. The research suggests, however, that people who come into contact with the police (e.g., to report victimization) are less satisfied than those who do not come into contact with the police.

The results of a special report on the police based on the results of the 1988 British Crime Survey (Skogan, 1990b) showed varying levels of satisfaction among members of the public who came into contact with the police in the past year. About half of members of the public who contacted the police through the "999" emergency system (52%) or by visiting the station (47%) said that they were satisfied with police performance during their most recent contact. However, this varied considerably by sample subgroup. Respondents aged between 16 and 24 years of age were less likely to say that they were satisfied with police performance (39% "999" and 30% "station") than those aged 45 years or more (60% "999" and 54% "station"). Overall, nonwhites were less satisfied than whites, inner-city dwellers were less satisfied than rural-area dwellers, and respondents who called about crime were less satisfied than those who called to give, or to get, information (Skogan, 1990b).

The survey also looked at the reasons people give for being dissatisfied. About one third of those with a specific complaint mentioned a seeming lack of interest by the police in their case and 42% judged that police did not do enough. Fifty-three percent of all those who complained mentioned a problem concerning "apparent lack of effort." This reason was given as the main source of dissatisfaction by respondents in nearly all demographic categories and relating to almost every type of contact.

It is uncertain what, precisely, people are thinking about when they record that they are satisfied or dissatisfied with the police. It is unknown, for example, whether people's comments reflect their orientation toward the police or toward authority in a wider sense. It is possible that people who say they are satisfied with the police are in fact giving their general support for the existing social order.

There is some evidence available that supports this view. Studies by Alpert and Dunham (1988) and by Albrecht and Green (1977) found a substantial correlation between people's attitudes toward the police and people's attitudes toward other social institutions, including the rest of the criminal justice system. They found that there was a strong correlation, for example, between people's attitudes toward the police and toward the courts. They argued that people have a wider "attitude complex" within which their attitudes to the police fall. Albrecht and Green (1977) conclude that attempts to improve people's attitudes toward the police by improving community policing may be misguided unless they address this larger attitude complex.

Overall, the research suggests that public confidence in the police is high, but appears to have declined over the past 10 years and may still be declining. One major problem identified by the research seems to be the nature of the contact between the police and the public during routine encounters. Skogan notes in his report that an important problem with these findings is that support for the police seems to be declining among those who have the greatest need for police service (Skogan, 1990b). In other words, dissatisfaction is greatest among the main customers of the police service and greatest in relation to functions that lie at the heart of traditional policing.

EVALUATION OF POLICE DELIVERY
OF COMMUNITY POLICING

The effectiveness of the police in delivering community policing can be observed by looking at research on the three main elements of community policing: (a) its philosophy, (b) its organizational structures, and (c) its operational strategies.

The Philosophy of Community Policing

The main method of evaluating the extent to which police in Britain subscribe to the philosophy of community policing is through surveys of police officers. There have been two national surveys in Britain that include information on police officers' attitudes.

The first study (Reiner, 1991) is a survey of almost all chief constables (93%) of police forces in England and Wales. The survey was based on arranging personal visits to each chief constable in turn and administering a semistructured interview schedule. The research findings showed that 50% of officers had a broad view of the police role (which included the idea that the police should be concerned with community and social issues), 13% held a narrow view of the police role (which included the idea that the police should be concerned only with crime control and detection), and 35% claimed to stand between these two views. When asked specifically about community policing, 55% declared some support for the notion, while 45% thought that it was a "meaningless expression" (Reiner, 1991).

The second national survey (Bennett & Lupton, 1992) questioned samples of community constables (area-based foot patrol officers) and general duty officers (reactive mobile patrol officers) using self-administered questionnaires. The samples were drawn from single police divisions within each of the 39 (out of a total of 43) police force areas that agreed to take part in the research. All officers within the selected division who were available for policing duties during the 2-week period of the research were requested to complete the questionnaire. Approximately 80% of both community constables and general duty officers returned completed questionnaires.

The results showed that both community constables and general duty officers thought that community policing work was important. General duty officers, however, ranked this kind of work significantly lower than did community constables. In addition, the survey found that the younger officers in each group were more likely than the older officers to perceive community policing work as less important. There was no significant difference in perceived importance in terms of the sex of the respondent.

In addition to the national surveys, there have been some small-scale and local surveys of police attitudes toward community policing. A study by McConville and Shepherd (1992) found that community beat policing was highly unpopular among police constables. A common complaint was that community beat work was boring, unglamorous, and disconnected from "real" policing. Many officers interviewed said that they did not want any closer involvement with the community as it would only give them more "hassle." Overall, policing was seen as a collective effort directed toward the restoration of law and order rather than servicing the particular needs of individual communities.

Overall, there is insufficient research evidence to arrive at a strong conclusion on the extent to which British police believe in a community-policing philosophy of policing. There have been no surveys to my knowledge that have investigated community policing philosophies specifically and in depth. The evidence that is available, however, suggests that, while the philosophy of community policing is widely and publicly proclaimed as a central principle of policing in Britain, it has not yet become fully integrated into police thinking and beliefs.

Organizational Structures

The most common organizational structure associated with community policing is decentralization, and the most common form of decentralization in Britain at the moment is sector policing. There are very few evaluations of sector policing in Britain. However, there have been two studies that have included both process and outcome evaluations as part of the research.

The first evaluation of sector policing was conducted in the early 1980s during a period in which the Metropolitan Police organized a number of pilot programs that were referred to under the general heading of "neighborhood policing." One of these schemes in Notting Hill in London was evaluated by the British Police Foundation (Irving, Bird, Hibberd, & Willmore, 1989). The study included a process evaluation that involved monitoring the effectiveness of the implementation of the program. The research found substantial evidence of implementation failure at almost every level of the program. The system of geographic responsibility was resisted by relief (reactive response) officers on the grounds that it undermined reactive cover and manning levels and by home beat officers on the grounds that allocating proactive tasks to relief officers undermined and confused their position. The implementation of graded response was also disliked by lower ranking officers and was eventually abandoned, along with the system of computerized management information, which failed to be used by the police to inform operational policing.

The research also included an outcome evaluation that examined the effect of the program on public attitudes and on victimization. The research showed that, following the implementation of neighborhood policing, there was no measurable change in public attitudes toward the police or toward the area in which they lived. The report also showed that, during the course of the experiment, the number of single and repeat victimizations within the area of the experiment increased substantially. The report concluded that the program failed to overcome the issue of police conservatism and the self-interest of the various policing groups and failed to overcome the strong inertia to change among frontline police officers and junior managers (Irving et al., 1989).

The second study that included both process and outcome evaluations of sector policing was conducted in the Thames Valley Police Force Area (Bennett & Kemp, 1994). The process evaluation included a number of methods designed to monitor the various stages of program implementation, including observations of steering group meetings, collecting documents, and interviewing key personnel at regular interviews. It was also evaluated by conducting repeated activity surveys and repeated self-administered question-naires among patrol officers. These were designed to test whether police behavior on the streets changed from the period before the implementation of sector policing to the period after. Two activity surveys were conducted in the posttest period to determine whether any changes observed were progressive over time.

The results showed that the amount of time spent on incident work declined slightly among shift officers and increased among area beat officers. As the main proactive work of the program was intended to be conducted by the area beat officers, this finding is in the opposite direction from that hypothesized. The results relating to type of work conducted showed that the amount of time spent on community-oriented police work (defined as foot patrol, crime prevention, and community involvement) declined overall among both shift officers and area beat officers. Again, this result is in the opposite direction from that hypothesized. The results relating to type of deployment showed that the amount of time spent by officers on vehicle patrol increased among both shift officers and area beat officers. Again, the finding is in an opposite direction from that hypothesized.

The results also showed that job satisfaction declined across the three survey periods among both shift officers and area beat officers. The percentage of officers who said that they were satisfied with their job reduced from 81% satisfied in the first survey to 65% satisfied in the third survey among shift officers and from 77% satisfied in the first survey to 67% satisfied in the third survey among area beat officer. Morale also declined among both types of officer.

The evaluation of implementation effectiveness concluded that area beat officers were generally more satisfied with the developments in sector polic-ing than shift officers. Shift officers experienced changes in policing that might be interpreted as undermining their situation. The shift officer strength was reduced in number as a result of area beat officers being drawn from their ranks. The change in job description of the sector inspectors meant that they spent less time with the shifts and more time with the area beat officers. Further, the philosophy of sector policing gave greater emphasis to proactive police work and the work of the area beat officers, which served to undermine the perceived value of reactive policing.

Outcome effectiveness was measured using pretest and posttest victimiza-tion and public attitude surveys and a separate repeated burglary victim survey using self-administered questionnaires. The results showed that during the pretest to posttest period there was no significant change in either the prevalence or incidence of victimization. There was also no evidence of any significant change in incident rates or fear of crime. The results also showed that only a small proportion of residents noticed any changes in policing over the experimental period. When asked specifically about the recency of sighting of a police officer in their area, residents in the experimental areas were significantly more likely than residents in the control areas to say that they had recently seen an officer on foot in the area. There was no change in public evaluation of the police in terms of whether residents thought police were doing "a good job." However, there was an improvement in public evaluation of the police in terms of their performance during specific contacts with residents.

The report concluded that there were some encouraging findings in terms of outcome effectiveness. However, there were a large number of findings showing no change and there was little clear pattern to the positive findings. On balance, the results suggest that some of the major obstacles affecting implementation effectiveness had not been overcome by the end of the evaluation and that there was little evidence of any substantial or meaningful program effect.

Operational Strategies

The most common and longest lasting operational strategy for implementing community policing on the ground is the system of community constables or resident beat officers. The work of community constables has been investigated in both national surveys and local surveys to determine the extent to which they deliver community policing in practice.

The national survey of community policing conducted in Britain described earlier included an embedded activity survey that was used to assess the work of community constables and shift officers (Bennett & Lupton, 1992). Although the time available for the survey did not allow an extensive activity survey, it was possible to conduct a limited survey of the nature of police work.

All officers were asked to record activities performed during each quarter of an hour of the last completed tour of duty. The self-completed questionnaire included a recording sheet and a list of activity codes. The respondent was asked to distinguish between activities conducted outside the station and inside the station. The results of the survey showed that community constables spent about one third (36.4%) of typical duty tours inside the station and two thirds (63.6%) outside. General duty officers spend just over two fifths of their time (43.1%) of typical duty tours inside the station and just under three fifths of their time (56.9%) outside. The difference in time spent by permanent beat officers and general duty officers on inside duties was statistically significant.

Three categories of the activity survey covered community-oriented police work ("community contacts," "patrol," and "preventative and proactive police work"). In order to obtain an estimate of the total amount of time spent on community policing among community constables, the three categories were combined in the analysis to form a single category referred to as "community involvement and preventative police work." The results showed that about one third (35.1%) of each tour of duty made by community constables was spent on community involvement and patrol.

An important current issue is the extent to which community constables are withdrawn from their beats to conduct other and often unrelated tasks. In order to examine this, respondents were asked whether they had been withdrawn from their beats during the last 20 days of service (effectively a working month). The results obtained showed that approximately two thirds (65.8%) of all permanent beat officers said that they had been withdrawn for at least 1 day during the last 20 working days before completing the questionnaire (respondents who said that they were withdrawn for less than 1 day were coded as zero days withdrawn). The mean number of days withdrawn out of the last 20 working days for the sample as a whole was 3.7 days. On average, community constables were abstracted from their duties for an average of about 20% of their working time. The mean number of days withdrawn among those officers who said that they had been withdrawn for at least 1 day over the last 20 days was 5.6 days.

EVALUATION OF PUBLIC INVOLVEMENT
IN ROUTINE POLICING

This section of the chapter concerns the effectiveness of the public in relation to the role that they play in routine policing. The main item investigated in this section concerns public involvement in making calls for service and their effectiveness in reporting crimes to the police.

The main research on crime reporting can be found in the national and local public surveys that examine public reporting rates and reasons for nonreporting. The reporting rates for different offenses found in the 1992 British Crime Survey showed substantial variations by type of offense. Victims gave a number of reasons for not reporting offenses to the police. In the 1992 survey,

55% of nonreporters said (as a reason for nonreporting) that the offense was too trivial. Twenty-five percent of nonreporters said that the police could do nothing about it. Thirteen percent thought that the police could not be bothered. The results of the 1996 British Crime Survey showed that the proportion of reasons for nonreporting concerning police performance had increased slightly. In 1996, 40% of nonrespondents stated that the offence was too trivial and 29% and 20%, respectively, stated that the police could do nothing or could not be bothered (Mirrlees-Black, Mayhew, & Percy, 1996).

While the quality of police service is often thought to be an important reason for nonreporting, it is clear that the public has other reasons for not reporting crimes to the police. There is some evidence that reporting is linked to the likelihood that the victim will receive some kind of loss reimbursement through an insurance claim. This idea is also given some support in a summary report of the 1994 British Crime Survey, which showed that reporting rates had declined since the 1992 survey (which marked a reversal of the gradual increase in reporting experience over the preceding 10 years) (Mayhew, Mirrlees-Black, & Maung, 1994). It was argued that the recent reduction in reporting rates might in part be an "insurance effect" as a result of recent increases in insurance premiums. The authors argue that if this were found to be true, it might have important implications for crime rates and detection. It seems plausible that any increase in insurance premiums will have a disproportionate effect on reporting in poorer areas. As these are also the areas with the highest crime rates, any decline in reporting due to an "insurance effect" would have a disproportionate overall effect on reporting rates as a whole. Hence, in this one particular area of public involvement in routine policing, the research suggests that the public provides information about crime to the police in a limited and uneven manner.

EVALUATION OF PUBLIC INVOLVEMENT IN COMMUNITY POLICING

This final section concerns the effectiveness of the public in the delivery of community policing. In practice, this involves looking at the evidence relating to public involvement in consultation and collaboration with the police.

Police-Community Consultation

The major research on police consultative committees in England and Wales has been conducted by Morgan and Maggs (Morgan, 1986; Morgan &

Maggs, 1985). The authors concluded that all police authorities had followed Home Office advice and implemented some kind of consultative arrangement in their police force areas. Most police forces had a number of consultative committees with, on average, one for each division (or subdivision) or (in the case of the Metropolitan Police) one for each borough.

The research examined in detail consultative committees in nine police subdivisions. The results showed that meetings generally were poorly attended. Further, some social groups were not represented at the meetings at all. Meeting attenders tended to be disproportionately male, middle-class, middle-aged, and existing community activists. Many of the members had little experience of the police or current policing issues and were fairly ignorant of day-to-day policing methods and procedures. As a result, the meetings typically took the form of the police educating the community representatives about policing. The majority of the time of the meetings was devoted to police reports about the state of crime in the area and the paucity of police resources. The police accounts were generally accepted by the members (who according to Morgan had no basis to challenge them) and the meetings were generally supportive and sympathetic to the situation of the police.

Hence, these results seem to indicate a general apathy among the general public to becoming involved in formal consultation arrangements arranged at the community level.

Neighborhood Watch

There is also some evidence that the public plays only a minimal role in policing when given the opportunity to do so. This can be argued most strongly in the case of Neighborhood Watch schemes. The results of a detailed study of two Neighborhood Watch schemes in London showed that, in many respects, the programs were not well implemented. One of the problems concerning implementation was the lack of involvement of members of the public. Apart from attending the launch meeting and displaying a Neighborhood Watch sticker in their windows, local residents typically played very little further part in the scheme.

Less than half of residents in each of the two experimental areas (47% in one area and 40% in the other area) said that they had watched for something suspicious even though this was the central component of the scheme. Of those who said that they had watched for anything suspicious, less than half (48% in Acton and 45% in Wimbledon) said that they had seen anything suspicious. Of those who said that they had seen something suspicious, about half said that they had reported the incident to someone. Of those who said that they had reported the incident to someone, just over half said that they reported it to the police. In total, only 9% of residents in Acton and 5% of residents in Wimbledon actually reported anything suspicious to the police in the previous year.

The results of the London evaluation showed that the programs had no impact on victimization rates, reporting rates, or police clear-up rates (although there was a reduction in worry about property crime in one of the neighborhood watch areas; Bennett, 1990a). The research concluded that the lack of program impact was a result (at least in part) of program failure and weak program design that resulted in limited public involvement in it.

CONCLUSION

The results of this brief review of some of the evaluative research conducted in Britain on the police and public involvement in community policing suggest that in many important respects the contribution of each has not been as great as might have been expected.

The research on community policing suggests that the police have not yet assimilated the philosophy of community policing into their routine thinking. Decentralization in the form of sector policing has been found to be hard to implement, and some research has shown that lower ranking officers have obstructed or sabotaged attempts to implement it. Community constables are widespread in terms of their numbers, but spend relatively little of their time conducting community-oriented tasks and are often withdrawn from their beats to conduct other policing duties elsewhere. The research on community policing also shows that public involvement in community consultation and in collaborative partnerships with the police is in some respects limited. Involvement and participation in community crime prevention involving collaboration with the police is generally low, and important elements of programs are often not supported or sustained.

The research on routine policing that involves some kind of contact between the police and the public, and that has been evaluated in terms of public satisfaction, has shown that there are important gaps in the quality of service provided by the police. It could also be argued, however, that the research has shown that there are also important gaps in the quality of service provided by the public to the police. Reporting rates for some crimes are fairly low and there is some evidence that reporting rates are beginning to decline further.

While these conclusions are to some extent based on a selective reading of the research literature, there is at least some cause for concern about the level of commitment of both the police and the public to the quality of service delivery in general and to community policing in particular. It is possible that this apparently weak level of involvement and commitment on the part of the police and the public might explain the relatively limited success shown in evaluative research for community policing programs. Future attempts to implement community policing should perhaps look carefully at some of the reasons for this apparent reluctance of the police and the public to take a more active role in the delivery of police service at the community level and to take these reasons into account when designing the programs.

7

EVALUATING SATISFACTION

Vincent F. Sacco

The movement from traditional to community-based models of policing has suggested to many observers a need to develop alternative methods for the evaluation of police performance (Chicago Community Policing Evaluation Consortium, 1995; Normandeau & Leighton, 1990). A narrow reliance on the use of measures such as response time or crime, arrest, or clearance rates is increasingly seen as inconsistent with the new policing philosophies, in large part because such measures fail to speak to the role of the public as the consumer of policing services (Couper, 1983; Skogan, 1994a). It is argued that, like all complex agencies involved in service delivery, it is important for the police to know how satisfied or dissatisfied their clients are. Moreover, it is important to discover the factors that affect citizen satisfaction and whether they are subject to manipulation within the parameters established by law and available organizational resources. It is in this context that public satisfaction with the police has emerged as a significant issue.

Judgments regarding public satisfaction are usually based on the findings of surveys of general populations or of more specialized samples such as crime victims or those who have had some other type of recent contact with the police. Respondents are typically asked in direct fashion how satisfied they are with their local police, how good a job they think the police are doing or how effective they perceive the police to be. Respondents who have had a recent encounter with the police might be asked if they were satisfied with the outcome; whether the officers with whom they had contact were "polite" or "courteous"; or if they behaved in a "professional" manner.

While surveys are not the only source of information about citizen satisfaction, they are generally thought to be preferable to many of the alternatives. Negative newspaper coverage, formal or informal complaints, the public forum, and the rhetoric of special interest groups provide a skewed and potentially misleading impression of the type and intensity of public feelings. In contrast, it can be argued that despite their own well-known limitations, surveys have an inherently democratic character in that opinions are solicited widely and weighted equally. In this way, surveys correct for the fact that many members of the public do not attend community consultations in order to express their views and that others do so selectively (Patterson & Grant, 1988).

Over the past several years, consumer-based surveys of policing have become a "growth industry" (Horne, 1992). Frequently, under the auspices of policing agencies, such studies are undertaken by researchers who are affiliated with universities or marketing firms and who claim an "arm's length" relationship to the problem at hand. In other instances, these studies are undertaken by police agency personnel or volunteers who, although they are less able to claim professional distance, maintain that they possess intimate insider knowledge of the issues that the survey is intended to illuminate.

For some cynics, the surveys themselves are best conceptualized as little more than a public relations exercise. It is suggested that, although they provide highly visible evidence that the police are engaging in "broad consultations" about service delivery, the surveys generate little information that is of real value.

Overall, surveys done in Canada seem to indicate that Canadians are highly satisfied with policing services. Cycle 8 of the General Social Survey asked a representative sample of 10,000 Canadians in 1993 if they thought their local police were doing a "good," "average," or "poor" job in several areas of service delivery. For all of the items except one, at least one half of respondents chose the most favorable response. The single exception was an item that asked about promptness in responding to calls, for which 46% of Canadians described police performance as "good."

A 1991 Gallup poll report indicated that close to 80% of Canadians approve of the performance of their local police and that the level of support has not changed substantially since the question was first introduced in 1969 (Bozinoff & MacIntosh, 1991). The results of the most recent round of the International Crime Survey indicate that overall satisfaction with the police is higher in Canada than in any of the other countries included in the study. The same survey found that about three quarters of the Canadian respondents who said that they had reported a crime to the police were satisfied with the ways in which the police responded (van Dijk & Mayhew, 1992).

These high ratings are particularly noteworthy when they are compared to those that are routinely associated with the courts or other components of the criminal justice system. For example, respondents to the 1993 General Social Survey were asked whether they thought the courts were doing a "good," "average," or "poor" job in the performance of four specific functions. For three of the items, fewer than one quarter of respondents gave the courts the highest rating. In the case of the item that asked respondents about the job that courts do in "protecting the rights of the accused," close to one half of Canadians expressed the view that the courts do a good job. It is unclear, however, given public concern about the assumed laxity of the court system, whether the high numbers in this case indicate approval or disapproval.

In view of the high levels of public satisfaction with the police described by such surveys, it is prudent to ask what these numbers really mean and what practical implications they have. The chapter addresses these questions through an examination of three broad issues. The first concerns the problematic character of the concept of satisfaction. The second focuses attention on the social factors—especially personal experience—that have been shown to have significant influence on public satisfaction. Finally, the community dimensions of public satisfaction with police services are explored. Based on a review of research in these areas, the chapter concludes with some practical observations about the potential benefits and liabilities associated with the use of satisfaction measures.

THE MEANING OF PUBLIC SATISFACTION

Like all such evaluative concepts, the term *satisfaction* proves to be ambiguous upon close examination. This ambiguity has several dimensions.

First, when respondents are asked about their degree of satisfaction with policing services, it is not necessarily clear that the questions are as meaningful to them as they are to those who sponsored the survey (Southgate & Ekblom, 1984). More pointedly, it is not always evident precisely what type of evaluation respondents are being asked to make. Do the questions relate to their views of the police as an organization or are respondents being asked for an opinion based on their cumulative experiences with individual police officers? Is the judgment to be made in terms of some absolute standard or in some relative way that makes implicit comparisons to other times or other places? Should the assessment take explicit account of the resources that the police have at their disposal or should it employ more general criteria for evaluating police performance?

Next, the range of responses provided to respondents does not necessarily reflect the range or the content of opinions among the public at large. In other words, it is not obvious that those who score highest on a relevant scale are expressing satisfaction in an absolute sense or simply expressing more satisfaction than is implied by the alternative response categories. Similarly, do low scores mean that people are dissatisfied or simply less satisfied than those who rate the police most highly (Garofalo, 1977)? Any such distinctions could have significant implications not only for public policy but also for the morale of the members of the policing agency.

In a related way, data from victimization surveys show that when victims who do not report crimes to the police are provided with a list of possible reasons for their decisions, they frequently indicate that "the police couldn't do anything about it" (Gottfredson & Gottfredson, 1988). While this response could be read as an indictment of the police or as an expression of a lack of confidence, it could also reveal, as has frequently been observed, that people are able to make relatively accurate and rational assessments of the investigative power of the police in certain types of situations.

Third, the gap between survey reports and incidents about which reports are provided may be substantial. In a fundamental way, expressions of public satisfaction or dissatisfaction with the police do not tell us how well things are working, but how well they are perceived to be working. Survey responses may reflect preexisting tendencies to be satisfied or dissatisfied rather than the quality of the service that is delivered.

In the context of specific encounters, dissatisfaction with what the attending officer did or failed to do does not necessarily imply inappropriate action. While crime victims may, for example, resent police attempts to establish the legitimacy of a claim of victimization, this does not necessarily mean that a different course of action should have been taken (Poister & McDavid, 1978). Citizens may forget what the officer did, or misunderstand or misjudge questions asked or actions taken by the police (Skogan, 1990b).

Alternatively, high levels of public satisfaction with policing can indicate approval of actions that may be inconsistent with other organizational standards. The vox populi character of satisfaction measures may mean that situations exist in which the police are allowed, for example, to ignore the rights of minorities and still get high marks from many members of the public (Normandeau & Leighton, 1990).

Fourth, satisfaction and other attitudes toward the police are complex and multifaceted rather than unidimensional phenomena. The various components of satisfaction—police demeanor, respect, effectiveness, professionalism, the use of police power—may be understood differently by different audiences (Lee, 1991; Munn & Renner, 1978; Sullivan, Dunham, & Alpert, 1987). Moreover, these attitudes do not exist in isolation but are bound up with perceptions of other aspects of the urban or political environment. Dissatisfaction with the police may reflect dissatisfaction with the delivery of urban services more generally (Charles, 1980; Greene & Decker, 1989) and more general attitudes to the police may be part of "a larger complex" that includes attitudes toward the courts and the legal system as well as political alienation and powerlessness (Albrecht & Green, 1977; Arthur, 1993).

Fifth, the relationships linking various forms of satisfaction are inadequately understood. How people feel they have been treated by the police in particular situations may be influenced by how they feel about the police more generally; although there is evidence to suggest that the reverse is also true (Mayhew, Maung, & Mirrlees-Black, 1993).

With respect to specific incidents, dissatisfaction with one aspect of the encounter may lead to dissatisfaction with other aspects. It is not necessarily the case that people neatly divide up their perceptions into the narrow categories about which interviewers ask them questions. Using data from the Winnipeg Area Survey, Forde (1992) found, for instance, that among consumers of police services, dissatisfaction with the police operator (who took the call) was related to dissatisfaction with response time and with the officer's investigation. In addition, those who were dissatisfied with response time were also likely to be dissatisfied with whatever investigation took place. "Halo effects" may also operate in some situations such that satisfaction with the way in which the police handle the later stages of an incident may encourage a retrospective interpretation of the degree of satisfaction with earlier stages of the contact (Poister & McDavid, 1978).

Even more generally, those who encounter the police in highly stressful or adversarial circumstances may not always be able to discriminate with respect to the source of their frustration. As a consequence, dissatisfaction with the situation may be displaced onto the police officer (Maxfield, 1988).

Finally, the relationship between satisfaction and expectations is rarely made explicit. Evaluative concepts like satisfaction with overall quality of service, and judgments about courtesy, effort, or professionalism imply the existence of some standards against which the judgment is made. These standards may be conceptualized as expectations that clients have about police performance generally or in specific situations (Erez, 1984). In the case of response time, for instance, several researchers have noted the important role played by expectations in the determination of satisfaction (Brandl & Horvath, 1991; Percy, 1980; Southgate & Ekblom, 1984). Yet while surveys tell us how people feel about the things that police do, they less often tell us what people expect the police to do or how they expect them to do it.

The relationship between expectations and satisfaction is not necessarily a simple one. Members of the public who have very high expectations of the police are likely to become frustrated when the police fail to meet these expectations (Carter, 1985). Such expectations may be rooted in what people believe they have a right to expect from the police or from the social service sector more generally (Erez, 1984). This link between expectations and notions of justice may result in the use of relatively stringent criteria in the evaluation of police performance and in higher levels of dissatisfaction in situations that are defined as violating these expectations. Alternatively, when past experiences encourage a downward revision of expectations, the result may be a more negative view of the police and greater dissatisfaction in the context of subsequent encounters.

It is reasonable to argue that expectations regarding policing are contextualized by group experiences and therefore reflect ethnic or class variations in the ways in which policing roles are understood. With respect to ethnic differences specifically, Erez (1984) suggests that treatment by the police can be viewed as symbolic of the respect to which groups believe they are entitled in a multicultural society. Thus, minorities that are attempting to become part of the cultural mainstream may be very aware of, and very sensitive to, police responses that seem to signal a lack of respect.

In a related way, the finding that crime victims (especially victims of serious crime) are less favorable to the police may demonstrate a tendency to have high expectations of the police and what they can accomplish in crime-related situations (Brandl & Horvath, 1991; Koenig, 1980; Yarmey, 1991). The growth of the victims movement over the past several years has probably contributed to the raising of expectations in this respect (Elias, 1993). Skogan's (1990b) analysis of the British Crime Survey found that levels of public satisfaction were generally higher in the case of calls for service that were defined as less urgent and that dissatisfaction was greatest regarding events that were most closely related to the traditional core of policing.

Undoubtedly, public expectations about how the police are expected to perform are shaped by mass media images. Skogan (1994a) found that those British Crime Survey respondents who identified television, radio, or newspapers as their major source of information about the police were more positive in their assessments and more likely to think that the police in their areas performed above average. Analyses of media content consistently demonstrate that of the various criminal justice agencies, it is the police who are most frequently and most favorably portrayed (Sacco, 1995; Surette, 1992). Comparisons, for instance, of the "clearance rates" in either crime news or television crime drama with the clearance rates provided by police data suggest that media images set very high standards for real-world comparisons.

THE DETERMINANTS OF SATISFACTION

As Reiner (1992a) has noted, early research generated broad generalizations regarding the social distributional character of public attitudes toward the police. Much of this research encouraged an understanding of satisfaction and other perceptions as a function of the personal characteristics of respondents. Notably:

1. In the case of age, research supports the view that positive assessments of the police are more likely to be expressed by older respondents (Garofalo, 1977; Murphy & Lithopoulos, 1988; Skogan, 1994a). In the Canadian General Social Survey, for instance, those between the ages of 15 and 24 were least likely to rate police performance favorably (Sacco & Johnson, 1990). There is some evidence that the effect of youthfulness on dissatisfaction varies between men and women such that the most negative views are expressed by young males (Forde, 1992).

2. The level of positive sentiment varies across ethnic and racial groups (Greene & Decker, 1989; Jefferson & Walker, 1993; Lee, 1991; Mayhew, Elliott, & Dowds, 1989; Mayhew et al., 1993; Skogan, 1994a; Smith, 1991; Waddington & Braddock, 1991). This is perhaps most clear in the context of American research that indicates that African Americans are less likely than whites to express satisfaction with police performance.

3. The relationships involving satisfaction and other key social and demographic variables such as sex, income, and employment are much less consistent (Decker, 1981; Klein, Webb, & DiSanto, 1978).

The factor that has received the greatest amount of attention in recent years is personal experience with the police. Because citizens may encounter the police in a wide variety of contexts (as victims, suspects, witnesses, seekers or providers of information, etc.), surveys generally show that the proportion of respondents who report a recent contact with the police is relatively large (Forde, 1992; Southgate & Ekblom, 1984). Fully 45% of the respondents to Cycle 8 of the Canadian General Survey indicated that they had experienced at least one professional contact with the police during the 12-month period preceding the survey.

Three factors complicate efforts to make sense of the relationship between public experiences with the police and satisfaction with the police:

First, the various forms of police-citizen contact cannot be studied with equal ease. The population survey, for instance, is probably better used to study public consumption of police services than to study the ways in which members of the public react as suspects or adversaries of the police.

Second, people who engage the police in one capacity are more likely to engage them in other capacities. Maxfield (1988) argues that those who meet the police as "beneficiaries" of police services (as victims of crime or as receivers of information) are also quite likely to meet them as "sufferers" (suspects). He suggests that victims have less positive attitudes toward the police at least in part because they are also more likely to have encountered the police in more adversarial circumstances.

Third, public experiences with the police are not randomly distributed in the population but are related to people's other social and demographic characteristics. The unemployed, for instance, may be more likely to have adversarial relationships with the police, while those of higher socioeconomic status are more likely to be consumers of police services (Southgate & Ekblom, 1984; Skogan, 1990b). Such findings have implications for community-level processes in that the greater the concentration of negative contacts in particular social groups, the more likely it is that hearsay and folk knowledge will contribute to negative views of the police (Southgate & Ekblom, 1984).

In all such encounters, the probability of citizen satisfaction or dissatisfaction is dependent on a variety of factors—most important, the nature of the incident that brings the police and the public together, the perceived appropriateness of the police officer's behavior, and the citizen's expectations regarding the situation and its potential outcome.

With respect to the first of these factors, a general distinction is usually made between voluntary and involuntary contacts with the police. The former type of contact is typically initiated by members of the public, while the latter type is typically initiated by the police. Voluntary contacts are usually consumer-oriented in that the public seeks policing services in the forms of advice or assistance, while involuntary contacts are much more likely to be adversarial in nature. In general, while voluntary contacts tend to be more common, involuntary contacts are more likely to contribute to negative views of the police (Dunham & Alpert, 1988; Jefferson & Walker, 1993).

The interpretations that members of the public make of the behavior of the police affect the degree of satisfaction that they are likely to express with respect to the encounter. In this respect, perceptions of courtesy, demeanor, level of interest, actions taken, professionalism, and response time importantly influence public satisfaction (Brandl & Horvath, 1991; Klein et al., 1978; Maxfield, 1988). Higher levels of satisfaction are also associated with face-to-face rather than more impersonal forms of interaction (Skogan, 1990b). Because police-citizen interactions are subject to highly variable interpretations, it is difficult to determine whether the greater degree of dissatisfaction that is expressed by minority group members reflects differential treatment by the police or the use of different standards regarding police performance (Mayhew et al., 1989).

Expectations regarding investigative efforts have been shown to be related to level of satisfaction, but more so in the case of property crime than in the case of crimes of violence. Victims of violence are less likely to expect intensive investigations since in the majority of cases, they are likely to know who the offenders are (Brandl & Horvath, 1991).

Public expectations about the potential outcomes of the interaction are also related to satisfaction, particularly in the case of crime victims (Poister & McDavid, 1978). Victims express greater satisfaction, for instance, when offenders are apprehended or when property is recovered (Skogan, 1990b). Data from the British Crime Survey indicate that victims who are insurance claimants are more likely to be satisfied with their encounters with police and that, overall, the highest levels of satisfaction are expressed by victims of breaking and entering, and of automobile and bicycle theft. The obvious interpretation of this finding is that in such cases, the police are seen as facilitators of insurance claims and thus helpful in bringing about a more favorable resolution of the incident (Mayhew et al., 1993). Of course, the ability to achieve desirable outcomes—in the form of property returned or offenders apprehended—is in many cases beyond the control of the police.

It has long been argued that public satisfaction with policing can be increased if the rate of informal but official, nonemergency contacts is increased (Scaglion & Condon, 1980). Consistent with this view, citizen contact patrols, mini-stations, foot patrols, and other types of programs that come under the umbrella of community policing have as their objective an increase in such contacts. Evaluations of several such programs do, in fact, indicate that public views of the police can be improved by proactive contact (Bennett, 1990b; Rosenbaum & Lurigio, 1994; Skogan, 1990a; Williams & Pate, 1987)—even when that is not the primary objective of the program (Bennett, 1991). Several caveats appear to be in order, however.

First, for some groups the effects of proactive contact may not be easily generalized to other experiences. Among young people, for instance, positive contacts with school liaison officers may promote positive views of the officer in question but may not defeat expectations about adversarial contacts with police beyond the school setting (Hopkins, Hewstone, & Hantzi, 1992).

Second, members of the public may have little interest in such contacts unless they believe that there is a practical reason for them (Brandl & Horvath, 1991). Otherwise, they may perceive the contacts as a waste of time or as an intrusion (Southgate & Ekblom, 1984).

Finally, as Skogan (1990a) has argued, in order to achieve program objectives, it may not be enough simply to provide the opportunity for such contacts as is frequently the case with mini-stations or community policing organizations, for instance. In such circumstances, the effects of these programs may spread to those who need them least (Rosenbaum, 1988). More desirable is an aggressive proactive program that does not depend on the public coming forward to engage the opportunities for interaction.

COMMUNITY DIMENSIONS OF SATISFACTION WITH POLICING

The research tradition linking attitudes to the police to such individual characteristics as age, ethnicity, or social class reflects the powerful legacy of public opinion research that views "the public" as a collection of disconnected individuals. However, this emphasis ignores the character of the local community context within which views of police performance develop and to which policing services are delivered.

There is, of course, no clear and unequivocal definition of local community either in the policing literature or in the more general literature of social science (Buerger, 1994b). To a considerable degree, as Leighton (1988) notes, community is in the eye of the beholder. Frequently in discussions of policing, "community" is used as a political concept to denote the nexus of local organizations that claim to speak for area residents (Buerger, 1993). In the present context, the use of the term is less political and more traditionally sociological. Communities in this sense are collections of people who are tied to particular places, who share common concerns, and who have available to them common lifestyles. The reemergence in criminology of ecological approaches and the developing interest in topics such as "social disorder" and "hot spots" suggest the relevance of community analyses of crime and policing (Bursik & Grasmick, 1993; Byrne & Sampson, 1986; Farrington, Sampson, & Wikstrom, 1993; Sherman, Gartin, & Buerger, 1989; Skogan, 1990a).

It has been argued that local communities develop "neighborhood cultures" that lend variable levels of support to policing activities (Dunham & Alpert, 1988; Greene & Decker, 1989). Such cultures reflect residents' accumulated experiences with crime, disorder, and the police. In some cases, they make available a "folk history" of unpleasant experiences with the police (Gaskell & Smith, 1985), and as stories about police misconduct travel through neighborhood networks, they affect the views of those who are exposed to them (Klein et al., 1978). Particularly notorious cases, such as the Rodney King incident, can exert a profound negative effect on the perceptions of members of the public, especially when the episode resonates with their own experiences (Lasley, 1994). In short, beliefs and feelings about the police do not form in isolation but as part of a social process rooted in the local area.

Given patterns of residential segregation, the influence of ethnic, racial, or socioeconomic factors is partially, at least, indicative of community effects. However, these relationships may involve interactions among ethnicity, class, and the local community such that the effects of ethnicity on perceptions of the police may depend on the community context (Murty, Roebuck, & Smith, 1990; Smith, 1984). Data from the Toronto Community Policing Survey, for example, found that while East and Northern Europeans provided consistently more positive ratings of the police, irrespective of neighborhood of residence, East Indian, Caribbean, and Italian residents tended to express more negative views, but the effects varied by neighborhood (Murphy & Lithopoulos, 1988).

Unfortunately, data gathered at the national, regional, or even the metropolitan level often mask such effects. National studies, for instance, are unable to tell us much about local communities and thus we learn little about how factors such as policing styles, press coverage of highly sensationalized cases, or recent changes in the local crime rate affect satisfaction with the police at the local level (Greene & Decker, 1989).

Research concerning the relationship between fear of crime and other indicators of the concern for personal safety and public perceptions of the police provides a useful example of the relevance of community context. Several studies have examined these relationships and the findings have been inconsistent (Baker, Nienstedt, Everett, & McCleary, 1983; Bennett, 1991; Box, Hale, & Andrews, 1988; Flanagan, 1985; Forde, 1992; Mirande, 1980; Murphy & Lithopoulos, 1988; Thomas & Hyman, 1977). No doubt, part of the problem rests with the wide variations in the ways in which fear of crime and satisfaction with the police are operationalized.

It is also likely, however, that whatever relationship does exist between perceptions of crime and personal safety on the one hand and perceptions of the police on the other is dependent on the character of the local community. Such relationships seem more likely to emerge when the local political culture links rising crime rates to police performance. In an early study that used crime rate data from 13 large American central cities, Skogan (1978) found that while in some communities, the relationship between perceptions of neighborhood safety and perceptions of the police were moderately related, in other communities they were practically unrelated.

Generally, data that are intended to characterize the views of a large population are of limited practical value since police resources are not deployed across entire populations but within local communities. Because policing must be responsive to the needs and concerns of cultural or class groups, contextualized by specific community settings, a detailed understanding of the community dimensions of public satisfaction is highly desirable.

While attention to the community dimensions of public satisfaction has distinct advantages for both researchers and policing managers, there are liabilities. Leighton (1991), for example, warns that a purely local perspective increases the risk of "sand-box policing" such that regional or national problems come to be seen only in terms of their local dimensions.

There are also problems associated with the recent grassroots movement toward the collection of community-based information about public perceptions of the police. These problems emerge out of attempts to balance the need for high quality, representative data with the costs and complexities of gathering such information.

Surveys are often preferred for this purpose because they are widely viewed as scientifically more rigorous than other approaches and because they produce "hard numbers." However, surveys are also resource-intensive undertakings that require accessibility to funds and expertise (Eck, 1984; Linguanti & McIntyre, 1992). In larger departments, this may be less of a problem than in smaller ones. Yet, the perceived need to use surveys either to document high levels of public satisfaction with police or to identify and correct low levels of satisfaction appears to be spread much more evenly than are the resources with which to undertake such projects. Inattention to problems of sampling, conceptualization, and the measurement of complex phenomena such as victimization, produces data that may not only fail to inform but that may mislead those who seek to use the information in a practical way.

CONCLUSIONS

This brief review of the literature on public satisfaction with the police suggests several tentative conclusions. First, general levels of public satisfaction with policing are very high in Canada. No other criminal justice component and few other social services enjoy such a high degree of public confidence (Bozinoff & MacIntosh, 1990). On the positive side, this can be seen as a source of pride for policing agencies—particularly in a period that has witnessed "crises of confidence" in many institutional realms. However, it is important to recognize that satisfaction is most apparent when survey questions are phrased most generally. As one moves away from this "warm and fuzzy" level, and as the questions become more specific, dissatisfaction with various aspects of the police begins to emerge. In addition, "sound bite" statements about overall approval ratings mask the greater degrees of discontent voiced by socioeconomic or ethnic minorities.

Second, the experiences of other countries indicate the need to be humble even in the face of overwhelming support. Such support can decline for a variety of reasons—only some of which are directly controllable by the police. On the other side, some factors such as Canadian cultural traditions and the routine processes of crime news production should continue to reproduce an environment conducive to widespread public support of policing. There is as well reason to believe that the media treatment of new policing initiatives as "good news" will further enhance press presentations of the police (McGahan, 1992).

Third, higher levels of public satisfaction with the police can be achieved through programs that increase the number of nonthreatening contacts with the public. In fact, improvements in attitudes toward the police seem to be among the more likely outcomes of community policing initiatives. In the absence of such contacts, it is argued the police have an inadequate understanding of public concerns and members of the public feel that the police are not really concerned with their welfare. For most segments of the population, however, it appears that general satisfaction is already at a high level. Where it is not, positive effects cannot be expected simply because opportunities for satisfying experiences are made available.

Fourth, the issue of public expectations of the police is to some extent a two-edged sword. On one hand, the high level of expectations associated with policing probably contribute to the high regard in which the police are held. On the other hand, such expectations create a gap between what people expect and what people feel they receive when policing services are delivered. Quite obviously we need a more detailed understanding of what people do expect from the police, as well as what police services they expect to be able to do without in the current fiscal climate. Survey findings can inform whatever public information strategies might be developed to speak to these expectations.

Fifth, despite their apparently unambiguous character, measures of public satisfaction with the police are of only limited utility for strategic decision making. It appears that those who use police services more frequently express less satisfaction. Moreover, satisfaction may rest upon assumptions about what the police can accomplish rather than upon what they actually are able to accomplish. Such observations indicate the need to consider the high levels of public satisfaction with the police in a context that also assigns high priority to other indicators of agency performance. Otherwise, improvements in satisfaction ratings can too easily become an end in themselves. This is particularly problematic in view of the fact that many community-based programs that are intended to improve police service (through the reduction of crime or of the fear of crime) may increase satisfaction even though the primary objectives of these programs are not met. While it is frequently argued that high levels of public support and satisfaction provide an important source of capital that can be mobilized in support of new policing initiatives, it is easy to confuse contentment with policing and enthusiasm about policing. Satisfaction does not imply that apathy ceases to be a problem (Grinc, 1994).

Finally, there is a need to encourage data collection efforts that assign priority to the study of community differences in public satisfaction with policing. National data collection efforts, like the General Social Survey, can provide broad standards against which local performance can be judged but these data prove to be of limited practical utility at the local level. However, the collection and analysis of high quality data relating to crime and policing at the local level can prove to be a resource-intensive undertaking. Policing agencies should not undertake such projects unless they are confident that appropriate methodological standards will be met. The results of such projects can be too easily dismissed or if used for planning purposes can prove misleading. Instead, such agencies are well advised to consider, as some have already done, the use of more qualitative (if less statistically representative methods) such as focus groups.

PART III

ISSUES IN ORGANIZATIONAL CHANGE

EVALUATING PLANNED CHANGE STRATEGIES IN MODERN LAW ENFORCEMENT
Implementing Community-Based Policing

Jack R. Greene

For nearly 10 years, community and problem-oriented policing ideas have captured the imagination of police officials, community activists, and even academics. The rhetoric of community policing now embodied in the passage of the U.S. 1994 Omnibus Crime Control Act and has even received presidential utterance. Today, the crime control agenda of the United States, and many other countries, includes a visible place for "community policing" and its derivatives.

Despite all the "hoopla," what we actually know about community and problem-oriented policing is minuscule in comparison to what we don't know.

AUTHOR'S NOTE: Parts of this chapter were originally presented at the 21st Century Policing Meeting, November 1993, sponsored by the National Institute of Justice, U.S. Department of Justice.

What we particularly don't know is how community policing is converted from an organizational philosophy or strategy to a set of coherent activities with measurable efforts, outputs, and results. In many community policing programs it is simply assumed that police officers can act in a "community orientation," that police organizations can support this emerging style of policing, and that communities can differentiate community policing actions from those of traditional policing. Such assumptions produce the illusion that it is relatively easy for police agencies to convert from traditional to community policing. Nothing could be farther from the truth. A growing body of research suggests that without proper implementation community and problem-oriented policing are empty concepts, raising public and police expectations without a real chance of success.

THE RISE OF COMMUNITY POLICING

> Community Policing has become a new orthodoxy for cops. Simultaneously ambitious and ambiguous, community policing promises to change radically the relationship between the police and the public, address underlying community problems, and improve the living conditions of neighborhoods. One reason for its popularity is that community policing is a plastic concept, meaning different things to different people. There are many perspectives on community policing, and each of them is built on assumptions that are only partially supported by empirical evidence. (Eck & Rosenbaum, 1994, p. 3)

It is perhaps understandable that policing is continually in the throes of critique and reform. Much of government finds itself in the same position. Since the early 1900s, American government, most particularly city government, has been in a perpetual state of political, social, and economic transformation. Such transformation has invariably involved questions of justice and the role of the state in shaping and controlling everyday life (Judd, 1988, pp. 83-117). Implicitly, and more often explicitly, the police have been part of this transformation.

Since their earliest inception, the police have struggled with being efficient, effective, and lawful. Rooted in Western political philosophies emphasizing equity, fairness, and justice (Critchley, 1967), modern policing must be concerned with controlling violence and civil unrest while reducing the public's fear of crime. In addition, in recent years the police have come under closer scrutiny for the quality and effect of their interactions with the public. Taken together, the historical premises underlying policing in a democratic society, coupled with current public concerns with crime, as well as the social, political, and community accountability of the police, have perhaps resulted in the broadening of the "impossible mandate" (Manning, 1977) of modern-day policing.

The newest in a long line of reforms, community and problem-oriented policing seek to redress concerns for police accountability, as well as the efficient and effective pursuit of crime control objectives. Community-based policing essentially seeks to form a stronger alliance and dialogue between the police and communities. Such an alliance, it is believed, produces greater mutual support and the co-production of crime control activities, while strengthening community resistance to the invasion of crime and disorder (Skolnick & Bayley, 1986). Problem-oriented policing, by contrast, focuses on the ends of policing—solving community problems that give rise to crime and disorder (Goldstein, 1990). Together, community and problem-oriented policing have been hailed as the new paradigm in policing, emphasizing improvements in police effectiveness as well as increased police accountability.

Community Policing: Basic Elements

Whether community or problem-oriented policing will increase police efficiency and effectiveness, or make the police more lawful, remains to be seen. The philosophies, strategies, programs, and tactics that have emerged in modern-day policing over the past 10 years, and that are tied to the community policing movement, suggest some common orientations.

Common "core" elements of community policing programs include a redefinition of the police role; greater reciprocity in police and community relations; area decentralization of police services and command; and some form of civilianization (Skolnick & Bayley, 1986). Each of these changes is viewed as a necessary condition to realizing greater police accountability to the community. At the same time, these efforts suggest that, if adopted, the police can become more effective and efficient.

The core elements in community and problem-oriented policing are replete with assumptions about changing people, attitudes, work routines, information, organizational structures, and interaction patterns. Many of these assumptions remain unexplored in the research on community policing, although there is a growing recognition that to be realized, community policing requires supportive institutional apparatus and thoughtful implementation.[1]

The collective assumptions embedded within community and problem-oriented policing are indeed complex. They include assumptions about:

(a) how shifts in organizational philosophies affect service delivery; (b) how organizations translate missions and values into clear job descriptions and on-the-job behaviors; (c) how organizations interact with their wider environments and the degree to which the environment can tolerate increased interaction; and (d) how changes in philosophy, structure, training, supervision, and technology impact community problems, disorder, crime, and fear. At a minimum, such assumptions require major changes to the institution of policing, not "tinkering at the margins."

The Rhetoric and the Reality

Claims and counterclaims not withstanding, it is difficult to understand the full impact of community policing on police organizations or on the relationships between the police and the public. This is in part due to the wide array of activities and outcomes falling under the community policing umbrella. Part is also due to the fact that most community policing efforts have not been rigorously evaluated (Greene & Taylor, 1988), and part is due to the fact that as more stringent assessments of community policing are undertaken, the likely consequence is finding no result.

In some agencies community policing is a specialist function, in others it is more generalized throughout all police activities. In some police agencies problem solving is patrol centered, in others investigators are being drawn into problem-focused efforts. In some communities fear of crime is the target; in others "problems," generally defined, are targeted for a wide range of police interventions. Under the community policing banner, police are now more likely to get out of their police cars and talk with citizens or to provide services from local mini- or substations, investigate a broader range of social behaviors, and attempt to tailor a response to the needed intervention. While many of the projects under way report favorable results, much of the research surrounding these interventions is bounded by the research design employed. As a result, research on these questions is of limited guidance.

Despite acknowledged shortcomings, the general findings of various studies suggest that the police have some effect on perceptions of crime and assessments of the quality of police service, if not on crime itself. Fear of crime is apparently affected with greater public visibility of the police, and programs that bring the police into greater interaction with the citizenry typically produce more positive assessments of police services (see, for example, Skogan, 1994b).

Other findings suggest that community policing has some effect on improving police officer job satisfaction and job attachment. In a review of 12 such analyses, Lurigio and Rosenbaum (1994) concluded that these studies reported "increases in job satisfaction and motivation, a broadening of the police role, improvements in relationships with co-workers and citizens, and greater expectations regarding community participation in crime prevention efforts" (p. 160).

During the first 5 to 10 years of research on community policing much of the evaluation effort has been focused on outcomes; crime, disorder, and fear of crime dominated this discussion. As previously indicated, the results of ongoing research suggest that crime is largely unaffected by these police strategies, but neighborhood "problems" and fear of crime are impacted by community and problem-oriented approaches. In one respect, community and problem-oriented policing can be said to be no less effective than traditional policing in regard to crime, and, perhaps, slightly more effective in terms of reducing community disorder and fear.

One consistent finding from nearly a decade of research on community policing is the intractability of police organizations in their adoption of community policing, and their capacity for curbing, minimizing, and defeating reform movements. Nearly every study on the matter concludes that the structure and culture of police organizations are the largest impediments to implementing community-based policing.

Such a recognition calls for a consideration of program implementation in police organizations and how planned change is conceptualized, implemented, and evaluated. Such an assessment provides the "missing link" to conventional research, which has been primarily focused on police and community outcomes.

PROGRAM IMPLEMENTATION IN POLICING: GENERAL CONSIDERATIONS

The history of social program implementation, including that of the police, is a history of unrealized expectations; broken promises; discarded beliefs, slogans, and ideas; and frustrated policymakers. To be sure, policing has come a long way from the days of the "watch and ward." In general, policing is more civil, humane, and thoughtful than it has been in the past. Nevertheless, modern-day policing resembles more its historical roots than its envisioned future (see Buerger, 1993). There are many reasons for the seeming stability in the formal and social organization of policing. In large measure, the failure of many reforms to "change" policing may be most attributable to the insularity of police organizations and their concomitant ability to change "changes" as they are being introduced into police agencies. For many years and in many places, changes sought of the police have had to adapt to the police organization and subculture, rather than the organization and subculture adapting to the change (see, for example, Greene, 1989; Kelling & Wycoff, 1978; Manning, 1977).

For the most part, reforms of policing have also been largely rhetorical and less than substantive. The "core technology" of policing—basic patrol and detective services—have changed only slightly over the years, despite a long list of programs aimed at service delivery reform. Currently, in most American cities the 911—call-response—call system, for example, continues to dominate police organizational, managerial, and operational decision making even with the recognition that the 911 system clouds the strategic vision of the police (Sparrow, Moore, & Kennedy, 1990). Similarly, mandated police training programs continue to stress administrative and legal dictum, rather than building the interactive and thinking skills police officers in the 21st century will need if policing does indeed change. Moreover, today most police agencies are not information intensive, they cannot identify problems very well, and they often lack the administrative and cultural flexibility to respond quickly to a rapidly changing environment. Even in the current political debate, the assumption that we need more police, rather than the idea that we might need to rethink what they do, attests to the dominance of the 19th-century model of public law enforcement that continues to undergird American policing.[2]

These are not the views of a cynic. Rather, they stem from the recognition that, despite protestations to the contrary, there remains great ambiguity over the role of the police; it is not clear what the police do, nor is it clear what effects the police have on crime, fear, and victimization (see Bayley, 1994, chaps. 1 & 2; Greene & Klockars, 1991; Sherman, 1993). Pressures to "control the police" compete with pressures for the police to be more community oriented (Mastrofski & Greene, 1993), and the perception of escalating violence, particularly among America's youth, has created a demand for greater police visibility and crime suppression activities—not necessarily for problem solving. At times community and problem-oriented policing have been taken as "soft on crime," although many have argued that disorder and crime are inexplicably linked and that the pursuit of safer streets will, of necessity, attack crime (see Wilson, 1993). Taken together, these and other forces complicate the implementation of any significant change in the institutional and social fabric of the police.

Much of the concern with community-based and problem-oriented approaches to policing has been with demonstrating results. This "results" focus has concentrated on whether crime, victimization, or fear of crime went up or down in the target neighborhoods for these "experiments." Whether the personnel within these police agencies had a *clear understanding of the goals and objectives* of "community policing" has been much less well documented or understood. Whether personnel were *prepared adequately* for the "new" role implied of community policing is equally less clear. Whether the *organizational systems within any particular police agency could support* a shift from traditional to community-based policing has also been generally overlooked in most of these studies.

Levels of Police Intervention

> We may view a social action program as a form of intervention which attempts to prevent certain undesirable effects or consequences from developing by a deliberate attack upon causes or antecedent events. . . . Employing the analytic model of intervening variable analysis, we may conceptualize the intervention process largely as one attempting to alter the causal nexus between the independent and dependent variable through manipulation of the intervening variables by means of which the cause leads to the effect, or which modify or condition the effect. (Suchman, 1968, p. 173)

Such a conceptualization results in the specification of a chain of cause and effect relationships that include "(1) the relationship between the precondition and casual variables, (2) the relationship between the cause and effect variables, and (3) the relationship between the effect and the consequence variables" (Suchman, 1968, p. 173). Illustrations of these relationships for policing are depicted in Figure 8.1.

As shown in Figure 8.1, the police have three possible points of intervention into situations producing fear, disorder, and crime. *Primary interventions* taken by the police include programs that seek to model behavior for youth and those that seek to involve the community in some form of self-protection or related community-building activities. These are preventive to the extent that they seek to intervene between the conditions that spawn crime and disorder, generally those rooted in individual motivation and the level of community cohesiveness, and the more proximate causes of crime and disorder such as youth delinquency and deteriorated neighborhoods. Here lies much of the rhetoric and programming of community policing. Neighborhood

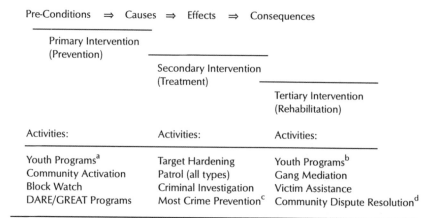

Figure 8.1. Levels of Police Intervention

SOURCE: Adapted from Suchman, 1968, pp. 171-175.

NOTE: a. Youth programs like Police Cadets, Police Athletic Leagues, or conflict mediation programs offered by the police and emphasizing "role modeling" attempt to intervene in lifestyle choices, making them preventive.

b. Youth programs dealing with gangs and "high risk" youth that emphasize mediation efforts are most focused on rehabilitation.

c. Most crime prevention programs focus on denying opportunity (a treatment) rather than focusing on motivation (a prevention).

d. Most dispute resolution programs seek to "repair" and/or rehabilitate the relationship between two or more disputants after a dispute has occurred and has failed to be resolved.

storefronts, beat officers, expanded block watch, community councils, and the like are aimed at reinforcing the community's ability, not that of the police, to resist crime. Other programs such as DARE and GREAT[3] seek to create alternative futures for youth so that they can more easily resist the temptation of drug use and gang membership.

Secondary interventions undertaken by the police include most of the "traditional" forms of policing. These include reactive patrol, follow-up criminal investigations, and most forms of crime prevention, including crime prevention through environmental design, that seek to deny opportunity rather than change motivation. Creating defensible space or analyzing crime patterns for "routine activities" are approaches seeking to intervene between proximate causes and immediate effects. Here the focus is on treating crime situations and events, through either the response of the police or the community. To be sure, there is some overlap among some police crime prevention activities, to the extent that they deter people from committing crimes in specific locations or at specific times. Yet to the degree that the police alone cannot be expected to affect the larger forces of society and personality that shape criminal intentions and behaviors, they too (the police) are a form of "social treatment" to the failures of larger social, political, and economic institutions.

It might be argued that much of "problem solving" falls under this secondary intervention level as well. Problem solving generally starts with the premise of analyzing historical and current behaviors and incidents, looking for some pattern. Crime analysis, for example, seeks to understand crime and disorder patterns. Once patterns are identified, strategies and programs designed to address the underlying problem are then brought to the forefront for implementation and evaluation. While the language of "prevention" is associated with the problem-solving activities of the police, pragmatically these activities are perhaps better associated with differing treatments.

Tertiary interventions pursued by the police tend to center on ameliorating a past victimization or dispute situation. Such interventions can be said to be rehabilitative in nature. Victim assistance and youth programs emphasizing "high risk" as a criterion for participation seek to intervene between the effects of crime and disorder and their consequences. Here, too, lie some of the newer community policing programs and efforts. Such efforts seek to broaden the role of the police to include supporting victims of crime, as well as trying to reclaim youth who might have already begun a minor criminal career. Gang mediation and community dispute resolution programs have been conducted by the police either alone or in conjunction with social rehabilitative agencies, typically those rooted in social work and education. Here the police are linking their efforts in the social rehabilitation arena to the extent that they concentrate effort on addressing the consequences of crime and disorder, not their roots or proximate causes.

The importance of understanding the basis of intervention in any particular police program—community, problem-oriented, or traditional—cannot be overstated. Knowing where in the causal chain the police are intervening provides a better understanding of the intervention program and its anticipated outcomes and effects. Without such a foundational understanding of intervention, evaluations are uninformed as to the purposes and anticipated consequences of police efforts. For example, preventions aimed at individual motivation or community activation are meant to be assessed differently from those emphasizing the reclamation of gang members or making victims whole again. Similarly, police treatments such as changes in patrol strategies should be assessed not for their prevention aspects, but rather for their ability to treat adequately a situation or problem.

Better specification of the level and type of police intervention will likely produce a broader range of police output and outcome measures. Rather than relying on crime, disorder, and fear measures alone, such issues as community cohesion; individual attitudes toward criminal behavior; victim readjustment; and problems solved, minimized, or otherwise reduced are potential measures of the impact and effect of police services. Such a broadening of impacts, by virtue of clearer specification of type and level of police intervention, would lead to better information on the following outcome-focused questions in policing as well:

1. What are the *Changes in Community Conditions Outcomes* thought to be associated with crime, disorder, and fear of crime outcomes? This includes the assessment of changes in community cohesion, willingness to work with the police, the level and type of information provided to the police in furtherance of crime prevention and/or suppression activities, community use of public places, and improvements to the physical environment, among many.

2. What are the *Changes in Police and Citizen Interaction Outcomes* thought to be associated with increased police and citizen partnerships in crime prevention and community stabilization efforts tied to community policing? This includes an assessment of changes in the frequency, duration, and quality of police and community interactions; the goal directedness of such activities; and public service networks created through such efforts.

3. What are the *Changes in Police Agency-Other Government Agency Interaction Outcomes* thought to be associated with improved problem-solving capability of the police? This includes an assessment of changes in the frequency, duration, and quality of police and other government agency interactions; the goal directedness of such activities; and public agency service networks created through such efforts.

4. What are the *Crime Reporting and Victimization, Disorder, and Fear of Crime Outcomes* thought to be associated with implementing a community and problem-oriented policing approach? This includes changes in the frequency, severity, concentration, location, and duration of crime; fear of crime; and disorder within a given community.

Such intervention specification would also begin to focus attention on the processes of converting interventions into outcomes. Here the focus is on program implementation within complex organizational, social, and political settings.

COMMUNITY POLICING AS PLANNED CHANGE

At the onset of any institutional change, symbolism often outstrips practicality (Edelman, 1977). The rhetoric of community policing, of necessity, preceded its coming to the police (Greene & Mastrofski, 1988). Yet like Mark Twain's death, the "success" of community policing may be greatly exaggerated.

This exaggeration is because most of the evidence concerning community and problem-oriented policing is limited. Rigorous studies of the collection of innovations subsumed under the rubric of community policing are few in number (Greene & Taylor, 1988). Rather, the study of community-based policing has rested on the use of limited case studies to define the complexity and effects of this program innovation (e.g., see Eck & Spelman, 1987a, and Trojanowicz & Bucqueroux, 1990). Such case studies are plagued with many problems that limit their credibility (see Cook & Campbell, 1979), and, hence, their ability to inform police policymakers.

Diagnosing Community Policing as an Institutional Intervention

To move from the anecdotal approach to assessing community policing toward a model of intervention and assessment more closely allied with "organizational development," it is necessary to understand interventions, like community policing, according to the level(s) such interventions seek to change. At least four intervention levels apply to community policing as an institutional change: (a) the environmental level, focused on organizations, groups, and other sources of influence that help define the sources of input for community policing, as well as being the ultimate consumers and evaluators of goods and services produced; (b) the organizational level, including concerns for the strategy, culture, and structure of the focal police agency; (c) the group level, including issues of task structure, performance norms, interpersonal relationships, and group composition among organizational work groups; and (d) the individual level, including concerns with police officer autonomy, feedback, task identity, and skill (see Cummings & Worley, 1993, pp. 84-109). Figure 8.2 presents a diagram of the potential relationships within these levels of institutional change.

By making explicit the levels of intervention and change, as well as the anticipated outcomes for community policing, we can begin the process of building effective monitoring and evaluation systems (to be discussed below). More important, such explication of desired results and their concomitant institutional changes provide police administrators and evaluators with a better understanding of the dynamics of change within and surrounding police agencies. Such an understanding can dramatically improve efforts to implement and evaluate community policing initiatives.

At the *environmental level,* community and problem-oriented policing interventions seek to engage the police and the community in a public safety co-production relationship. Such programs are likely aimed at stabilizing neighborhoods, increasing neighborhood bonds and communication, increasing the capacity of the neighborhood to mediate in conflict situations, and ultimately strengthening neighborhood cohesion.

All of these activities are rooted in the notion that cohesive neighborhoods are more crime resistant. Such activities, if properly implemented, should reduce fear of crime; increase neighbor use of public spaces, thereby increasing neighborhood surveillance; reduce neighborhood disorder; and ultimately reduce crime and victimization in neighborhoods.

At the *organizational level,* community policing interventions must address several police department issues. First, these interventions must confront the police agency's technology, or the way in which the department converts inputs to outputs. This includes how (or if) the department currently defines and solves problems and how it values what it produces. Community policing interventions must also consider the department's structure, or the way the organization divides labor and differentiates its parts, and how (or if) that structure supports community policing initiatives. These interventions must also address the organization's culture, or the values, beliefs, symbols, and assumptions that undergird organizational life, as well as the department's human resource systems, or the mechanisms for selecting, training, rewarding, and socializing personnel toward community policing objectives.

Finally, community policing change interventions must address the police agency's effectiveness assessment mechanisms, or the systems internal to the police organization that gather, evaluate, and disseminate information about how the organization is doing. If community-based policing is to become a lasting strategic intervention (Kelling & Moore, 1988; Moore & Stephens, 1991), it will need to confront several macro-level organizational change issues, particularly if it intends to replace or modify the structure and culture of traditional policing.

In addition to organizational-level issues, community policing as a change intervention must also address several issues associated with the *group level* within police organizations. This will include the establishment and clear communication of group performance norms consistent with community policing outcomes. Such outcomes include building and supporting crime

Level of Intervention	Change Issues Confronted	Anticipated Community Policing Outcomes
Environmental →	Linkage with: →	*Reduced Crime/Fear*
	External organizations and groups	Cohesive neighborhoods
		Increased public safety
	Political and economic support	Greater public support
	Define and maintain an organizational set	Reduced hazard/violence
		Community problems solved
Organizational →	Technology →	Reduced crime/fear
	Structure	Cohesive neighborhoods
	Culture	Increased public safety
	Human Resources	Greater public support
	Effectiveness	Reduced hazard/violence
	Assessment	Community problems solved
Group →	Performance norms →	Team cohesiveness
	Group composition	Task consensus
	Interpersonal relations	Quality decisions
	Task definition	Group effectiveness
Individual →	Task Identity →	Increased police officer effectiveness
	Autonomy	Increased performance
	Feedback	Increased job satisfaction
	Skill(s)	Broadened role definition
		Greater job attachment/investment

Figure 8.2. Levels of Change for Community Policing
SOURCE: Adapted from Cummings and Worley, 1993, p. 90.

resistant, cohesive neighborhoods; reducing public safety hazards within communities; and increasing public safety and public support. Such outcomes are not consistent with current approaches to defining desired police outcomes, for example, reducing crime, disorder, and fear.

Beyond creating and communicating group performance norms, the community-oriented police agency must specify group composition in terms of the knowledge, skill, and functions of police groups operating within community settings. Similarly, the police agency will need to improve interpersonal communications and information sharing within the agency, especially across groups defined under a community policing philosophy and structure. Finally, if community policing is to become the vanguard of change within police agencies, it will need to clarify task definition among groups of police officers.

In the relatively brief history of community policing, police officer tasks have been rather ambiguous. The tension between crime control, order maintenance, and service tasks of the police have often been accentuated but not resolved in much of community policing programming. Greater task clarity and specification will have to become a major issue in the refinement of community-based policing or else everything the police do could be considered community oriented (of course, the obverse is also true—nothing they do is community oriented).

Community-based policing also has several implications for *individual-level* change within police agencies as well. In terms of individual-level outcomes, community policing anticipates changes in police officer effectiveness, primarily through the mechanism of problem solving. In addition, police officer performance, job satisfaction, and job attachment are anticipated to increase through attachment to community policing initiatives. Finally, police officer role definitions are expected to broaden under community policing. Such outcomes presume greater task identity (and consensus) among officers, greater officer autonomy in decision making, job enrichment and job enlargement, increased feedback to officers regarding their community and problem-focused activities, and increases in the depth and range of skills officers are trained for and employ as part of their community policing methodology. Such anticipated changes and outcomes, at the individual level, are complex and will require much attention to individual police officer adoption of community policing philosophies, strategies, methodologies, and tactics.

Once we acknowledge and specify the differing levels of organizational change implied by community policing, assessment of the appropriate "fit" among levels of organizational change can then be made. It is not enough to specify the differing levels (environmental, organizational, work group, and individual) of change, but rather to examine how each complements and supports the other. In fact, these levels of organizational change are "nested" with one another; for example, work group changes are greatly affected by macro-level organizational changes, and individual-level changes are affected by those occurring within work groups. Individual and work group changes also affect the achievement of macro-level organizational change. The "fits" among these changes, and their implications for a police department emphasizing community-based policing, should occupy much policy making and evaluative time to assess implementation fully.

In regard to the measurement of change as implied in community policing efforts, Figure 8.3 provides an overview of the measurement focus, unit(s) of analysis, and measurement constructs for varying levels of community polic-

Measurement Focus	Unit(s) of Analysis	Measurement Construct(s)
Environmental →	Communities →	Internal Cohesion Neighborliness Community stability Conflict mediation capacity Order/Disorder/Fear/Crime
	Organizational →	Service delivery network capacity Agency interaction and exchange Joint programs/Information sharing
	Customers →	Use patterns Satisfaction with service Problem solved/reduced

Organizational →	Technology →
	    Structure
		Information Quality/Flow/
		    Use in decision making

	Culture Human Resources Outputs	Level of decentralization Level of specialization Organizational values Extent and quality of training Rewards/Sanctions Services produced Activities undertaken
Group →	Work groups → Teams Task forces Performance	Team participation Work group cohesion Information sharing Group problem solving Group Values
Individual →	Police officers → Civilians	Job-related feelings/Sentiments Job-related knowledge/Skill

Figure 8.3. Change Measurement in Community Policing

ing intervention. Figure 8.3 extends the consideration of level of change by examining what evaluators might measure if they were fully to assess the implementation of community policing as well as its effects.

At the *environmental level,* measurements are taken for communities, organizations, and aggregates of customers. For communities, the focus is on issues of cohesion, neighborliness, stability, the mediation of conflict, and traditional measures of outcome including disorder, crime, and fear. For

organizations, issues surrounding the creation and sustenance of interorganizational networks focused on public safety, joint programming, and information sharing come to the forefront of evaluation concerns. For customers,
measurement of patterns of use, satisfaction with services received, and extent
of problems ameliorated are a reasonable starting point for assessment.

At the *organizational level,* changes across a wide array of internal police
agency dynamics should be the focus of evaluation and measurement. They
include the quality, flow, and use of information within the organization and
by organizational incumbents; the level of decision making and available
resources to support that decision making; the structure of the organization,
including concerns with hierarchy and specialization; the values of the organization and subcultural values within the organization that compete with or
support community policing; human resource development processes that
support or detract from community policing objectives (includes formal and
informal sanctioning systems, formal and informal socialization, and the
modeling of appropriate behavior); and the range of services and activities
produced and valued by the organization. The units of analysis in these
assessments include the technology structure, culture, human resources, and
outputs of the agency in question.

At the *group level,* assessments of the implementation of community
policing need to focus on the dynamics, interactions, decisions, and outputs
of work groups, teams, and task forces as they are created and encouraged.
Here the concern is with team cohesion, information sharing, group problem
solving, and group values, among other things. Much of traditional policing
has focused on the behavior of individual officers. By contrast, community
and problem-solving policing tends to stress the importance of groups. If this
is true, then measures of group, not individual, performance will need to be
used in the assessment of community policing.

At the *individual level,* implementation assessments need to concentrate
on job knowledge and performance, as well as the feelings and sentiments of
police officers and of civilian employees. This, of course, will require that
community policing job behaviors be made explicit and measurable. In terms
of feelings and sentiments, building a better understanding of the symbolic
and subjective meanings police personnel attach to organizational life is an
important starting point for implementation assessment efforts.

This brief overview of the levels, range of changes, and measurement issues
anticipated in community and problem-oriented policing points to the very
real need to exercise great care in evaluative pursuits. While these issues may
seem obvious to some, much of what passes as community policing innovation

relies on specialized or "experimental" groups that are distant from the "key" or central organizational, work group, and individual dynamics necessary for sustained change, as discussed above (see, for example, Kelling & Bratton, 1993, for a discussion of middle-level management and community policing).

All too often, community policing is adjunct to "real" policing done by the majority of the police department. Such adjunct status, if allowed to continue, will resign community policing to the same place in history that "team policing" currently enjoys—a reform that failed.

Monitoring and Managing Community Policing Change Interventions

From the perspectives of policy making and evaluation, the monitoring of community policing change within police departments is a necessary condition to assuring appropriate implementation, as well as linking implementation to outcome measurement. Such monitoring will in all likelihood be a full-time undertaking, perhaps initiated and sustained by a planning and research function within the police agency, perhaps supported by external evaluators.

Many methodologies for conducting applied organizational analysis are available for such monitoring efforts (see Seashore, Lawler, Mirvis, & Cammann, 1983, and Van Mannen & Dabbs, 1983). They include quantitative tools for examining such issues as work flow, employee perceptions and cultural attachment, and environmental demand for and satisfaction with services provided. They also include qualitative tools for assessing the contextual dimensions of organizational life, for assessing the content of official pronouncements and directives, and for understanding information necessary for effective community policing decision making, among other things.

Together, such methodologies provide a rich amount of information relative to ongoing changes within police agencies. Yet the collection of this information alone is insufficient for increasing the likelihood of community policing being institutionally adopted by the police. What is necessary is the development of information feedback to better inform the implementation process.

Feedback during the implementation process provides the opportunity for correcting oversights or deficiencies in implementation along the way. To be of any impact, such feedback needs to be timely, relevant, and understandable to the persons who must use this information to inform their actions. The development of such feedback will require that those who will need the feedback participate in structuring and monitoring these implementation processes. Such involvement should provide a climate for using feedback data toward purposeful ends. Feedback allows police administrators and evaluators to monitor the process of moving the police agency from its current state, through a transition state, to a future desired state, that of being a community policing agency.

Feedback provides the vehicle for managing the change process as it unfolds within the police agency. Effective change management is information dependent. Change management requires feedback information to motivate and sustain change, to identify sources of resistance to change, to create a change vision, to develop support (internal and external) for the change agenda implied of community-based policing, and to manage the transition from traditional to community or problem-oriented policing. Without such information, evaluators and police administrators, even those with good intuition, can go awry.

CONCLUDING REMARKS

In recent years much has been made of reinventing government services (Osborne & Gaebler, 1992), including those of the police. In law enforcement academic and administrative circles the ideology and language of "community" has crept into the most recent reform era. Coupled with a problem-solving methodology, community policing has emerged as a rather loose collection of philosophies, strategies, goals, programs, and tactics, all of which seek greater police and citizen interaction, more involvement of citizens and police officers in public safety decision making, and greater emphasis on the effectiveness of police interventions.

While the language and some programming of community policing have begun to take some hold in policing, the implementation of this police reform has been less examined, and is certainly less assured. Community policing, like its predecessor reforms, will in all likelihood be modified and diluted by rather intractable police organizations unless implementation assessment and monitoring are made integral to the reform movement. Such is not the case today.

Implementation questions are far ranging. They focus on many environmental organizational dimensions at several levels of analysis. They will produce much information about the inner workings of police agencies; information that will be essential if meaningful, sustained planned change is to occur. The implementation evaluation and change management processes associated with introducing community policing into any police agency should, at minimum, address the following issues.

1. What is the *Institutional Capability* for initiating and sustaining a community policing change? This includes an assessment of the fit between the organization; its environment; its technology, work flow, and structure; its systems for measurement and reward; and its internal culture.

2. What is the *Personnel Capability* for initiating and sustaining a community policing change? This includes an understanding of personnel strengths and weaknesses, socialization and training patterns, work group definitions, task definition, and individual commitment to varying definitions of police work.

3. What is the *Information and Support Service Capability* for initiating and sustaining a community policing change? This includes the organization's current and projected measures of effectiveness; the system for collecting, analyzing, and communicating this information to those inside and outside the police agency; and the other aspects of the organization that will need to support community policing initiatives.

4. What is the *Strength of the Treatment* for initiating and sustaining a community policing change? This includes an explication of the things the police are to do under a community-oriented mode of operation, as well as the ways in which organizational members and functional units contribute to community policing outcomes.

5. What is the *Community Capacity to Accept and Use the Treatment* for initiating and sustaining a community policing change? This includes a thorough assessment of the environmental demands for community-oriented police services, as well as the ability of community partners (civic, business, and political) to use the community-oriented services provided by the police.

The implementation of any complex change, such as that implied by advocates for community policing, in a resistant institutional setting, such as that identified in many police agencies, will require more attention to the organizational medium within which these changes occur. The glacial change we have witnessed in the core technology and values of policing attest to the importance of designing change strategies that are well thought out, are monitored, and that provide feedback to police administrators attempting to implement community policing.

NOTES

1. For example, see Part III, "Police Organizational Reform: Planning, Implementation and Impact Within the Agency," chapters 4 through 8, in Rosenbaum (1994); Buerger, (1993); and Williams, Greene, and Bergman (1992).

2. The passage of the Omnibus Crime Control Act of 1994, and the continued political debate surrounding crime control, is rooted in a belief that more police is better. Walker (1989) calls this the "mayonnaise" theory of policing, suggesting that at some point more mayonnaise can actually ruin the sandwich. The current federal proposal calls for 100,000 more police on the street. What these police are to do, or how police organizations are to make them work smarter, are questions largely unaddressed.

3. DARE (Drug Awareness and Resistance Education) is focused on drug awareness and resistance, while GREAT (Gang Resistance Education and Training) is focused on youth developing a resistance to joining gangs. Both seek to model behavior for youth by teaching them reasoning and decision-making skills emphasizing alternatives to drug use and gang membership. As such they seek to change fundamental motivation among participating youth.

COMMUNITY POLICING AND POLICE ORGANIZATION STRUCTURE

Stephen D. Mastrofski

Community policing brings to North America the promise of a "quiet revolution," "paradigm shift," "sea change," and "new blue line." The hoped for results are safer, happier, and more socially integrated communities. Some reformers argue that police must do things they have never or rarely done (Goldstein, 1990). Others suggest that community policing does not really introduce new strategies and tactics, but only finds more effective ways

AUTHOR'S NOTE: An earlier draft of this chapter was delivered at the Workshop on Evaluating Police Service Delivery, sponsored by the Centre for Comparative Criminology, University of Montreal and the Solicitor General of Canada, Montreal, November 2-4, 1994. The author appreciates the comments of R. Richard Ritti, Herman Goldstein, Jerome McElroy, Roger Parks, and Dennis Rosenbaum, none of whom are accountable for the views expressed or limitations of the arguments.

of promoting the best of what has always been with modern democratic police forces (Braiden, 1988). Whether community policing's methods are old or new, there is a premise that police organizations must be restructured in fundamental ways.

Here I describe the nature of the transformations called for by community policing reformers and speculate on their prospects for achieving the desired results. I identify four structural features of community policing reform: debureaucratization, professionalization, democratization, and service integration. I then apply two models of organization to understand the emergence of these changes and their consequences: a technical/rational model and an institutional model. My conclusions are these: Most of the community policing structural reforms do not enjoy strong prospects of successful implementation in the foreseeable future. Even if the structural transformations do occur, they are unlikely to produce the desired results absent some fundamental changes in both the technology and environment of police organizations. I suggest that rearranging the structure of policing without a better understanding, application, and development of police technical capacity is placing the cart before the horse. For reforms to fulfill the technical promises of safer, happier, more socially integrated communities, the structural changes must flow out of an environment that enables and demands such performance from police.

THE PROMISES OF COMMUNITY POLICING

Community policing is a general term capturing a potpourri of social and political trends that have converged at about the same time. It has emerged in reaction to problems that became highly visible in the past three decades (Fogelson, 1977, chap. 11). Its direction is determined largely by contemporary fashions in politics, government, and business (Manning, 1984, 1994, 1995). The frustration of those who search for a single definition of community policing is understandable precisely because community policing at present represents the confluence of many streams of reform that produce cross- and countercurrents. To build momentum, and to make sense of this complexity, some try to offer coherent descriptions of community policing (Eck & Rosenbaum, 1994; Goldstein, 1990; Skolnick & Bayley, 1986; Sparrow, Moore, & Kennedy, 1990; Trojanowicz & Bucqueroux, 1990; Wilson & Kelling, 1982, 1989).

A careful historical analysis of this reform movement would map the many tributaries of its major streams, identify their sources, and show their influence on the flow of police practice. For my purposes, however, it is sufficient to note such complexity before focusing on only those features currently enjoying widest popularity. My sense of this popularity is based on impressions gleaned from the rhetoric of reform: books and articles advocating community policing, presentations given at conferences, press accounts, conversations with police and public leaders, and field observations of departments. The four selected themes have roots in earlier reform eras.

Debureaucratization

For most of the 20th century, police organizations have been bureaucratizing (Reiss, 1992). They have been territorially centralized; their workload is managed centrally; the number of special bureaus and specialist employees has grown tremendously; personnel matters and operational policies are governed by myriad rules; they have become hierarchically elaborated as the number of mid-level supervisors and administrators has grown; and their operations are buffered from political interference by lengthy chains of accountability that make it difficult for outsiders to penetrate the organization.

Community policing reformers have taken a bead on many of these trends, considering them dysfunctional, out of touch with the times, and impediments to the accomplishment of the police mission. Territorial centralization has put key decision makers in the organization out of touch with their "clientele." The centralized communications operation has become obsessed with response time but thereby keeps the organization from making any long-term advances in solving problems. Remote communications personnel decide how the bulk of the department's resources are committed, rather than line personnel who may have the greatest insight into community problems. Heavy reliance on specialist units makes the organization less flexible, requires more coordination, and creates interunit turf problems. Obsession with formality, rules, and red tape is disparaged as counterproductive and is thought to sap morale. The elaborated hierarchy contributes little to productivity, but obstructs any innovation that might bubble up from below. In response, some advocate "streamlining" or "delayerization"—making "leaner and meaner" police organizations with "flatter pyramids" that put key decisions in the hands of those supervisors closest to the work itself (Greene, Bergman, & McLaughlin, 1994, p. 92; Robinette, 1989; Weatheritt, 1993a, p. 78).

By the 1970s many inside, as well as outside, American police agencies felt that the legalistic and bureaucratic reform movements of the first half of the 20th century had come to a "standstill" (Fogelson, 1977). The goal of perfecting bureaucratic objectives had displaced the proper goals of police, which were to identify and solve the *community's* problems (Goldstein, 1979). Contemporary police reformers borrow as heavily from the corporate sector's current organization development gurus (e.g., Peters & Waterman, 1982) as earlier progressives did in their time (e.g., Taylor, 1911). Contemporary reformers do not advocate a return to the highly politicized, decentralized, informal, and undifferentiated police organizations of the late 19th century (e.g., see Kelling & Moore, 1988b), but they call for a reversal of the powerful trend to bureaucratize, proposing to replace it with a number of structural alternatives.

Professionalization

Since the late 19th century, professionalization has served as a rallying cry of police reformers, and it continues to do so today. Commentators on the history of American police note, however, that it was mostly lip service that earlier progressives paid to professionalization (Klockars, 1988; Reiss, 1971, 1992; Walker, 1977). Police have made some advances in certain elements of their professional status: a strong service mission, increased education and training, and more extensive checks of personal background for moral defi- ciencies (Mastrofski, 1994). Yet other elements of professionalization remain virtually undeveloped: autonomy for individual practitioners and a highly developed scientific knowledge base.

Community policing reformers call for the creation of a truly professional police force, one that draws even more heavily from the college-educated and one that commits even greater resources to training (Carter, Sapp, & Stephens, 1988). More important, they call for officers whose discretionary powers are no longer ignored or disavowed, but are celebrated as essential to the practice of a profession, just as a physician is expected to exercise discretion in diagnosing and treating patients. Professionals become "results oriented." Department managers institutionalize these results in the form of organiza- tional "values." Yet rather than perpetuating a rule-bound bureaucracy, they encourage subordinates to exercise judgment and to innovate. The rank and file take a more active role in formulating policies and strategies, while those up the chain of command change from rule givers, form checkers, and petty controllers, to leaders, coaches, and facilitators. Police no longer *assume* that core technologies and tactics are efficacious; they submit them to scientific test. Adjusting subsequent efforts according to the results, they engage in what Sherman (1992b, p. 251) calls "smart" policing.

Democratization

Democracies give citizens important roles to play in governing police and in policing itself. The history of municipal police in the United States post-bellum to the second decade of the 20th century shows the many ways in which police agencies were "democratized" in the Jacksonian sense—penetrated by political factions that made police employment dependent upon political connections. It is often thought, perhaps with more romance than evidence, that the machines also offered immigrants and the working classes greater access to police services. There can be no doubt, however, that the machines contributed a degree of economic and social entrée to these groups by providing police jobs through a patronage system that produced little security and a high degree of amateurism (Monkkonen, 1981). Historians have documented the efforts of late 19th- and earlier 20th-century Progressives to buffer police departments from the vagaries of political influence, and, by most accounts, the reformers were successful, perhaps too much so, by the 1960s, when police were widely portrayed as too remote from those they policed.

Nothing has more powerful public appeal than the promises that can be placed within the category of democratization. "Partnerships" with the public are pledged in which the police consult the community for guidance on purposes, priorities, policies, and practice, and enlist the public in jointly "co-producing" police services (e.g., community crime prevention programs, policing and regulating disorders in one's home, neighborhood, or place of business; Buerger & Green, 1994). The impetus for democratization has at least two sources. First is public dissatisfaction with police unresponsiveness under the now "traditional" reform model. Second is the pressure to respond to expanding demands for service with resources that do not keep pace. Community consultation takes place through such mechanisms as public opinion surveys, citizen advisory councils, and input from special interest groups (representing businesses, victims, neighborhoods). Co-production can be organized individually (e.g., target hardening of one's residence to prevent burglary) or collectively (Neighborhood Watch; Rosenbaum, 1988). In most of its forms, the citizen's contribution is limited to the provision of information (reporting crimes and suspicious circumstances), but in some cases it can amount to volunteer labor in some police program (staffing a mini-station, data entry and record keeping, research), and, in very rare cases, the direct delivery of service to the public (Givens, 1993).

Service Integration

Services delivered by local governments, especially in large metropolitan areas, have become highly specialized. Although that specialization may increase service delivery capabilities, it also creates a multitude of problems among the various government units that provide the services: turf battles, lack of coordination, and an inability to concentrate efforts strategically. A neighborhood's decline into crime and disorder is viewed as not just the worry of police, but of many other agencies, such as code enforcement, public housing, alcoholic beverage regulation, transportation, sanitation, health, education, welfare, employment, and so on. Social and economic decline is seen as closely intertwined with crime and disorder (Wilson & Kelling, 1982), so much so that to prevent or reverse decline, governments must treat neighborhoods "holistically." They must enlist a broad range of public (and sometimes private) organizations in a coordinated effort (Eck & Spelman, 1987b; Wilson & Kelling, 1989). Advocates argue that the police must take a major, and often *the* lead role in identifying problems and mobilizing other organizations to tackle problems (Mastrofski & Uchida, 1993). Structurally, this dovetails with decentralization (serving the interests of a neighborhood or some specific area) and democratization (listening to the people to learn their needs and helping them mobilize to get the rest of government to assist them; Goldstein, 1990).

TWO PERSPECTIVES ON ORGANIZATION STRUCTURE

Two very different perspectives on organizations can help us understand the impact of the structural changes reformers envision. The first is called the rational/technical (hereafter called technical) model of organizations. The second is an institutional model of organizations. Each of these models suggests reasons that organizations develop particular structures and suggests what purposes those structures serve for the organization.

Technical Model of Police Organizations

The technical model posits that organizations are contrived to accomplish specific goals. Organizational structures (procedures, programs, personnel, and policies) are rational to the extent that they realize their objectives efficiently. These objectives are predetermined and precisely defined; structures are formalized (precise, explicit, visible, not contingent upon the particular participants in the organization). An example in policing is the goal of crime control. A number of organizational structures have been widely implemented to accomplish this with what is expected to be maximum effectiveness: 911 reporting systems, geographically dispersed patrol officers engaged in preventive patrol, criminal investigations and forensics specialists. Police effectiveness is measured in arrests and ultimately crimes known to the police and, more recently, victimizations reported in public surveys. Of course, evidence emerges that shows that some organization structures are ineffective. The police department behaving according to the technical model will then attempt to find structures that more effectively or efficiently achieve crime control. Some organizations will fail to search for new structures and others will search but fail to find them. Ultimately, these organizations will disappear or will seek a niche in some other line of work.

The technical model frames our understanding of the emergence of community policing and helps identify its impacts, at least those intended by its advocates. For example, Kelling and Moore (1988) argue that police in the United States are entering an era of "community" policing because of acknowledged failures of previous reform structures to reduce crime and calm citizens' fears. Leighton (1994, p. 211) makes the same argument for Canada. Similarly, Sparrow et al. (1990) argue that the "market share" of public police is shrinking due to encroachment from private security companies, and that more effective "corporate strategies" are necessary to make police organizations sufficiently flexible and efficient to remain competitive (cf. Manning, 1992b; Shearing, 1992). According to the technical model, the pathway to police organization survival and success (resources, domain, and other means of support) is by delivering tangible improvements in public safety and social integration. Ultimately, the technical approach is predicated on the notion that the organization's environment (market demand and competition) impel it to be as productive as possible. Not surprisingly, then, the evaluation of community policing structures, programs, strategies, and tactics is likely to become a growth industry in the United States, as Crime Bill funds for community policing are disbursed over the next several years. These evaluations search for evidence on the effectiveness of a variety of reform structures for accomplishing the formalized objectives, such as reducing crime, disorder, fear of crime, and other threats to the quality of life (see, for example, Skogan, 1994b).

Institutional Model of
Police Organizations

The institutional model begins from a very different set of assumptions about the nature of the organization's environment. For many organizations, the most salient feature of their environment is not the demand to be efficient, but rather the demand to respond to widely held beliefs about what such organizations *should* be and do—even though these beliefs cannot be verified. Schools, mental health agencies, courts, law firms, and a host of public service agencies that operate in a noncompetitive context fall into this category, including police. It is virtually impossible to verify what these kinds of organizations "produce." It is difficult to specify their goals in ways that can be readily measured, and it is even more difficult to establish the impact of these organizations' efforts on those goals. To survive, such organizations institutionalize structures and processes that have come to be accepted as right, true, and correct for that type of organization—even though they have not been validated in a technical sense. These institutions are constituted as "rationalized myths"—rules that stipulate what is required to achieve the desired end and that are accepted, not "because of rational pressures for more effective performance but [because] of social and cultural pressures to conform to conventional beliefs" (Scott, 1992, p. 118).

In the case of police, the various crime control structures and methods listed in the previous section were effective in securing external support for police organizations as long as they were perceived by important constituencies as the "right" way for police to go about their business (Crank & Langworthy, 1992). They appealed to the myth of the police officer as an enforcement-oriented, legalistic crime-fighter, highly trained and effectively controlled by paramilitary, bureaucratic structures. This was a myth that police themselves had perpetuated, but that was effective because it appealed to social and economic fashions growing popular in the first half of the 20th century (Fogelson, 1977; Walker, 1977). Empirical research on police that began to emerge in the 1960s suggested that the reality of everyday police work was at odds with the crime-fighter image, and by the mid-1960s there were increasing doubts about the "rightness" of this mythic vision, culminating in a crisis of legitimacy that extended into the early 1980s (Crank, 1994, p. 327). The crisis was triggered by a number of factors: a perception of a rapidly rising crime rate, urban rioting, corruption and brutality scandals, and public alienation from a police who seemed uncaring and unresponsive—especially to social and economic outgroups. With the assistance of federal grants and progressive think tanks, American police forces began to experiment with new or revitalized structures and strategies, such as team policing, foot patrol, directed patrol, crime analysis, community crime prevention, and victim assistance programs. In this context, American police began to respond to powerful social sentiments evoking a lost sense of democracy, small-town "community," and local autonomy.

Emerging from this context, a new—or rather, revitalized—metaphor for policing began to take hold as the standard against which to measure police organizational structures: the police officer as the "watchman" or keeper of community morality who maintains public order and protects the community from crime (Crank, 1994, p. 335). Building upon a nostalgia for 19th-century communities recalled as safe and orderly, and an image of the watchman as a skilled craftsman who can strike a balance between both conservative and liberal perspectives on crime control, community policing has become a cause of entrepreneurs from both ends of the political spectrum. Conservatives see in it the opportunity for aggressive order maintenance to reestablish moral order and safety, to repel the criminal invasion of neighborhoods. Liberals see in it the opportunity to get at the underlying causes of crime and other social problems, to revitalize communities, enhance citizen participation, and improve the responsiveness of their police, as well as other local government agencies (Crank, 1994, pp. 342-345).

To Crank's analysis, I would add that the structural forms gathered under the community policing umbrella are precisely those au courant among progressive corporations and management consultants: decentralized decision making (power to the precinct commander), client-responsive service structures (neighborhood advisory boards), autonomy and entrepreneurship (professionalism and rank-and-file bottom-up initiatives), quality circles (problem solving), and leaner management staff (see, for example, Goldstein, 1990, chap. 9; Sparrow et al., 1990, p. 144). In the 1980s, these kinds of structural changes became widely accepted among progressive businesses and organizational development consultants as the "right" way to revitalize private and public sector organizations (Deming, 1986; Osborne & Gaebler, 1992; Peters & Waterman, 1982). Evidence on the effectiveness of these reforms is pretty thin (Bleakeley, 1993; Manning, 1995; Pinder, 1977; Walters, 1992; West, Berman, & Milakovich, 1995), and many of the businesses that adopted them have since either fallen on hard times or moved on to other reforms. Nonetheless, these forms seem well on their way to institutionalization as the accepted way to organize police departments in North America (Leighton, 1994; Trojanowicz, 1994).

The institutional model acknowledges that organizations such as the police will pay obeisance to technical mandates, such as crime control or (more recently) order maintenance, because the mere adoption of such goals associates the organization with widely and intensely held societal aspirations (Klockars, 1988; Manning, 1977). The institutional model also posits that police agencies cannot reliably demonstrate their success in technical terms (demonstrations that they have reduced crime, increased public safety and order, and stimulated social harmony), but they can adopt structures that have come to be recognized as hallmarks of those accomplishments. This constitutes a displacement of the ostensible ends of the police organization by the means that are presumed to achieve them (Warner & Havens, 1968). Thus, in lieu of a demonstration of police effectiveness in reducing drug crime, police leaders tout their special units, programs, and efforts to arrest and disrupt drug traffickers and steer children from a life of drugs. In lieu of producing greater interethnic group harmony, police departments feature community picnics, form community advisory panels, and strengthen ties to various grassroots groups.

Failure in institutional terms occurs when organizations do not catch the wave, do not conform to dominant expectations of what constitutes the "right" forms and methods. In police departments, institutional failure is usually celebrated by the sacking of the top leader and the search for someone who will embrace the dominant or rising structural forms. It is conceivable that police organizations could disappear or decline because of institutional failure, but the more likely route is institutional transformation, akin to the kinds of metamorphoses that mainstream American political parties experience in response to long-term social and economic change. They divest themselves of old institutional forms and select those that allow them to survive and prosper. That accounts for the phenomenon of "institutional isomorphism" (DiMaggio & Powell, 1983)—a kind of "copycatism" that over the years has achieved epidemic proportions for a variety of reform fashions in criminal justice, not just community policing.

Technical and Institutional Models Reconciled

Both the technical and the institutional models are premised on the notion that organizations generally try to act in ways that benefit themselves by acquiring or keeping resources, domain, and other forms of environmental support. The technical model assumes that organizations are structured to do this by seeking technical effectiveness in an environment that obliges them to do so. The institutional model assumes that organizations are structured to secure support by appearing to be and do what is widely accepted as correct and that they respond to an environment that pressures them to do so. Theorists argue that some types of organizations fit the technical model, while others fit the institutional model. That is because of the construction of their environments (Scott, 1992, chap. 6).

There are two dimensions to each organization's environment, one technical and one institutional. Some organizations have environments that are well-developed technically but not institutionally—general manufacturing firms, for example. Here the organization's product is well defined and the methods to manufacture it are well established, and the organization's structures and practices are understandable from a rational model perspective. However, there are also organizations that exist in an environment that is only weakly developed technically, yet strongly developed institutionally. Many public service agencies with ill-defined "products" and weakly validated methods fit in this category, including police departments. Here the elaboration of institutional forms enacts those highly developed expectations from external constituencies. Also, there are some organizations that operate in environments where both technical and institutional dimensions are well developed: utilities, banks, and hospitals, for example. All produce services that are quite tangible and are supported by highly elaborated technologies, yet they must also respond to certain symbolic forms that are accepted as right—regardless of their technical utility (e.g., medical malpractice review panels that signify professional accountability).

From the perspective of technically versus institutionally elaborated environments, we can develop a richer appreciation of community policing's promises and prospects. Some might take the view that community policing represents a shift from one set of institutional forms to another (Crank, 1994; Klockars, 1988). Others, however, suggest that community policing—or at least certain elements—also provides a structural mechanism to achieve technical performance and accountability: to prevent crime and restore order, for example (Goldstein, 1990; Sparrow et al., 1990). Even these advocates acknowledge that the technical effectiveness of community policing reforms in their current state is undemonstrated, but that these structural changes are necessary to develop the organizational flexibility and innovativeness necessary to evolve into technical effectiveness (see also Goldstein, 1994; Moore, 1994; but cf. Manning, 1992b). For the long range, however, reformers advocate that police agencies become more highly developed in a technical sense. That no doubt accounts for the frequently expressed aspirations that police agencies become more like some in the health care field (Sherman, 1995, p. 343).

CONSEQUENCES OF STRUCTURAL REFORM

Based on the preceding discussion, we should anticipate the consequences of structural changes in police departments at two levels: the technical and the institutional (Parsons, 1960, pp. 63-65). In what follows, I will select a few of the many structural changes promoted by community policing reforms and consider their likely impact in both technical and institutional terms.

Delayerization: Thinning the Hierarchy

One popular way to debureaucratize and streamline organizations is to reduce the number of middle managers (Peters & Waterman, 1982). This not only frees up resources for direct service to clients, it also forces top management and line personnel into a closer working relationship and more efficient lines of communication. It is difficult to conceive that this streamlining will have much impact on the everyday work and accomplishments of police officers, however, because middle management and staff now have relatively little impact on the work of line operations in all but small departments. Reiss (1992, p. 72) observes that middle managers in large agencies spend most of their time coordinating the work of their units with other units and dealing with constituents and other service providers outside the department. Middle managers, such as the deputy in charge of patrol, expend relatively little time on the governance of street-level practice, a function left mostly to the sergeant (Muir, 1977, pp. 235-248; Van Maanen, 1983). Of course, middle management *can* play a role in the formulation of policies and the review and correction of operational unit performance, but this occurs far away from the "action" and has only a tenuous relationship to practice in the field.

There are good reasons why this is so. First, there are simply too many officers and too much activity for them to play a timely hands-on role. Even the line supervisor is rarely present for most police activities and encounters with the public (Allen, 1980). Second, as Reiss notes, the increasing specialization of police departments requires more attention to intra-agency coordination. Third, as departments pay more attention to "partnerships" with agencies and groups outside the organization, even more demands are placed on middle management. Of course, the rank and file may be expected to attend community group meetings and work with outside agencies, but there are limits to the amount of time they can give to this and still perform their core functions: responding to calls for service and looking for situations that require their intervention. Middle managers, then, perform an important "buffering" function, protecting the "technical core" of line units from turbulence from their environment (Reiss, 1992, p. 82; Thompson, 1967). Indeed, the rank and file tend to value middle managers in direct proportion to their success in buffering them from outside interference, while they are devalued to the extent that they themselves attempt to take a direct hand in the governance of street-level decision making. Those who do choose an interventionist (as opposed to protectionist) role run the serious risk of demoralizing subordinates and diminishing unit productivity (Van Maanen, 1984).

This is not to say that streamlining is *necessarily* a bad idea from a technical perspective. It depends upon the department and the middle managers. Some departments might benefit by reallocating resources from staff to line operations because their need for line resources is greater than the need for the performance of staff functions. It also matters who serves in middle management positions. As top police executives attempt to implement the many reforms of community policing, they often meet resistance from middle managers who achieved their status by pursuing another model of police organization, or who are threatened by the uncertainty of changing the status quo, or who have superiors who cannot conceive or articulate a useful role middle managers might play. One way to eliminate this resistance is to eliminate the middle ranks. In terms of more technical productivity (e.g., crimes solved, crimes prevented), however, the additional resources reallocated to street-level operations can be at best only modest. That is because even the largest departments with the most people in middle-management positions already display rank "pyramids" that are already pretty "flat." The ranks of middle management (between lieutenant and chief) account for between 5% and 10% of the sworn force of the nation's largest (and arguably most hierarchically elaborated) police agencies.

In terms of the police agency's institutional environment, delayerization offers a mixed blessing. If, indeed, delayerization has become *the* proper way to structure police departments, then the chief can feature this as an important indicator that his or her department is in the mainstream of progressive improvement. This would seem particularly apropos in the current political environment that rewards officials who appear to reduce the size of government. It has the added virtue of not being too disruptive to routine operations. There is a downside to streamlining as well. Because police departments, with their flat rank structures, already have so few opportunities for upward mobility, eliminating middle-management positions reduces even farther this incentive for long-term organizational commitment among those with career ambitions.

Of the many structural changes proposed under community policing, delayerization appears to be one of the most feasible, since it requires little disruption of existing structures and routine service delivery practices. Whether departments that engage in this can resist the temptation to "relayer" their organizations is another matter.

Professionalizing the Force:
The Officer as Clinician

Social scientists have observed that police exercise great discretion significantly decoupled from hierarchical controls (Lipsky, 1980; Muir, 1977; Reiss, 1971). Community policing reformers acknowledge this and attempt to restructure the organization to help officers exercise their judgment in ways that are most likely to bring about the desired results ("values" promoted by the leadership). This means that the lower ranks must be given the freedom to make decisions about how best to achieve these organizational objectives and the skill and support to make the best choices. By shelving "bureaucratic" methods that give only the appearance of control in the minutiae of police work, managers are expected to gain greater influence over the direction of practice and ultimately improve results. The literature on problem-oriented policing best captures this vision of the work of the rank and file as neighborhood clinician—screening the neighborhood for problems, diagnosing them, analyzing them, treating them, and assessing the results (Eck & Spelman, 1987a; Goldstein, 1990; Sherman, 1992b, p. 186). Many of these activities are done in close collaboration with the "patient." The initiative for identifying problems and finding solutions is nested among the rank and file and their immediate supervisors. Supervisors and higher level managers provide general guidance, monitor progress and results, and, most important, support the efforts of the problem solvers.

Depending upon how far the department takes the cop-as-clinician model, the impact of its implementation could range from undetectable to profound. Departments around North America are beginning to adopt a "problem-solving" orientation, but at this stage not much has changed in the activities of the typical police officer. Problem-solving projects are encouraged in most of these innovative departments; systems for monitoring these projects are being developed; and a few departments are even requiring that officers engage in and document their problem-solving efforts. Still, problem-oriented policing tends to be limited to special units, or it occupies only a small portion of the time of generalist community policing officers, who still expend most of their time patrolling, responding to calls for service, and making ad hoc interventions as they observe the need (Capowich & Roehl, 1994; McElroy, Cosgrove, & Sadd, 1993; Wilkinson & Rosenbaum, 1994). This is not to make light of departments' efforts to innovate, but only to note the difficulties in making even modest changes. Rather than try to assess the impact of these early efforts, I will speculate on what we might expect from a radical transformation to the police-clinician model.

From an institutional perspective, the cop as clinician has tremendous appeal, the same as that of the family practitioner in medicine: someone known personally, readily accessible, caring, and responsive—as well as professionally competent with an array of methods for diagnosing our problems and correcting them. Even as this model of the family practitioner in health care is rapidly approaching extinction (Starr, 1982), the yearning for that kind of service delivery—in public safety as well as health care—is quite strong. Furthermore, although Americans are renown for placing the highest priority on finding what works in a technical sense, the aspect of the cop-clinician that seems most appealing is not the officer's ability to cure the patient, but his or her "bedside manner." In this regard, the prospects of problem-oriented policing seem quite good. Much is known about what is needed to improve the "bedside manner" of police. Permanent assignment to the beat, developing knowledge of and familiarity with its denizens, showing concern for the quality of life of those who are regularly on the beat, and a willingness to account for one's decisions (Goldstein, 1990, p. 159; Mastrofski, 1983; Muir, 1977).

At a technical level, the prospects of the officer-clinician seem far more precarious. This is so because problem-oriented policing does not offer a new, improved, or validated strategy that will reduce specific problems. Rather, it offers a framework to search for strategies that *may* work and, through trial and error, learn whether they *do* work (Mastrofski & Uchida, 1993). The technical core of policing—those things that the police do to produce and process information (Manning, 1994; Reiss, 1992, p. 82)—remains untouched by community policing reforms. Indeed, effective problem-oriented policing would require a substantial upgrading of the information production and processing capacity of police. The capacity to scan for problems, analyze them, search for and select alternatives, and evaluate results calls for a much greater resource commitment to research and development than currently characterizes American police forces (Goldstein, 1990, p. 161; Reiss, 1992). It may go too far to expect every police-clinician to have the requisite research skills to do all these things, but American police agencies lack, for the most part, a well-developed habit and adequate staffing in a research and development unit to do what must be done to learn what works and under what conditions. Police managers often do not know how or where their officers spend their time, despite having elaborate computer aided dispatch systems that account for every minute of an officer's workday. They are developing a capacity to track problem sources (the offending patterns of people and places), but most do not do these things on a routine basis (Taxman & McEwen, 1994). The greatest obstacle to developing stronger clinical-based knowledge is the absence of follow-up data (Bayley & Bittner, 1984). Unlike medical care institutions, police do not conduct systematic follow-up assessments to learn what happens after a "treatment"—whether it is a lone officer responding to a domestic dispute or a task force sweep of a drug retail area. The success or failure of innovative efforts is usually determined with vague impressions, anecdotes, or a simple pre-post comparison of crime data. Rigorous evaluation is exceedingly rare (Sherman, 1992a).

Ultimately, for the clinician model of policing to produce more public safety, officers must know what is likely to work in a given situation and must have the departmental support to see that it is delivered. Both of these things are in short supply at present, due in no small part to factors beyond police control. Here I will address only the need to develop a stronger police knowledge base of what works.

For all the hopefulness of police professionalism since August Vollmer, the state of police science at the end of the 20th century is not much advanced over what it was at the beginning, the principal difference being that today we know a bit more about what does *not* work. That is not to say that the police are irrelevant to the control of crime and disorder, or that some police are not exceptionally skilled at doing whatever police can do to make communities safer. What is clear is that the storehouse of knowledge that is scientifically based has a lot of unused room. Much of what appears to be the best in the craft of policing remains unvalidated (Bayley & Bittner, 1984). Those few instances where the impact of police tactics has been rigorously examined—for example, handling domestic violence—have failed to test the best that the police craft has to offer (Mastrofski & Uchida, 1993, p. 341), and the mixed results raise more questions than they answer (Sherman, 1992b). This is not surprising for an applied science in its infancy, but, for example, it can hardly be reassuring to police who want to be "results oriented" to hear that the tactic that seemed so promising in 1984 for reducing domestic violence (arrest) was a few years later implicated as likely to increase the risk of repeat violence in many cases.

Taken in a literal sense, the notion of the problem-*solving* police-clinician seems to carry a promise on which police cannot yet deliver. There simply is an insufficient knowledge base and infrastructure to produce technical success on a regular basis. Given the fragility of these experimental efforts in a political environment that demands instantaneous success the first time out, it is understandable that some are fearful that rigorous inquiry into these efforts would likely contribute to their premature abandonment (Goldstein, 1994, p. ix; Moore, 1994, p. 298). The risk of not conducting such inquiries seems even greater, however. Without rigorous validation of what works and why, police will not be in a position to make timely corrections and to pursue more promising methods. What needs changing is the political environment in which such experiments are conducted. Adept police officials and elected leaders can promise to look for solutions without having to have invested a priori in what is being tested. There is precedent for this in other applied fields, such as medicine.

Democratizing Policing:
The Police as Partners With the Public

In an institutional sense, the movement to recast the police and public as partners in public safety appears nothing short of a smashing success. Not only does it appeal to currently popular themes of citizen responsibility for self-help and government responsiveness to citizen needs (Osborne & Gaebler, 1992), it also adjusts the criteria for success from public safety to developing a sense of community and a perception of a caring government (Bayley, 1988, p. 228). Whether participation in Neighborhood Watch has the desired effect on crime, the mere existence of such programs and joint participation by police and public may be counted successful. Even if citizen advisory councils serve more to ratify *police* policies and practices than to shape them (Buerger, 1994a; Mastrofski & Greene, 1993), they convey a sense of access, participation, and ownership of this powerful agency of local government.

The major threats to the institutional integrity of police-public partnerships will come from corruption scandals. Police officers or citizens who take advantage of these closer working relationships for personal gain will activate another powerful set of institutional imperatives: that government be fair and lawful. Although this "good government" sentiment seems dormant in the current political climate, chiefs would be ill-advised to underestimate its power if a corruption issue becomes highly publicized. Another potential hazard for police-community partnerships is the eruption of social and economic conflict among different groups of citizens that is so severe that partnership with one party to the conflict is viewed by the other as a hostile alliance. "Defended neighborhoods," the very kind that seem most needful of police-community linkages, are prime candidates for acrimonious disputes that make it difficult for the police to appear to be fair and neutral arbiters, even if that is their intention (Mastrofski, 1988).

The technical aspects of police-public partnerships are fraught with problems, as many observers and researchers have noted (Buerger, 1994a; Friedman, 1994; Mastrofski, 1988; Rosenbaum, 1988; Skogan, 1990a). These fall into two general categories: difficulties in implementing "partnership" programs, and whether or not, if implemented, they actually work to make communities safer (Rosenbaum, 1987). Depending upon the evaluator, the current state of affairs seems to be either that (a) we have insufficient evidence to draw conclusions about the effectiveness of these programs, or (b) some programs work sometimes under certain conditions—usually in areas that are not the most afflicted with crime, disorder, and poverty.

The most popular partnership programs have as their ostensible purpose the "co-production" of public safety by providing information about crime and other problems to police (e.g., Neighborhood Watch). Although it is often difficult to develop and sustain a high degree of resident participation in these programs, police have learned a great deal, especially from others with much experience in community organization. Except in the most alienated, disorganized, and dispirited neighborhoods, getting significant public involvement is not the major challenge confronting police nowadays. They can be remarkably successful in getting citizens to provide information through these programs and hotlines. A less-explored structural problem is that most departments lack the ability to analyze the citizen-provided data and get this analysis to decision makers who can use it in a timely fashion.

The net effect of activating a Neighborhood Watch program should be increased calls to the police to report suspicious or undesirable situations and increased direct contact with the beat officers to apprise them of the same. Although this may well produce more valuable tips, it will also generate many false leads and unreliable information. Police need to develop more effective methods for sifting through this information and making sense of it. Calls for service are routinely recorded on computerized information systems and could form the basis of a routine "hotspot" analysis that searches for problem patterns associated with geographic areas. At the street level, problem-solving clinicians should receive daily printouts of this sort of analysis for their patrol areas and should be able to receive special analyses on demand. Line supervisors and middle managers could use this information to make strategic decisions about how to allocate scarce resources most effectively. Criminal investigators need to be able to sift through a tremendous amount of information to develop accurate intelligence files about criminal activity. The technology is available for handling large amounts of such data (Institute for Law and Justice, 1994; Maltz, Gordon, & Friedman, 1990; Sherman, Gartin, & Buerger, 1989), but few police departments use it, and fewer still make such analyses available to their officers and staff in a user-friendly format and on a timely basis. Of course, timely citizen tips can be handled efficiently using current police information systems, but these are designed for incident-focused, reactive responses. An entirely different approach is required for preventive, anticipatory problem solving. Furthermore, if citizens begin to see that their information does make a difference at the strategic level, it may be easier to sustain their commitment to participating in partnership programs.

There is more than a little of the technophile's "Tom Swift" image imparted by the information systems envisioned above: informed middle managers cleverly deploying their officers in a high-tech contest with the elements of crime and disorder. There is cause for skepticism. They can be no more effective than the underlying assumptions police use to decide what data to gather and how to compile them. Police of all ranks presently fail to use this information even when available. It is rarely offered in a manner compatible with their own understanding of beat problems. Officers tend to place greatest faith in information personally communicated by informants whom they know and whose reliability they can assess from prior experience. Police custom is to avoid sharing crime intelligence widely, a norm that limits the utility of even the most sophisticated information management system. Supervisors and managers are unaccustomed to making strategic resource allocation decisions, having been socialized to accept the simple bureaucratic imperative of the dispatcher's assignment. Whatever the technical merits of harnessing the routine input of "citizen partners," one of the greatest challenges remains convincing police to use it.

Integrating Services: Holistic Government

One of the most enticing promises of community policing is that it will return local government to the early 19th-century American vision of what *policing* meant to municipalities: according to Webster's dictionary, "the internal organization or regulation of a political unit through exercise of governmental powers especially with respect to general comfort, health, morals, safety, or prosperity." Long before there were police organizations as we know them today, American governments were providing such "policing" through general, undifferentiated structures that were eventually fragmented as specialist occupations arose and governments began to compartmentalize into separate service-providing bureaus (Lane, 1992, p. 5). The pathologies of this aspect of bureaucratization are well documented (Sayre & Kaufman, 1960): turf battles; service agencies responsive only to narrowly defined constituencies; and uncoordinated, inefficient government that cannot mobilize to address important problems.

The appeal of correcting this state of affairs is so great that some cities have replaced the notion of community *policing* with community *government*—to stress that all parts of local government share a joint responsibility for the welfare of the citizenry. Community policing advocates suggest that police can and should play a central role in bringing about holistic government. Police are called upon as a last resort, they are typically the most numerous and accessible of public servants, and the nature of their work gives them a large investment in making life better for those who live and work within their realm of responsibility. They can do this by identifying problems in which other agencies should have a hand; they can mobilize and prod those agencies into action; they can coordinate their efforts; and they can activate the public and other puissant forces when greater political pressure must be brought to bear.

Because it is widely thought that the condition of a neighborhood's public safety depends upon the condition of its economic vitality, physical condition, and the general health and welfare of its residents, this approach makes tremendous good sense to the public. In the abstract, cooperation to achieve these ends seems incontrovertibly "correct." If the police can stimulate visible inter-agency cooperation where there was none before, that may well produce a significant augmentation of public goodwill, even if it fails to live up to technical expectations. When demands for cooperation move from the general to the specific, however, that is when service integration loses its appeal. Schools are wary of routine police involvement in their security and order maintenance problems; the priorities of housing authorities are most influenced by the demands of their funding sources; public works has its own system for deciding what work gets done when; and union officials are quick to object when management wants something done that is outside the contract.

This is not to say that these problems are insurmountable, but they are inevitable, and the greater the project's scope, the harder they will be to overcome (Benson, 1975). That is because each of these agencies has developed its own specialized set of constituents whose influence as interest groups tends to be narrowly focused (Lowi, 1969, p. 201). If the integrated problem-solving effort requires a substantial departure from what these interest groups value, the consensus on the particulars of a given project will rapidly dissipate without artful persuasion and negotiation. In such a conflicted environment, the institutional value of integrated service delivery is greatly diminished.

From a technical perspective, placing the police at the axis of integrating other municipal services is a high-risk venture, at least from the police department's viewpoint. First, the police are rarely given the authority to compel other agencies to cooperate, and they are often in a weak position to offer attractive incentives to potential partners. Second, in many local jurisdictions, the resources available to other municipal services have dwindled, making it particularly difficult for them to be responsive to police initiatives. Third, the crime reduction capacity of these programs (such as midnight basketball, trash cleanup, and increased lighting) are yet undemonstrated, and in many cases, effects are observable, if at all, only in the long term (e.g., drug and sex education programs). Of course, police can pursue inter-agency service integration at a modest ad hoc level, and a number of anecdotal accounts of success are available (Eck & Spelman, 1987b; Goldstein, 1990). Even major endeavors are reported to have met with success, although they do not appear to produce enduring service-integration practices. Failures are rarely reported (and understandably so), although they are instructive, because they show that the most daunting task may be implementation (Tien, Rich, Shell, Larson, & Donnelly, 1993, pp. 6.7-6.9). It may be that service integration would be as effective as advocates hope, but that there will be few opportunities to test major initiatives. As compelling as public safety may be as an organizing objective for service integration, it may not be strong enough to overcome bureaucratic inertia and political alliances that are well entrenched in the local political scene.

Finally, there are limits to how much American society will tolerate a truly integrated system of government services organized around such objectives as crime and disorder reduction. Taxpayers want drug-free, safe schools, but they also want many other things from these schools, the pursuit of which increases the risks of substance abuse, theft, and violence. They want municipal services coordinated at the neighborhood level, but they also expect citywide standards in roads, sanitation, and code enforcement. Americans may yearn for the kind of holistic public service small towns are alleged to provide, but they also want corporate development, which requires responsiveness to a very different constituency on a much broader scale than the neighborhood. With all of its limitations, fragmented interest group-dominated public bureaucracies produce a complexity of responsiveness that enables local governments to endure and prosper (Long, 1968).

THE PROSPECTS OF STRUCTURAL CHANGE

A candid appraisal of the current state of the structural reform of police in North America must surely yield the conclusion that little has changed with the advent of community policing. Objective case studies of recent efforts are replete with descriptions of the difficulties of achieving structural change, which is understandable, because reforms by their nature occur in small increments over long time periods (Greene et al., 1994; Sadd & Grinc, 1994; Wilkinson & Rosenbaum, 1994). A recent study of 236 municipal police agencies with 100 or more sworn officers examined structural changes between 1987 and 1993 (Maguire, 1997). This sample showed no significant change in the degree of formalization, administrative density, or civilianization. There was a significant decrease in organizational height (showing a "flatter" hierarchical structure) and a significant (and continuing) increase in functional differentiation (specialization). Notably, the trend toward increasing specialization is contrary to the direction of mainstream community policing reform, and even more important, neither of these two structural trends were statistically attributable to a department's implementation of community policing.

Structural reform takes time, and one might therefore temper short-term skepticism with long-term patience. However, there is evidence that leads one to expect that the engines of *structural* reform are unlikely to be stoked by police leaders. A 1993 survey of municipal and county police and sheriff's departments (very small to very large) asked top police administrators in each agency to describe their views about community policing (Wycoff, 1994). Ninety-eight percent of respondents agreed that community policing is a concept law enforcement agencies should pursue. Seventy-two percent said that every aspect of law enforcement would benefit from a community policing approach. Nearly half reported that their agencies had or were implementing community policing, about 9 of every 10 large departments saying this. Despite this level of enthusiasm, 47% said that what community policing means in practical terms is *not* clear. Most tellingly, only about half of the respondents said that community policing would require major changes in policies, goals, mission statements, or training. Only 27% said that it would require extensive reorganization of police agencies. Despite the profusion of community policing rhetoric calling for fundamental structural changes, it appears that police agency leadership is not a driving force for accomplishing it.

More fundamentally, there is cause to wonder just how much top police leadership can effect fundamental structural changes, even when that is their top priority. Most of the reform literature is pitched to police managers. This material evokes an image of a jockey astride a headstrong steed, artfully guiding it around the track. One more apropos, especially for leaders of large urban departments, is that of the rodeo cowboy who with great skill manages merely to stay astride his bucking bronco until the bell sounds. The analogy underscores the reality of the many constraints placed upon those in police leadership roles. As useful as the heroic vision of the leader may be to buttress performance and accountability in the institutional domain, it is perhaps time to take a more hardheaded look at what students of organization call the "romance of leadership" (Meindl & Ehrlich, 1987).

Instead, a careful analysis of the structural impact of government reforms over the past century or so might lead one to conclude that "successful" movements were those able to catch the wave of broad and powerful forces of demographic, economic, social, and technological change. Successful reformers were able to anticipate or follow the implications of these broader, powerful forces and thereby helped the targets of their efforts to adapt to them. Applying this Darwinian approach to police history in North America encourages analysts to pay more attention to those broader forces and give less credence to the impact of reformers' Herculean efforts to transform their organizations singlehandedly. It helps us understand why some strands of reform wither and die out, while others survive and even prosper. We are thus impressed less with the impact of August Vollmer, O. W. Wilson, and J. Edgar Hoover on the trajectory of police structural change in the 20th century than we are with their insights about what a successful organization structure should look like.

Here we must be careful to note that successful structural adaptations are those that allow the organization to survive and prosper. Thus, for police of the 20th century we note that structural adaptations have succeeded to the extent that they demonstrated effectiveness in institutional, not technical terms. Yet it is the hope and promise of much community policing reform that its effects will produce benefits of a technical sort. Such a transformation would indeed be profound, and to some unimaginable. It may nonetheless be useful to speculate on what would need to happen to be able to make police agency structures responsive in terms of technical, rather than institutional, performance.

TECHNOLOGY AND ENVIRONMENT: THE MISSING ELEMENTS IN THE EFFICACY OF STRUCTURAL CHANGE

Community policing defines technical performance variously, but ultimately it boils down to reducing crime and disorder and, for some at least, increasing social harmony or "community." This is akin to defining performance of health care organizations in terms of decreasing disease and injury. The comparison to health organizations is apropos, because strengthening the technical capacity of police agencies would make them much more like health organizations today. The police mission becomes easing particular problems, such as convenience store robbery, drunk driving, disorderly youths in public places, and spousal violence. Much as medical professionals know quite a bit about how to reduce the risks of heart disease and how to ease the problems it causes, reformers hope that police will be able to do the same for assorted crimes and disorders experienced in broader social arenas. A police chief wants to produce an X percent decrement in convenience store robberies and knows that he (and the stores) can apply strategies A, B, and C, which will yield a Q percent probability that robberies will be reduced between F and G percent. This is very much like a public health expert's advice on how to reduce heart disease by changing diet and exercise habits.

Police organizations today are unable to demonstrate anything close to this kind of technical capacity. Some leaders are quick to claim technical prowess in a time of declining crime rates (Pooley, 1996), but few chiefs are willing to tie their own job security to such results in the long run. We simply lack the kind of knowledge about police technology to speak with confidence about its efficacy. Thirty years ago, Wilson (1968a) described this situation; his description remains apt today:

> The difficulty in managing the police arises, in my view, less from the quality of men recruited or the level at which authority is exercised and more from the nature of the police function. Mental hospitals provide a useful comparison to the police in this regard. Like the police, they are regarded as essential; like

the police, they are routinely and repeatedly condemned for failures and inadequacies. . . .

In an incisive review of the literature on mental hospitals, Perrow concludes that the reason for the failure of reform has not been bad men or low budgets or improper organization or incompetent management (though all these things may exist); the central problem is that we do not know how to cure mental illness. The problem is not one of ideology, but of technology. The hospitals are given a task they cannot perform, yet they must try to perform it, for the alternative (doing nothing) seems even worse. The most important recent improvement in mental hospital care was the result of an advance in medical technology—the development of tranquilizer drugs. Changes in organization, leadership, and in the men recruited to hospital tasks have rarely produced significant or lasting results from the patient's point of view.

The parallel with the police is striking. . . . (pp. 410-411)

Determining whether and how much police methods produce the desired results is still an act of political divining, not something demonstrated with anything approaching credible empirical validation of the sort we have come to expect from the health care industry.

Taking technical performance seriously means first and foremost learning more about the efficacy of current crime and disorder control technology and seeking knowledge about how, if possible, to improve it. We have limited evidence about the efficacy of traditional police methods, such as preventive patrol, arrest, and counseling. It may well be that the greatest advances in the technical capacity of the police will come, at least in the near future, from learning how to apply old methods to greater effect. This requires a stronger basic knowledge base about what works (Sherman, 1992a), plus more effective application of rapidly expanding information technology to target police activities in the field. There are, of course, developments in other arenas— weapons and use of force, forensics, surveillance, and noncoercive persuasion —but advances in information technology appear to hold the greatest potential for realizing the goals underscored by community policing (Manning, 1992b, p. 329).

Calls for more research and development to understand and expand police technological capacity can be found in much of the current reform literature. Devoting more resources to assessing and developing police technical capacity would undoubtedly stimulate knowledge about how to be more effective in crime and disorder control. Compared to the public resources devoted to medical and other health research, those devoted to crime and disorder control are minuscule (Reiss, 1992), but even if massive resources are given to R and D, the newly acquired knowledge will be insufficient to transform police agencies so that they actually employ those technologies to accomplish technical results. The environment of policing must change as well.

Increasing the technical capacity of police requires that these agencies operate in an environment that rewards and punishes on the basis of technical, not institutional, effectiveness. Police leaders will give the pursuit of technical effectiveness a higher priority than institutional effectiveness when they experience considerable pressure to do so. When a chief's job and a department's budget depend upon technical performance, then there will be serious incentives to pursue technical effectiveness. Some law enforcement leaders have recently moved to stimulate public expectations of technical effectiveness in crime control, former New York City Commissioner Bratton's being the most visible. This may be the harbinger of a movement to change the technical environment of police. Whether these efforts endure in New York and proliferate elsewhere, and whether powerful forces in the police environment condition their support on performance to these standards remains to be seen. Presently, however, leadership in the law enforcement industry does not experience accountability of a technical sort.

Another environmental condition that could stimulate the quest for technical performance is a more competitive market for the delivery of police services. Such a market might be viewed in limited terms, as greater competition among public agencies for the provision of public policing services, an argument found in the public choice school of policy (Ostrom, 1972). The extent to which public police agencies in U.S. metropolitan areas actually compete for business is not well documented, although there is some evidence of interjurisdictional contracts, agency consolidations, and other transfers of government functions (Mastrofski, 1989). The relative infrequency of these events suggests that local police agencies seldom compete with each other, although it is possible that the perception of competition with proximate agencies stimulates potential rivals to higher levels of technical performance. Citizens "vote with their feet" when they decide where to live (and pay local taxes), and the quality of police services may be an important consideration in many cases, but it is difficult to determine the extent to which police agencies feel and respond to this kind of competitive pressure.

Public police agencies may experience a more profound form of competition with providers of private security. The extent to which private security competes with or merely complements public police is a matter of debate. Shearing and Stenning (1981) discuss evidence on both sides. They note that public police of today are beginning to emulate private security by seeking a more proactive, preventive model of intervention rather than the reactive and corrective one that has come to characterize public police work in the late 20th century. This might represent a move to become more competitive with private security. The strong interest in managing the police calls-for-service workload might even be uncharitably interpreted as a move that divests the organization of less desirable customers and invests more resources in preventive, "community-related" services for customers who are able and willing to pay higher taxes for them. Police departments survive despite high levels of crime and disorder in their jurisdictions, and police chiefs rarely lose their jobs for these reasons. They are lost because the organization fails to fulfill expectations about the "correct" institutional forms. The most politically compelling part of the 1994 Crime Bill is not the promise of safer streets, but the promise of greater police presence, which is widely equated with "good" police service.

Despite the widespread belief that public police agencies enjoy a near monopoly on police services, there are some indications of at least sub rosa competition. Yet even a cutthroat market would not necessarily demand performance in technical terms. It is only when there is pressure for technical performance *and* a competitive market to provide these services that one may expect significant movement *inside* the police organization to develop and harness its technical capacity. Although politicians campaign against rising crime rates, disorder, and the dearth of community, there is no obvious indication that important constituencies really hold them or police leaders responsible for solving these problems. Police and other public officials who take the technical performance aspects of community policing rhetoric seriously, walk a very narrow line nowadays. They must nurture the technical capacity of the police, while at the same time they must encourage their constituents to hold them accountable for results, such as crimes reduced and problems solved. The former requires bold new approaches and a fairly forgiving political environment, one that tolerates the trial and error necessary to learn what works and what does not. The latter requires frequent, rigorous, and objective evaluation that concentrates on results. Combining the two produces a volatile brew, more likely to poison than profit the careers of police and other public leaders in the chain of accountability.

IMPLICATIONS FOR THE FUTURE OF REFORM

The great architect, Louis Sullivan, offered the dictum that form should follow function. That is an apt one for those who wish to improve policing by changing the structure of its organizations. The selection of the right forms should follow from an analysis of the functions we expect police to fulfill. I have argued that these functions are shaped by the technologies available to the police and by what environmental forces pressure police to perform. Given the uncertainties about what police technologies are most effective, and therefore what the technical capacities of police are, those who wish to improve the police technically would do well to examine popular reform assumptions carefully about what structural forms work best under what conditions. For example, there are some approaches to crime prevention that would seem to work best with a decentralized decision-making system, while others would seem most likely to achieve optimal performance with a centralized structure. Whether police pursue a "security guard" approach (reducing immediate risks) or a "public health" approach (reducing long-term risks) to crime prevention could have profound implications for how decisions about resource allocation and field tactics are made (Sherman, 1995). The former would seem to require decentralization and the latter centralization. We need to know a lot more about how well each of these technologies performs under different degrees of centralization before declaring that there is a one true and effective structure for policing (Mastrofski & Ritti, 1995).

If police departments are to advance in the pursuit of the technical promises of reformers, a great deal must change. The current obsession with implementing the "right" structures (an impulse that serves institutional objectives admirably) must give way to one that seeks not consensus, but delights in disorder. Law enforcement agencies must experiment with technological innovations and evaluate old ones. This should be done in different structural contexts and service conditions so that we can learn more about what structures facilitate the effectiveness of a given technology in a given type of service environment.

This requires experimentation and risk taking by police leaders, while at the same time calling for a degree of technical accountability to which the police and public are heretofore unaccustomed. The current environment of policing in America is quite hostile to the pursuit of experimentation, risk taking, and results-oriented accountability. This is especially so, given that the American public has been primed to expect government to deliver the quick fix. It works against long-term knowledge development about what works and conducting rigorous assessments of technical results. Politicians avoid association with policy failures, but because of the need for trial and error, failure is essential to the development of technology. This makes innovation and objective assessment very risky for police agencies—from top management on down to the rank and file, for they are and must be responsive to their political environment, one conditioned to accept institutional performance. Add to this an enduring political environment where elected officials offer simplistic solutions to complex crime problems and excoriate their opponents whose misfortune it is to have sponsored a policy or decision that produced even one publicized misadventure. One of the principal functions of police chiefs (and mayors) remains ceremonial: taking the heat when things go awry (Crank & Langworthy, 1992, p. 359). The kind of risk taking required to develop the technical performance of police under these conditions seems a low-probability event.

If reformers want to move toward a policing that is technically developed, they should strive for ways to make the police environment more hospitable to experimentation, risk taking, and objective evaluation. Funding support for such efforts is always welcome in times of tight budgets, but what is even more important is having a public sufficiently demanding of technical performance that it is willing to give their police license to experiment, fail, learn, and grow. Stimulating that kind of environment calls for practical, inspirational leadership of the highest order.

PART IV

PERSPECTIVES AND CONCLUSIONS

10

LATE MODERNITY, GOVERNANCE, AND POLICING

Les Johnston

The main contention of this chapter is that policing in late modern societies is undergoing a fundamental structural shift. In what follows, the main features of that restructuring are outlined and their implications considered. Though most of the discussion that follows focuses on developments in Britain and, to a lesser extent, the rest of Europe, the processes identified are universal ones whose impact is widespread. Indeed, many of these developments are more advanced in North America than elsewhere. The chapter is divided into three sections. Section One outlines some of the key changes arising in late modern society. Section Two considers the implications of these changes for policing, concentrating on the processes of sectoral and spatial restructuring. Section Three considers some of the issues raised by the structural shifts described earlier. What is the relationship between policing and security? What implications are raised by the generation of an apparently "infinite" public demand for security? To what extent is late modern policing open to public evaluation? How should it be governed? How should one theorize the relationship among policing, state, and society in the 21st century?

SOCIAL CHANGE IN LATE MODERN SOCIETY

Restructuring is a theme that has been at the center of much analysis of contemporary social change. Though the terminology used to describe that change varies ("late modern," "post-modern," "late capitalist," "post-capitalist," "post-industrial," etc.), there is general acceptance that a number of key structural shifts are at work in the contemporary period. For present purposes, four such shifts are of particular significance:

Economic Change. Contemporary economic change involves several elements, including high levels of unemployment; the growth of female, casual, and part-time work; the expansion of "mass private property"; and the growth of the service economy. One of the most significant changes concerns the structure of enterprise itself. Here, many commentators have observed a shift from "Fordist" modes of production (those based on mass production, scientific management, and "top-down" organizational hierarchies) to "post-Fordism." Unlike previous management styles, post-Fordism gives greatest priority to "innovation, quality, customised products and the flexible machinery that such customisation requires" (Murray, 1991, p. 25). In order to achieve those ends three conditions have to be met. First, an appropriate work culture must be inculcated. Second, key elements of the organizational structure must be decentralized. Third, the organization must become "flexible" in order to face new competitive challenges. These last two conditions—decentralization and flexibility—are, in fact, inextricably linked. Aglietta (1987), for instance, claims that the increased use of microelectronics in industry permits a new flexibility to occur: one that "enables the *centralization* of the planning of production but the *decentralization* of the units of production" (Bagguley et al., 1990, p. 20). Other versions of the flexibility thesis focus on the emergence of "dual labor markets." According to this argument the "flexible firm" is one in which a distinction develops between "core" workers (those permanent employees with high levels of skill) and "peripheral" workers (part-time and casual employees with lower levels of skill).

Economic restructuring along these lines is by no means restricted to the private manufacturing sector. Bagguley et al. (1990) note that many of the processes identified in restructuring theory can be found in public sector services. Among the most notable of these processes are the "flexibilization" of labor input; the replacement of existing labor input with cheaper labor; the "materialization" of the service function, so that the service takes the form of a material product that can be bought and sold like any other; the emergence of "partial self-provisioning"—providing services for oneself; and the expansion of subcontracting. In addition to that, a number of strategies for the restructuring of state services are identified, three of which—intensification, commodification, and concentration—are particularly noteworthy:

> Intensification will result from the "managers" in the organisation being given clearer, specific objectives and being expected to meet them by managing their unit, and especially their professional workers, more intensively; commodification will entail a variety of attempts to mimic markets, including the centralised specification of financial targets; concentration will involve the relevant minister and/or outsiders to that service being much more powerfully placed to "manage" it. (Bagguley et al., 1990, p. 70)

Globalization and Localization. The concept of globalization has been used to describe "those complex processes operating on a global scale, which cut across national boundaries, integrating and connecting communities and organisations in new space-time combinations" (Hall, 1992, p. 299). To that extent, the logic of globalization suggests a process of uniformity. National identity is eroded by the internationalization of capital. Space and time are compressed by the effects of supersonic travel and instantaneous tele-visual communication. Globalization, however, is a contradictory process, itself giving rise to countertendencies of "localization." At the cultural level, some national identities are reinforced by the very process of resistance to globalization. At the economic level, service-oriented management ideologies aim to direct tailor-made products to particular groups of consumers, rather than standardized products to mass markets. At the political level, the supranationalization of the state generates its own nationalist backlash. Globalization is accompanied, then, by an unstable combination of tendencies: centralization and decentralization; internationalization and nationalism; homogeneity and diversity; fragmentation and consolidation.

Changes in the Stratification System. The dominant form of stratification in modern capitalist societies is stratification by class. Late modern societies are, however, subject to more diverse forms of stratification. Although class persists as a key element in social structure, other significant social divisions come to the fore: race, region, religion, gender, nationality, ethnicity, age, and so on. One of the consequences of that shift to heterogeneous divisions is a diffusion of social conflict along plural lines. The existence of simultaneous plural fronts of conflict poses new problems for agencies of social control whose practices have been forged under a more homogeneous stratification system.

Political Change and the State. Given the structural changes already described, it is clear that the state, itself, is likely to undergo a process of structural transformation. Various terms have been coined to describe this process. Bottoms and Wiles (1994), for example, refer to the "stretching" of the state under the dual impact of globalization and localization tendencies, the state being pulled simultaneously in contradictory directions. Crook, Pakulski, and Waters (1993) prefer to speak of the "unraveling" of the state, a process that involves several elements: the redistribution of power from the state to autonomous and decentralized agencies; the privatization of state enterprises; and the shifting of responsibility for national state functions to supra-national bodies. The net effect of this process is to undermine traditional Weberian conceptions by which the nation state is perceived as an organization enjoying a monopoly of the legitimate means of coercion within a territorial jurisdiction. There are two further critical issues at stake here. First, the extent to which the state has lost power to nonstate bodies—the view adopted by post-modern commentators such as Crook et al. (1993). Second, the extent to which under contemporary conditions the conceptual distinction between state and nonstate bodies becomes problematic (Johnston, 1992).

POLICING IN LATE MODERN SOCIETY

For present purposes, attention will focus on two elements of restructuring—sectoral and spatial change—though at various points in the chapter the pertinence of the other aspects of change discussed earlier will be apparent.

Sectoral Restructuring and the Police Role

Although, in Britain, recent proposals have been put forward to privatize certain "ancillary" police tasks (Home Office, 1995), the government has done little to initiate informed debate on the topic of privatization. In the absence of that debate, market forces and consumer demand have begun to redefine the balance between public and private policing. This process has occurred in three ways. First, there has been privatization of functions previously undertaken by public police forces. Examples would include the privatization of the

Port of London Constabulary and the rapid growth of private security street patrols in many towns and cities. Second, there has been the expansion of the role of "hybrid" policing organizations: those whose precise sectoral status is a matter of contention. Finally, there has been an expansion of "civil policing": activities ranging from citizen street patrols to the informal justice imposed by vigilante groups.

Such developments are by no means exclusive to Britain. The expansion of the private security industry and its increased involvement in the policing of public space was first apparent in North America (Cunningham & Taylor, 1985; Kakalik & Wildhorn, 1972; Shearing & Stenning, 1987). In Europe, rapid expansion first took place in the 1970s. By the late 1980s, it was estimated that about 96,000 private security guards were employed in France (Ocqueteau, 1987); about 13,000 in the Netherlands—where government projections anticipated an expansion to 30,000 (Hoogenboom, 1989); almost 70,000 in Spain (Allen, 1992); and 190,000 in Germany (de Waard, 1993). In recent years, events in Eastern Europe have also encouraged private penetration of policing. In both Poland and Russia, former state security personnel have been involved in the establishment of private security firms and, latterly, Western security companies have, themselves, entered the Eastern market. In Poland, the Ministry of the Interior has encouraged businesses to sponsor local constabularies to disastrous effect. A case recently reported from Poznan tells of a private detective agency that was, itself, employed to collect evidence of corruption against the local police chief (Borger, 1994), thereby putting a new slant on the old problem, "who polices the police?"

It is not only private security that has expanded its role, however. In all jurisdictions there is a tendency toward the growth of "hybrid" policing (Johnston, 1992) or "gray" policing (which involve forms of cooperation between different social control agencies outside the boundaries of criminal law and for which traditional modes of accountability seem obsolete; Hoogenboom, 1991). In Holland, it is estimated that the welfare system has over 40 regulatory bodies employing some 20,000 officials with a variety of different police powers. In Britain, it is estimated that during the mid-1970s more than 57,000 people—excluding private security personnel—were engaged in various forms of policing and regulatory activity (Johnston, 1992; Miller & Luke, 1977). Developments since then have swelled that number. For example, in Britain, the field of commercial crime control has spawned bodies like the Serious Fraud Office, which employs civilian accountants and lawyers to initiate and direct police enquiries, despite their lack of formal police powers.

It is at street-level, however, where the sectoral restructuring of policing has become most evident. In Britain there are at least half a dozen agencies, apart from the public police, engaged in street-level policing:

1. *Private security patrols:* In circumstances where police resources are limited—and Home Office proposals for reallocation of funds between forces suggest that some will, in future, face harsher limitations (Rose, 1994)—private security companies are securing contracts for street patrol and for the protection of residential property.

2. *Private security employed by a municipal authority:* In some cases, local authorities have contracted private security companies to undertake street patrols and protect municipal property on their behalf.

3. *Municipal security:* Many local authorities, such as those on Merseyside and in London, have long-established security organizations—bodies of unsworn, uniformed personnel whose function is to protect council property (houses, schools, markets, etc.). Some have now established similar organizations to undertake general patrol of streets and other public places, duties traditionally the prerogative of public police.

4. *Municipal constabularies:* Local authorities have, since the 1800s, employed bodies of sworn constables whose police powers are limited to a given jurisdiction—typically a park or some other public place. In recent years, several London boroughs have established constabularies of this sort to enforce bylaws and other local acts, and there has been some dispute between them and the Metropolitan Police regarding powers and jurisdiction (Johnston, 1993). In August 1994, Wandsworth Borough Council failed to secure the Home Secretary's approval to have the jurisdiction of its Constabulary extended in order to enable its officers to undertake 24-hour anticrime patrols on housing estates.

5. *Activated Neighborhood Watch:* Though Neighborhood Watch is a comparatively passive mode of crime prevention, in recent years some groups have engaged in antiburglary street patrols. Although, in the past, the Home Office has refused to authorize such activities, in October 1994 the Home Secretary announced a new crime prevention initiative, one element of which supported the formation of neighborhood watch street patrols.

6. *Vigilantism:* Vigilante action is, of course, the ultimate expression of private (noncommercial) justice, and there is some evidence that vigilantism is on the increase in Britain (Johnston, 1996b). Those engaged in such action usually justify it in terms of the inability of the police to meet public demand for security, or because of the courts' alleged failure to punish offenders sufficiently.

The public police's response to this process of sectoral restructuring has been, on the whole, defensive. One fear is that commercial, municipal, and popular provision of street-level "social service" functions will reduce the police to a reactive public order force, thereby undermining their legitimacy. According to this view, a "two-tier" system of policing is developing in which "hard" policing functions are undertaken by the public police, while "soft" policing functions are captured by the private sector. Critics also maintain that a second type of duality is emerging, the better-off purchasing private protection, leaving the poor to rely on an increasingly depleted public sector. Though these concerns are certainly justified, the two-tier model upon which they are based is inadequate for several reasons. For one thing, it ignores the fact that service quality will vary within sectors as well as between them. To put it simply, some who purchase private protection will be able to buy a better quality product than others; for those with the least resources, noncommercial private solutions ("do-it-yourself" policing) may be adopted. This suggests that there will be many more than two tiers of service in the future. Indeed, the examples described in the previous paragraphs indicate that in many British towns and cities policing is already "multi-tiered," rather than "two-tiered."

Not all police responses to these changes have, however, been defensive. At least two British chief constables have proposed that public police organizations be permitted to establish their own security companies in order to compete at a local level with the private sector. Such companies, it is suggested, might be set up as trusts, all revenue being plowed back into public police authority budgets. One proponent of this view (Blair, 1994) notes that its successful implementation would require the Home Office to make various policy changes. First, the police would need the authority to deploy patrols consisting of police auxiliaries—uniformed personnel with less training, fewer powers, and lower pay than regular officers. In addition, Blair suggests, consideration should be given to allowing police authorities the right to hire private security firms to work under police direction. Second, police authorities should be allowed to generate income from the many services that are, currently, offered free to the public, such as crime prevention advice. Instead of providing a free call-out service for activated burglar alarms, Blair asks, why should the police not market and fit alarms themselves? By becoming strategic partners with private companies in the sale of home security equipment, driver training, personal security, or drug awareness, the police could guarantee service standards and generate the income from which additional street patrols might be funded. By these means, Blair maintains, the public police would, at least, maintain a monopoly over the control of private patrols, thereby ensuring an acceptable level of public accountability.

Debates on the future development of street patrol are by no means peculiar to Britain. In Holland, a key element of crime prevention policy has been the attempt to maximize the "functional surveillance" of public space. This policy has generated a number of initiatives: the employment of uniformed "VICs" (roughly translated as "safety, information, and control agents") to counteract fare dodging and vandalism on public transportation; the appointment of "social caretakers" to patrol housing estates; and the recruitment of the long-term unemployed as "City Stewards"—unsworn persons employed by the police or the local authority to prevent crime and to interact with the public (Hesseling & van den Hul, 1993; Van Andel, 1989). The shortcomings of this last development encouraged the police to initiate a system of "police surveillants." From the police's point of view, the City Stewards initiative had two limitations. First, though providing a response to the public's demand for increased street surveillance, its personnel possessed only citizen powers. Second, the Stewards initiative, when combined with other developments—not least the steady expansion of private security—"made it more difficult for the police to control and direct the supervision of public space" (Hesseling & van den Hul, 1993). The police's solution has been the deployment of police surveillants: regular officers with full police powers, though with limited training, whose role is to interact with the public and engage in low-level conflict resolution. From the public's point of view, surveillants meet the demand for an authoritative police presence on the streets. From the police's standpoint, they ensure the organization's continued "ownership" of street policing.

Sectoral restructuring and the multi-tiered system of policing that accompanies it, forces consideration of how the increasingly fluid boundaries between public and private provision are to be governed. At present, in Britain, there have been three alternative answers to that question. The first—a position held by "new right" ideologists—argues that policing, like any other commodity, should be bought and sold in the market place. According to this view, the governance problem is a pseudo-problem, since the "invisible hand" of the market ensures that only providers of quality service survive. Public agencies, such as the police, thus have no legitimate right to seek a monopoly of control over multi-tiered policing. Nor, it is said, do they have any right to act as "ringmasters" over the provision of justice, since free markets are, by their very nature, deemed to be "just" (Hayek, 1960). A second approach —that adopted by the Home Office (1995)—is marked by short-term pragmatism. Though the Home Office Enquiry was keen to demarcate between "core" and "peripheral" police functions in order to satisfy Treasury demands for reduced public expenditure, it was less inclined to discuss the principles by which "consumer conflicts" might be resolved—in particular, how in an increasingly diffuse policing market, coordination of operations, regulation of service quality, and standardization of justice might be assured. A third approach does, thankfully, try to establish some principled basis for dealing with a pluralistic policing system. The Independent Committee of Inquiry Into the Roles and Responsibilities of the Police, a body established by the Police Foundation and the Policy Studies Institute, proposed an integrated policy to avoid the "anarchic emergence of unregulated self-help and private police/ security services in the hands of sectional interests" (Police Foundation/Policy Studies Institute, 1994). Though the proposals were based on the principle that only sworn officers should have the right to arrest, detain, bear arms, and access criminal records (Police Foundation/Policy Studies Institute, 1996), the legitimacy of a plural system of policing was accepted in principle. In that system, officers might be supplemented by "designated" patrol personnel authorized to exercise limited street powers (like the Dutch "surveillants") or by "accredited" patrol officers operating under license to the constabulary, to the municipality, to community groups, or to security companies and subject to a binding contract monitored by the police (a refinement of the Blair, 1994, proposals).

Spatial Restructuring in Britain and Europe

Though police fears about legitimacy, justice, and service standards under conditions of sectoral restructuring are surely justified, the two-tier model on which they are often premised is simplistic. Policing in Britain and elsewhere is, increasingly, subject to the complex processes of fragmentation and consolidation associated with late modern society. These processes generate a multiplicity of policing tiers and are as much a product of spatial as of sectoral restructuring. In order to consider the impact of such restructuring, let us examine those spatial changes that have occurred in Britain alongside processes arising in Europe during the past 30 years.

Britain: Stage One. British policing has been undergoing a process of centralization for more than a century. In recent decades, however, the pace of that centralization has been increased by two factors. First, legislative changes (the 1964 Police Act and the 1972 Local Government Act) led to the amalgamation of forces. In the mid-1960s, there had been more than 150 police forces in England and Wales. There are now 43. A second factor was the political and industrial unrest that spanned the period from the early 1970s to the mid-1980s. The culmination of this period of conflict occurred with the Miners Strike of 1984-1985, during which time mutual aid arrangements between forces were such that, effectively, a national police force was said to exist for public order purposes.

Europe. Centralization in Britain has been accompanied by coordination in Europe. Debate about the prospects of and the need for a European Police Force has gone on for more than 20 years. Justification for European police cooperation has been expressed in several ways (Walker, 1993). The most common of these has emphasized the increased mobility of criminals and the growth of international crimes such as terrorism, drug trafficking, and money laundering. More recently, it has been suggested that the relaxation of internal border controls will exacerbate these problems, further increasing the need for cooperation. Another view is that in-migration by the poor of Southern and Eastern Europe, if not checked, will generate serious economic, political, public order, and crime problems.

Since 1976, there has been formal cooperation between governments through the Trevi Conferences, which were instigated to counter the terrorist threat. In 1985, Trevi broadened its brief to include issues of international crime and, in so doing, put policing issues back at the center of European debate. The goal of European police integration was further enhanced by the signing of the Schengen Agreement in June 1990 by Germany, Belgium, Luxembourg, the Netherlands, and France (there are now nine signatories, Britain, Denmark, and Eire being the exceptions). By the terms of that agreement, police checks at the frontiers of signatories were abolished, hot pursuit across borders was permitted, and coordination and sharing of computerized information was encouraged. Finally, the Treaty of Maastricht, signed in February 1991, brought policing issues under the jurisdiction of the European Union, Article K.1. 9, establishing a European Police Agency (Europol).

Initially, Europol will develop a system of information exchange for combating terrorism, drug trafficking, and serious international crime. Member states are also committed inter alia to the creation of new databases, the exploration of supra-national initiatives in crime prevention, and the provision of a central analytical facility for the planning of criminal investigations. There has, however, been no attempt to address the question of whether Europol might, at some future date, become a fully operational police force whose personnel enjoy full police powers.

The emergence of Europol raises a number of questions. How, for example, will Europol relate to Schengen? Concern has been expressed in Britain that the Schengen signatories, far from being subsumed under Europol, might come to represent the "fast track" in a two-speed development (Clark, 1994). A second question concerns the matter of effectiveness. In part, that question relates to the previous one, for if there is duplication of effort and lack of coordination, there can be no effectiveness. There are, however, other sides to this question, not least that of whether evaluations of effectiveness might be overridden by calculations of political expediency. Walker (1993) suggests that the case for European police cooperation is often based upon evidence that, though unclear, is difficult to falsify. Frequently, complex social problems about migration, economic dispossession, and political oppression are reduced to problems of security, then given a criminogenic twist: for example, the migrant as embodiment of a European crime wave. Walker (1993) suggests that the dynamic of cooperation is neither a product of crime itself, nor of any rational process in which the specific benefits of cooperation are evaluated. Rather, it arises from a populist political discourse of "internal security." If this is the case, of course, one is left with an uncomfortable question: What would constitute empirical evidence of "good practice" and "effectiveness" in European policing?

Finally, there is the matter of the accountability of Europol. Walker's (1993) assessment of the adequacy of existing mechanisms is a pessimistic one. Not only are the formal modes of accountability limited, the diversity of European police organizations, policing philosophies, and organizational structures will make it, paradoxically, easier for the police to play the "professional expertise" card on matters of accountability. The invocation of expertise will, moreover, be given added justification by the supposedly specialist nature of "Eurocrime." In fact, the position on accountability is, if anything, more worrying than Walker suggests. The diversity of European policing is not, after all, encapsulated in Europol alone. It should be remembered that the internationalization of private protection has proceeded rather more quickly than the "Europeanization" of public policing. Lilley (1992) has described the speed with which international consortia—many of whose members have a background in defense production—have, as a consequence of the "peace dividend," penetrated the private corrections market. The fact that there is a "Euro-melange" of public and private policing agencies adds to the difficulties of establishing adequate mechanisms of public accountability, particularly as interaction between the sectors increases.

Britain: Stage Two. One fact that is increasingly evident is that the centralization and consolidation described previously is, by no means, a uniform tendency. Spatial restructuring is a process of uneven—perhaps even contradictory—development. Reiner's (1992b) vision of post-modern Britain sees diverse policing as a corollary of increased social fragmentation. One facet of that diversity is its spatial polarization (what Reiner calls an "organizational bifurcation" within the police). On the one hand, there are a small number of centralized (and increasingly coordinated) police agencies at regional, national, and supra-national levels. On the other hand, there are a large number of decentralized (and probably fragmented) police agencies at local levels. Clearly, given the preceding discussion, that bifurcation will also consist of a complex of public, private, and hybrid bodies intersecting at different spatial levels.

To some extent, this model was implicit in the White Paper on the police (Home Office, 1993a). Here, it was recognized that future rationalization of the structure of forces might be necessary if there was to be a coordinated regional, national, and supra-national response to crime. Though amalgamations were not proposed, the machinery for bringing them about was put into place. This commitment to rationalization was combined with two others. First, there was renewed encouragement for police forces to engage in the contracting out of services. Second, there was commitment to financial decentralization and operational devolution through the establishment of "basic command units": "the main responsibility for local policing must go [to] the local commanders who are in touch with their local communities" (Home Office, 1993a, p. 3).

Arguably, then, "big" policing policies (on drugs, terrorism, or organized crime) will be determined at national, supra-national, and transnational levels. So, does this mean that local policing matters will be decided locally? Perhaps, though not necessarily. Although operational devolution is well under way in British police forces, the central state—itself being remodeled under late modern conditions—continues to play a dominant role in the formulation of policies that impact at local levels. If genuine devolution does not occur, however—whether because of internal organizational resistance or because of external interference by the central state—the customer may look for alternative providers: through do-it-yourself policing, through the private sector, or through the newly resurgent municipal sector (Johnston, 1993). In this last case, it was noticeable that the Chief Officer of the Sedgefield Community Force—a municipal police body composed of officers without police powers—saw the main justification for its establishment to be "local policing under local control."

Finally, it has to be recognized that sectoral and spatial restructuring are inextricably linked. Such linkage begs a question. Are we moving toward a future in Britain that combines two equally problematic tendencies? On the one hand, an increasingly centralized policing structure whose relationship to national and supra-national government will, effectively, stifle any real decentralization of decision making to the locality? On the other hand, a local system of policing subject to partial privatization and, increasingly, characterized by fragmentation of structure and unevenness of quality? In other words, a system in which privatization produces neither enhanced choice for the consumer nor a reduction in the power of the central state. Clearly, that begs important questions about the future governance of policing.

FUTURE CONSIDERATIONS

Policing, Security, and Commodification

One of the inferences that might, justifiably, be drawn from this chapter is that policing is difficult to define. If, under late modern conditions, policing becomes a complex patchwork of diverse elements, all attempts to equate policing with "the police" are, by definition, untenable. This suggests that any definition of policing has to be a functional one, rather than one based on the activities of particular personnel. Existing attempts to produce such a functional definition have produced prolonged debates about whether that function should be defined in terms of law enforcement (Kinsey, Lea, & Young, 1986), social service (Punch & Naylor, 1973), or order maintenance (Wilson, 1968b). In addition to that, there has been dispute about whether the exercise of such functions should be maximal/proactive (Alderson, 1979) or minimal/reactive (Kinsey et al., 1986). To a certain extent these already complex debates are complicated further by their tendency to conflate description (of what police do) with prescription (of what police should do). Predictably, having worked through them, one is left with the unsettling conclusion that the police function is simply a multifarious one. This view is, in fact, reflected in Bittner's (1980) famous declaration that the police function consists of "dealing with all sorts of problems" while in possession of a legitimate capacity to coerce.

Bittner's definition raises important issues. For one thing, it is sufficiently flexible to incorporate not only the multifarious duties that the police now undertake, but also the broad range of moral and administrative tasks that they undertook in the past (Johnston, 1992). Yet the inference that a legitimate capacity to coerce is a necessary precondition for "doing policing" poses problems. For, by so restricting the definition, most private, hybrid, and popular forms of activity are excluded from consideration. This restriction produces two difficulties. It draws a rigid and unwarranted distinction between activities carried out by police and comparable—even equivalent— activities carried out by nonpolice bodies. It also appears to invoke a "Weberian" concept of policing in which the police officer is the personification of the state's monopoly of legitimate coercion. Yet, given what was said earlier about the impact of late modern social change on the state's exclusively "public" character, this model has surely been superseded by events. It is not merely that private agents, nowadays, routinely exert powers in the public sphere, but that the public sphere is, itself, an ambiguous category. That is not to say that Bittner's definition, or a similar one, might not be adapted to suit late modern conditions. For that to be done, however, the concept of legitimation would have to be uncoupled from its exclusive location in the public sphere.

From what has been suggested so far, it would seem that policing is a multifunctional activity whose content and form are variable. Shearing (1992) has suggested that the multifunctionality of policing can, in fact, be encapsulated in the concept of "security." This is a novel suggestion since it cuts across those, somewhat sterile, approaches that try to demarcate the police function from the security function (e.g., Cunningham & Taylor, 1985). Shearing contends that security is a generic category that can, itself, incorporate the activities of both public police and private security organizations, as well as popular and hybrid forms of policing. Security, he argues always implies the preservation of some "established order" against internal or external threat, the question of what constitutes a threat depending on the character of the established order in question. The essence of security, however, lies not so much in the presence of protection as in the absence of risk. As Spitzer (1987) puts it, "[s]ecurity is said to exist when something *does not* occur rather than when it does" (p. 47). Security, in other words, requires assurances. Thus, policing consists of a series of practices through which some guarantee of security is given to subjects.

The notion of policing as security can be applied in various ways. Consider, for example, what was said earlier about the apparent concerns of Europol to monitor population movement. Here, it would seem that certain elements of European society may be offered guarantees of security against the threat posed by "outsiders." There are, in other words, signs that "Euro-policing" may come to reflect traditional 19th-century concerns about the management of "problem populations," though this time on a global scale rather than a national one. One of the most striking—yet least researched—aspects of this process is the extent to which transnational responsibilities now lie in private hands. Global population movement—through travel, tourism, and migration—is, more and more, policed by the commercial, rather than the public sector. Airline security, in particular, has become a virtual private monopoly, governments having passed on responsibility to the private sector during the past two decades (Kirby, 1993).

In that respect, the most significant feature of security under late modern conditions is its increasing "materialization" or "commodification." Nowadays, security is bought and sold like any other commodity, yet the character of security affects the impact of commodification in two ways. First, as the earlier comment from Spitzer (1987) suggests, security occurs when "nothing happens." Second, it has a dual quality: "security in an objective sense measures the absence of a threat to acquired values, in a subjective sense, the absence of fear that such values will be attacked" (Wolfers, cited in Freedman, 1992, p. 731). The problem is that these two features conflict with one another. Those who sell security commodities aim to assure purchasers of their objective effects. Yet the peculiar character of security (an absence) ensures that there is always a discrepancy between security-as-object and security-as-subjective-experience. For this reason Spitzer, following Marx, depicts the security relationship as one of "commodity fetishism": a relationship in which the consumer's dependence on the commodity is exacerbated by the very consumption of that commodity. In short, a situation where "the more we enter into relationships to obtain the security commodity, the more insecure we feel" (Spitzer, 1987, p. 50).

The process of commodification gives a perverse slant to Shearing's (1992) equation of policing and security. For whether one accepts this equation or not, the police are inextricably linked to the security sector through the commodification process. Commodification has produced an apparently infinite public demand for security services. Or, to put it another way, commodification generates an insatiable demand for "more policing." Public police organizations—no less than the private security companies that have done so much to generate that demand—are, more and more, obliged to respond to public expectations. After all, the provision of a "quality service" to "consumers" is the key element of late modern managerial theory. That is why more and more police effort is devoted to programs whose purpose is to give "assurances": fear reduction schemes, victim schemes, community safety initiatives, watch schemes, surveillance programs—many of them in partnership with the private and voluntary sectors. Whether "more" policing will increase the sum of subjective security, however, is another matter.

Commodification also raises complex issues of legitimation and evaluation. As to the first of these, one body of opinion maintains that commodified policing can be legitimized through market and quasi-market mechanisms— the "uncoupling of legitimation from the state" referred to earlier. In neo-liberal and libertarian philosophy (Hayek, 1960; Rothbard, 1978), as in commercial practice, "sovereignty" resides neither with the state, nor with the public, but with the consumer. For the commercial security company, as for any other participant in the free market the ("sovereign") consumer's satisfaction is proof enough of legitimacy. After all, in a free market, successful companies are supposed to thrive while poor quality ones go under. In that respect, performance evaluation is both a means to achieve "quality service" and, simultaneously, the mechanism through which public (consumer) legitimation is assured.

Two things may be said about this. First, existing modes of evaluating services may not be very effective. Second, it is clear that, on occasions, the customer receives very poor service. Ironically, some of the worst examples have occurred when the state, itself, has been the consumer. A notorious example occurred in Britain some years ago following the terrorist bombing of a military barracks in Kent. A subsequent Select Committee of Defence investigation into private guard contracts at military installations (House of Commons, 1990) demonstrated that the Ministry's decision to use price as the determining factor in selection ensured low wages and a correspondingly low level of service. Later attempts by Bruce George, M.P., to gain information on guarding contracts entered into by Departments of State (firms, numbers employed, size of contract, etc.) were resisted by ministers in Parliament on grounds of commercial confidentiality. The problem here, once again, is the very invisibility of relations between the state and the private sector.

Despite shortcomings in the "consumer sovereignty" model of legitimacy, however, public police forces in Britain are, more than ever, committed to it. Many have developed force-specific performance indicators to complement those required by the Government's "Citizens' Charter" and Her Majesty's

Inspectorate of Constabulary. Cleveland Constabulary, for example, operates a battery of 33 performance indicators under 6 separate headings—Call Management, Crime Management, Traffic Management, Public Order Management/Public Reassurance, Community Policing Management, and Resources/Costs (Cleveland Constabulary, n.d.). There is, however, concern among some senior police officers about the wider context of performance assessment. Sir John Smith, former DepCommissioner of the Metropolitan Police, has made a particularly telling criticism in that regard:

> The imposition of national objectives, league tables and performance targets will probably result in resources and efforts being diverted away from local people and towards doing the tasks that will be measured. We support local policing objectives and, where suitable, local performance targets, together with a published local policing plan. But we can't afford to concentrate just on those areas that are easily measured. (Smith, 1994)

Policing Futures, Governance, and the State

In the past, social commentators have tended to take the public-private divide for granted. The instability of that divide is, however, nowhere more evident than in the sphere of policing. In North America there is routine exchange of personnel and information between public and private policing sectors (Marx, 1987). In Britain it is now relatively common for public police to be "complemented" by commercial security when policing certain types of protest activity. Though this falls short of formal collaboration or cooperation, it raises serious issues of accountability, legality, and ethics. Such examples also raise questions about the very constitution of the public (state) and private (market) spheres in circumstances where policing is differentiated in structure and pluralistic in form. In that uncertain context various attempts have been made to predict the future character of plural policing, some seeing the future as benign, others seeing it as pathological (see also Shearing, 1992).

The Complementarity Model. Proponents of this view (e.g., Cunningham & Taylor, 1985) regard the private policing sector as the "junior partner" of the public police. The private sector expands because public police agencies cannot cope with increasing public demand for their services. According to this view, the public and private sectors maintain their distinction but complement each other (similar assumptions may be found in British Home Office literature on the benefits of "multiagency" and "partnership" approaches to crime prevention and community safety). The "junior" status of the private sector ensures, however, that the sovereignty of the state is maintained. This position is an unconvincing one, given the long-term changes to the late modern state already described.

The Integrated Model. This model pushes complementarity a stage farther to suggest that all agencies that contribute to the maintenance of community order should be encouraged to develop strategic partnerships. This view implies, as Shearing (1992) suggests, that the community and the state are integrated into a single unified system. Effectively, since there are no apparent contradictions between the parties, "the private becomes the public and the public the private" (Shearing, 1992, p. 419) (again, one can find this view reflected in British official crime prevention literature). Though this position takes into account the erosion of the public-private divide, its assumption that that erosion eradicates all public-private contradictions is unconvincing.

"One Big Police Force." Contrary to the previous models, this one sees the integration of public and private policing as a pathological development. Flavel (1973), for example, sees the development of systematic links between public and private police as expressions of "an increasingly coherent security ideology" (p. 15). Like the previous model, this one assumes that a fusion has occurred between the public and private sectors of policing. In this version, however, that fusion is seen as a threat to civil liberties, rather than as a guarantee of communal order. Paradoxically, however, this model still assumes that a reconstituted state maintains sovereignty and hegemony, assumptions that in late modern conditions are increasingly doubtful.

Corporate Pluralism. This concept was first formulated by Shearing and Stenning (1987). A recent and revised version describes it as a situation in which corporations cooperate with each other and with the state as "relatively autonomous guarantors of peace." The effect is to shift responsibility for policing from state to private hands, thereby challenging state power and redefining state-corporate relations (Shearing, 1992). Hence, the idea that the state resides at the top of a power hierarchy is supplanted by a decentered conception of power. This differentiates the position from the previous one which, though recognizing the fusion of public and private sectors, regards them as merging into a single, unified, hegemonic "lump": the "one big police force." Proponents of "corporate pluralism" share with the previous position, however, the fear that the process may be pathological. In a world where governance is "unlikely to be . . . monopolized by state" (Shearing, 1992, p. 427), there is a possibility that it will come to rest in the hands of local communities. More likely, however, is a situation where the decentered structure of power gives way to outright corporate domination: "one in which the economy infuses governance more completely than even the most instrumental Marxist theories have proposed" (Shearing, 1992, p. 427). The "corporate pluralism" thesis takes into account the impact of late modern change on the state, assuming that the eventual outcome of that change will be a "re-centering" of power along corporate lines and, presumably, a corresponding reimposition of social order.

"Beyond Blade Runner." This thesis shares many of the assumptions of the previous one, differing, however, in its estimation of likely outcomes. Whereas "corporate pluralism" presupposes a degree of social order—albeit in pathological form—Davis (1992) predicts only a state of continuing urban chaos: a war of "all against all" overseen by a repressive police force. For Davis (1992), Los Angeles is the model for the future city: a city in which the landscape is militarized, public space is privatized, city life becomes ever more "feral," video-surveillance is endemic, vigilantes roam freely, and those residents who can afford to do so retreat to homes protected by state-of-the-art security technology and private armed-response units. Davis (1992) describes an urban structure that is spatially, as well as sectorally, segmented. In effect, the urban ecology of the Chicago School is reproduced in late modern form, new territorial divisions being imprinted as "concentric rings" on the urban landscape. The outcome is an "ecology of fear" in which groups of residents are segregated from each other by razor wire and security cameras, the police cleansing the streets of problem populations on behalf of an increasingly militarized state apparatus.

Multiple Orders. In this last case, a degree of stability is sustained not through the imposition of any singular "social order," but through the application of plural "multiple orders." Rose (1996) has recently argued that rationalities and techniques of government have emerged that "seek to govern without governing *society*" (Rose, 1996, p. 328). In these circumstances government is effected through the "regulated choices" of "discrete and autonomous actors" in communities. In Rose's (1996) view, the social has ceased to be an objective of governmental strategy and we are witnessing its "death" as a focus for political objectives. Government through "society" and "the public sphere" is giving way to government through "communities" of voluntary actors and commercial consumers. In those circumstances inequality would continue to fuel dissent and disorder, yet there would be no singular social foundation upon which order might be reestablished and through which conflict might be resolved equitably.

The last three models, though reaching different conclusions, are all informed by an understanding of late modern social change. They also pose a legitimate problem of governance. *How, in a fragmented social order with a diverse policing structure, can one avoid the pathologies of corporate domination, chaos, and inequity?* The traditional answer to governmental problems of this sort has been to invoke the state as the essential guarantor of public interests. Interestingly, this view is implicit in Bayley's (1994) critique of market-based forms of policing: what he calls "private policing for the rich, coupled with a 'poor police policing the poor' " (Bayley, 1994, p. 144). Here Bayley maintains that the state cannot be removed from policing without undermining domestic order and, with it, the very legitimacy of government. This argument is, of course, true, though with two important qualifications. First, the provision of domestic order need not be effected exclusively by state institutions, a fact confirmed by our earlier references to the exchange of personnel and to an emerging functional complementarity between the policing sectors in both Britain and North America. Second, the very fact that the state combines with the private sector in the maintenance of domestic order indicates that, with late modernity, the state itself undergoes a transformation. Thus, although it may be true that the state cannot be removed from policing, "the state" in question may bear little resemblance to "the public sphere" of the past. Contrary to what Bayley says, the state, in its traditional sense, has been removed from policing, the foundations of domestic order and legitimacy being redesigned in the process.

The growing ambiguity of the state can be seen in many different contexts. At the local level it has already been noted that policing, far from being a state monopoly, consists of a diverse complex of intersectoral relations. Shearing (1994) argues that any attempt to construct a democratically accountable system of local policing has to confront this fact. Policing should be seen not as the prerogative of state police, but as the responsibility of "local security networks," themselves constituting the locus of democratic governance. Given that assumption, it is difficult to conceive "public interest" as the preserve of the traditional "public sector." Rather, democratic governance is predicated upon the existence of diverse communal mechanisms—formal and informal; contractual and noncontractual; voluntary and commercial—operating within the interstices of civil society and the state and, by their very actions, further eroding the boundaries between the two.

The state's transformation is not merely apparent at the local level, however. Shearing's governmental "networks" and Rose's (1996) "communities" of government can also be seen to operate at the global level.

> What globalization means in structural terms . . . is the *increase in the available modes of organization:* transnational, international, macro-regional, national, micro-regional, municipal, local . . . crisscrossed by *functional networks* of corporations, international organisations . . . two interactive worlds with overlapping memberships: a state-centric world, in which the primary actors are national, and a multi-centric world of diverse actors such as corporations, international organisations, ethnic groups, churches. (Nederveen Pierterse, 1995, p. 50)

CONCLUDING COMMENTS

In this chapter it has been suggested that the structural changes arising under late modernity transform the character of policing and the state. Inevitably, those changes demand new ways of thinking about the accountability, legitimacy, and evaluation of policing. As for evaluation, the core theme of this book, three general observations may be made.

First, evaluation is not merely a technical exercise. In one sense this is obvious, a point confirmed by Sir John Smith's warning against the collection and analysis of technically valid but substantively worthless evaluative data. More than that, however, this chapter has argued that questions about evaluation (or accountability or legitimacy) have to be understood in their sociopolitical context. In other words, without an understanding of the characteristics of late modern policing, meaningful evaluation is impossible. In order to illustrate this point, consider a basic question: What is to be evaluated? The answer to this question may seem obvious: Policing. Yet, this raises a problem. Are we to assume that the rudiments of late modern policing are the same as those of the earlier period? Modern police forces were established a century ago to deal with matters of law enforcement, crime prevention, and order maintenance—all of these being part of the state's "public" mandate. Late modernity transforms the state, uncoupling it from that traditional mandate. This process occurs partly through the commercial penetration of the state and partly through the growing dominance of neo-liberal modes of thinking. Critically, these developments have a significant impact on the character of policing, "post-Keynesian policing" becoming more and more preoccupied with matters of risk management, hitherto the prerogative of the commercial security sector (O'Malley & Palmer, 1996; see also Ericson, 1994). It is not that contemporary policing is unconcerned with its traditional, crime-oriented, "public" mandate. Rather, police philosophy, practice, and organization are, increasingly, oriented to the management and minimization of risk. This is no more evident than in community policing where, communal rhetoric notwithstanding, the communities in question are composed of autonomous, aggregated individuals (Rose, 1996). Whereas, in the past, states managed risks through socialized means such as social insurance, neo-liberalism individualizes risk, people bearing greater responsibility for their own health, education, and security. Those who evaluate policing need, therefore, to be mindful of two interconnected changes. On the one hand, there is the movement from public/client-based to individual/consumer-based modes of service delivery. On the other hand, connected to that movement, there is a change in the character of policing itself: a relative shift from publicly focused crime-oriented policing toward individually focused risk-oriented policing.

Second, there is the question: Who is being evaluated? The existence of diverse networks of policing at local, regional, national, and transnational levels finally explodes the myth that policing is a public monopoly. Once this is admitted, however, it becomes impossible to evaluate "the effectiveness of policing" in terms of the "effectiveness of police." If, as this chapter has suggested, the future of policing lies in diverse "networks," evaluative techniques capable of penetrating the dynamics of those networks have to be developed. That, in turn, is predicated upon effective and accountable governance of those networks.

Finally, there is the most difficult question of all: What is evaluation for? Again, the answer to this question might seem obvious. Services are evaluated to make them more effective, efficient, and responsive. Yet, this tells us nothing about the underlying objectives to which a service is oriented. Here, there is one overriding issue. Is policing to be evaluated according to the degree of satisfaction expressed by its individual consumers? Or is evaluation also to be underpinned by wider collective concerns? And, if, as Rose (1996) suggests, "the social" and "the public" are in retreat as rationales for defining governmental objectives, what mechanisms can be put in place to ensure that policing retains such a collective focus? One thing is certain. Without that focus, the collective worth of policing will be evaluated in terms of the aggregated costs and benefits accruing to its individual consumers. If so, neither policing nor justice will have been well served.

THE ASSESSMENT OF POLICE PERFORMANCE

Conclusions

Jean-Paul Brodeur

Late in 1994, a group of persons involved in policing at the practical level met in Montreal with a group of researchers in order to advance a dialogue between practitioners and academics. This dialogue had begun before, the attempt to integrate policing theory and practice being an incipient feature of community policing. It is also a precondition for problem-oriented policing, which rests on the identification and thorough analysis of the problems to be solved. The growing importance of technology in policing also necessitates a partnership between practitioners and researchers.

It is not possible, nor would it be helpful, to reduce the papers presented at the conference (many of which resulted in the chapters of this book) and the debates they generated to a few conclusions. I will instead give an account of the debates that can only hint at their intensity; the chapters in this book speak for themselves. It is therefore without any pretence of being comprehensive that I offer some thoughts on what might be drawn from the workshop papers and the resulting exchanges.

HIGHLIGHTS FROM THE DEBATES

Because of space limitations, I cannot cover all of the points brought up during the debates, but there are two issues that I feel should be singled out. One is police unionization, which, despite its overwhelming importance, seems almost to be taboo in the literature on implementing community and problem-oriented policing. Everyone felt strongly that winning the support of police labor organizations was one of the necessary keys to having the rank and file committed to reform. As Reiner's description of the events that followed the Sheehy Committee report in England show, it is close to impossible to bring about change in police organizations if there is hostility from staff associations. One of the most sensitive questions for these associations is, of course, the issue of individual performance assessments, which are vital to a successful career. There is a striking contrast between (a) the great amount of space that police researchers devote to stressing that the obstacle to reform is the structure of police organizations, and (b) the much smaller amount that considers the weight of police labor unions in fostering or hindering change.

The other issue—interagency cooperation—must be resolved to avoid undermining one of the foundations of community and problem-oriented policing. The results of a research program undertaken by the Vera Institute were reported by Wesley Skogan during the workshop. He noted that

> one of the implications of expanding the police mandate to cover new and much broader ranges of neighborhood problems inevitably involves community police officers in having to mobilize the resources of other city agencies, other private organizations, and basically find other people to do the work and solve the problems. What happens is that this expansion—the police mandate that goes with community policing—really begins to drive the capacity of the larger government to respond to a broad range of neighborhood problems. The Vera Institute in New York recently conducted an evaluation of community policing programs in eight American cities, and what they found was that this process failed in seven of the eight cities. Only in one of the eight cities were the police able to actively involve other municipal bureaucracies in problem-solving efforts.
>
> In seven places, what happened was that the inevitable problems of interagency coordination, different priorities, claims for lack of resource, different political agendas, in particular, a strong tendency of other city organizations, other city bureaucracies to think that community policing was the police depart-

ment's problem and not their problem, and they simply refused to cooperate. Not on their budget, thank you.

In the present climate of budget cuts, this result is not surprising, particularly in view of the pervasive tendency of bureaucracies to divide social territory into separate turfs that do not allow for any no-man's land. There is something to be learned from the sobering—and even jolting—character of this finding. Instead of debating the real or rhetorical character of community policing reform, we might want to distinguish between two phases of reform. The first phase, which is essentially programmatic, is characterized by an idealistic "ends over means syndrome," to take up *a contrario* Goldstein's dictum. The second phase, which is implemental, starts with a realization of the constraints that limit implementation and may even impede it. An exclusive fixation on implementation may lead reformers to replace their "ends over means syndrome" with a "means over ends syndrome," either by entering into partnerships that are purely formal or by retreating back into law enforcement isolation. In so doing, they fall back into practicing what was diagnosed as the main problem of police organizations.

POLICING REFORM:
LOOKING FOR ITS SECOND WIND

Saying that a set of research papers raises more questions than they provide answers can be seen as too predictable and jejune. Nevertheless, the description is appropriate. With respect to evaluation research on the *outcomes* of community and problem-oriented policing, only Wesley Skogan's and Dennis Rosenbaum's chapters bring news that is relatively good. Conversely, Skogan's analysis of interagency cooperation quoted above is not particularly good news. Vince Sacco reports that the Canadian public's satisfaction with the police is generally high, but this is not really news, since the level of satisfaction is generally high in Canada. All the other writers report evaluation findings that are more or less negative and at some distance from the present reforms (Brodeur, Greene, McElroy, Mastrofski), this distance being in some cases considerable (Bennett, Reiner). Yet even where evaluation findings are reported to be less than encouraging, no one calls for giving up on reform or for changing the course that has been followed for the past decade. Actually, the view from the practitioners of community and problem-oriented policing is in many instances more optimistic in the assessment of its results than the findings of evaluation research are. However, the enthusiastic mood that is a feature of new programs has given way to a realization of the complexity of the issues involved and of the fact that resistance to change is greater than was anticipated, particularly in the present context of budgetary restraint. Police reform is still proceeding, but it appears to be looking for its second wind before regaining momentum.

TAPPING INTO FRONTLINE POLICE EXPERTISE

From whence will this second wind come? Writing in 1973 about bringing the police into the second half of the 20th century, Egon Bittner declared that

> police research has demonstrated that police work, far from being the kind of low-grade occupation it is thought to be, in fact involves the exercise of judgment and skill in handling problems of great complexity and importance. But in order for the police to become fully equal to the tasks of our times, they must install study and research into their mandate. Only in this way can the police hope to advance and retain control of the direction of their efforts.
>
> From nowhere but from the ranks of the police will come the people who will undertake to discover, describe, systematize, codify, innovate, teach, and so on, the body of knowledge and skill that goes into doing a good job of policing. (Bittner, 1973, reprinted in Bittner, 1990a, pp. 320-321)

This view of policing is echoed in several chapters of this book (e.g., those by Reiner, McElroy, Mastrofski). It can also be found in David Bayley's research and notably in his latest book (Bayley, 1994). The main theme is the assertion that the police have accumulated through their work experience a large body of knowledge of the problems that confront them in the field. The most knowledgeable police *are* frontline officers whose expertise is not put to the use it deserves by high-ranking administrators who generally make the decisions and determine policy. This body of knowledge may be underutilized because it has so far remained largely intuitive, submerged under layers of personal police experience and unformulated in any explicit and systematic way. Performance evaluation might be instrumental in tapping into this body of knowledge and in giving it an external formulation that could increase its accessibility and the possibility that it would be shared among the different agencies involved in the co-production of security as well as among members of the community.

THE SCOPE AND DEPTH OF
PERFORMANCE ASSESSMENT

There are a number of conclusions that the chapters of this book underscore: (a) Performance assessment has been fascinated by outcomes, (b) some of these "outcomes" (e.g., the number of arrests) are poor indicators of the external impact of policing in respect to problem solving, (c) evaluation should also focus on other dimensions of performance, (d) but it must develop the tools, tools only partially available now, to do so.

Three dimensions of police performance can be identified for the purposes of evaluation. These three dimensions are present in all police performance, though they are more explicit in collective performance within the framework of a community or problem-oriented policing program. The first is the use of *expertise* and broadly consists of researching a problem. This is done through phases of problem identification and definition and the planning of a set of measures that will lead to solution. It implies a set of assumptions that are seldom explicit. This dimension, like the following one, may imply consultation with the community and interagency cooperation. The second dimension is *implementation,* and the third is *impact.* These latter dimensions of police performance are more familiar than the first, so there is no need to characterize them further.

There are several weaknesses with performance evaluation as it is presently conducted. The dimension of expertise, which coincides with the initial phase of performance, is rarely taken into account, as numerous parts of this book demonstrate. This weakness can be confirmed independently of the research findings presented here. For example, Bayley (1994) concludes that "modern policing must be reorganized so that thinking takes precedence over reaction" (p. 157). Yet of the 34 current performance indicators that Bayley lists, only the last one—"police knowledge of communities," which is called "soft"— has any relation to police expertise (p. 97, Table 5.2). This absence of expertise indicators would tend to justify his judgment that "the evaluation of police performance is narrow and superficial" (p. 161).

Second, there is no systematic attempt to depict relations among these different dimensions of police performance when they are evaluated. Finally, a related point needs to be stressed. In a famous argument with an atheist, a parish priest tried to refute the claim that the existence of a benevolent God was put into dispute by the pervasiveness of evil. The priest argued that there was nothing wrong with Christian morality except that it had never *really* been tried. Even if we resist introducing the jargon of evaluation research into theology, the point can be made that there are limits to repeatedly faulting implementation in order to save a theory. Despite its apparent soundness, a theory should be assessed on the basis of its implementability if it consistently fails to produce results.

It is crucial that all three of these weaknesses of performance evaluation be remedied if evaluation is to play its proper role in generating a sound basis for good policing.

PRODUCING SECURITY VERSUS
REPRESSING CRIME AND DISORDER

It bears repeating that one of the reasons the assessment of problem-oriented policing is difficult is that a significant part of the problems confronting the police admit of no definitive solution. As Durkheim repeatedly told us, a society free of crime and disorder is unthinkable. There will always be events that, however benign, will be labeled criminal and disorderly. Hence, even if we could eradicate serious crime and disorder—which we know we cannot— certain actions would still be perceived as criminal and disorderly. What greatly compounds this problem of the intractability of crime is that we are committed on moral grounds to being intolerant of crime. If crime is what we claim it is—an act that is morally repellent—then, on grounds of moral principle, even one crime will always be one crime too many. Therefore, the suggestion that we ought simply aim to maintain crime at tolerable levels will always be considered morally reprehensible.

There may be a way out of this predicament. We can redefine *in a positive way* the police mandate to prevent and repress crime by calling instead for the *production of security*. The crucial difference between the production of security and the prevention or repression of crime is that there is no moral commitment to produce *absolute* security, as there must be to eradicate crime absolutely. It is not even certain whether the notion of absolute security makes any sense, security being entirely a matter of degree. Yet even if security is relative, it allows for the possibility of rationally determining a threshold under which "not enough security" means in reality "no security," and above which "enough security" means the enjoyment of a reasonable quality of life. It is conceivable that we could provide an "objective" definition of "reasonable" security in comparing levels of the empirical probability of being victimized by crime or serious disorder, to the levels of probability of being noncriminally victimized (e.g., health hazards), which are not only often significantly higher, but generally found by the community to be acceptable risks. The provision of security in this sense is not an intractable problem for the police. It is a goal that can and ought to be met, providing that it does not disqualify the pursuit of such values and ideals as justice.

FACT AND VALUES

I have just argued in favor of the determination of a policing goal that can be empirically defined, and suggested that the goal be the provision of security, as opposed to a moral ideal that compels us to pursue the unattainable. It would be totally misguided, however, to consider all commitment to moral values as empty posturing or to try to eliminate justice from policing. In this regard, the growth of private security agencies is part of a tendency toward a lay control of policing that might result in what I call utilitarian fundamentalism. This tendency reaches its breaking point when it is claimed that our notions of security should limit the prosecution of criminals if criminal sanctions "do not work," whereas our notions of reasonableness should limit the expectation for protection of potential victims. This lopsided view of security is unpalatable to the professional culture of the public police, a group deeply permeated by notions of retribution—or, to use more modern language, permeated by the perspective of just deserts, a position with sturdier roots among police than among even the culture of sentencing magistrates. This is not to say that utilitarian fundamentalism ought to be resisted, but rather to make the more limited claim that it is in fact antithetical to deeply embedded features of the professional culture of criminal justice practitioners.

THE LOGIC OF PUBLIC VINDICATION
AND PRIVATE MANAGEMENT

Whether the retributive bent of the public police ought to be altered is, of course, an appropriate question. I believe that the proper framework for discussing it could be provided by comparative studies of public and private policing. The logic of private policing is managerial and utilitarian, mostly because private agencies are accountable to private businesses or concerns. The public police, however, are accountable through elected officials to the general public in its present vindictive mood.

Les Johnston's chapter provides an example of a study that contrasts public with private policing. By presenting different models of the relationship between public and private policing, Johnston raises some of the most significant questions regarding the future of policing. The neglect of private policing agencies in discussions of community and problem-oriented policing is both striking and relatively surprising. Although the development of partnerships between the police and other agencies is strongly advocated in such discussions, community and problem-oriented policing is considered almost entirely in the context of public policing. "The community" is very loosely conceived as the general public, in which only nonprivate groups such as ethnic minorities, elderly citizens, and sections of the underclass are considered as distinct. In the same way, "interagency cooperation" usually means coordinating the actions of different public departments and rarely addresses the question of integrating parts of the public and the private sectors.

Whether the future of policing can be better predicted using models depicting different interfaces between public and private policing, rather than through variations on the theme of integrating private policing with public policing, is a very open question. It is also one that deserves much more attention than it has received in discussions of community and problem-oriented policing.

REFERENCES

ACPO. (1990). *ACPO strategic policy document: Setting the standards for policing: Meeting community expectations* (Report of an ACPO Working Party). London: ACPO.

Aglietta, M. (1987). *A theory of capitalist regulation.* London: Verso.

Albrecht, S. L., & Green, M. (1977). Attitudes toward the police and the larger attitude complex—Implications for police-community relationships. *Criminology, 15*(1), 67-86.

Alderson, J. (1979). *Policing freedom.* Plymouth, UK: McDonald & Evans.

Allen, D. N. (1980). *Street level police supervision: The effects of supervision on police officer activities, agency outputs and neighborhood outcomes.* Doctoral dissertation, Indiana University, Bloomington.

Allen, S. (1992). *The a-z guide to European manned guarding.* London: Network Security Management Ltd.

Alpert, G. P., & Dunham, R. G. (1988). *Policing multi-ethnic neighborhoods.* London: Greenwood.

Anderson, D. C. (1978). Getting down with the people. *Police Management, 8,* 240-256.

Arthur, J. A. (1993). Interpersonal violence, criminal victimization and attitudes toward police use of force. *International Review of Modern Sociology, 23*(1), 91-106.

Audit Commission. (1990). *Effective policing: Performance review in police forces.* London: HMSO.

Audit Commission. (1993). *Helping with enquiries: Tackling crime effectively.* London: HMSO.

Bagguley, P., Mark-Lawson, J., Shapiro, D., Urry, J., Walby, S., & Warde, A. (1990). *Restructuring: Place, class and gender.* London: Sage.

Baker, M. H., Nienstedt, B. C., Everett, R. C., & McCleary, R. (1983). The impact of a crime wave: Perceptions, fear, and confidence in the police. *Law and Society Review, 17*(2), 319-334.

Bayley, D. H. (1988). Community policing: A report from the devil's advocate. In J. R. Greene & S. D. Mastrofski (Eds.), *Community policing: Rhetoric or reality?* (pp. 225-238). New York: Praeger.

Bayley, D. H. (1994). *Police for the future.* New York: Oxford University Press.

Bayley, D. H., & Bittner, E. (1984). Learning the skills of policing. *Law and Contemporary Problems, 47*(4), 35-60.

Bennett, R. R. (1983). *Police at work: Policy issues and analysis* (Perspectives in Criminal Justice, Vol. 5). Beverly Hills, CA: Sage.

Bennett, T. (1990a). *Evaluating Neighbourhood Watch.* Aldershot, UK: Gower.

Bennett, T. (1990b). Getting back in touch. *Policing, 6,* 510-522.

Bennett, T. (1991). The effectiveness of a police-initiated fear-reducing strategy. *British Journal of Criminology, 31*(1), 1-13.

Bennett, T. H., & Kemp, C. (1994). *An evaluation of sector-based problem-oriented policing in Thames Valley Police Force area* (Report to the Home Office Research and Planning Unit). Cambridge, UK: University of Cambridge, Institute of Criminology.

Bennett, T. H., & Lupton, R. (1992). A survey of the allocation and use of community constables in England and Wales. *British Journal of Criminology, 32*(2), 167-182.

Benson, J. K. (1975). The interorganizational network as a political economy. *Administrative Science Quarterly, 20,* 229-249.

Bittner, E. (1974). Florence Nightingale in pursuit of Willie Sutton: A theory of the police. In H. Jacob (Ed.), *The potential for reform of criminal justice.* Beverly Hills, CA: Sage.

Bittner, E. (1980). *The function of the police in modern society.* Cambridge, MA: Oelgeschlager, Gun & Hain.

Bittner, E. (1990a). *Aspects of police work.* Boston: NorthEastern University Press.

Bittner, E. (1990b). Florence Nightingale in pursuit of Willie Sutton. In *Aspects of police work* (pp. 233-268). Boston: NorthEastern University Press.

Blair, I. (1994, October 1). Let the police fund their own expansion. *The Times.*

Bleakeley, F. R. (1993, July 6). Many companies try management fads, only to see them flop. *Wall Street Journal,* p. 1.

Bloch, P. B., & Anderson, D. (1974). *Policewomen on patrol.* Washington, DC: Police Foundation.

Bloch, P. B., & Specht, D. (1972). *Evaluation report on Operation Neighborhood.* Washington, DC: Urban Institute.

Bloch, P. B., & Specht, D. (1973). *Neighborhood team policing.* Washington, DC: Government Printing Office.

Blumstein, A., Cohen, J., & Nagin, D. (Eds.). (1978). *Deterrence and incapacitation: Estimating the effects of criminal sanctions on crime rates.* Washington, DC: National Academy of Sciences.

Blumstein, A., Cohen, J., Roth, J., & Visher, C. (1986). *Criminal careers and "career criminals"* (Vol. 1). Washington, DC: National Academy of Sciences.

Bootman, J. L., Rowland, C., & Wertheimer, A. I. (1979). Cost-benefit analysis: A research tool for evaluating innovative health programs. *Evaluation and the Health Professions, 2*(2), 129-154.

Borger, J. (1994, March 14). Polish police face sponsorship row. *The Guardian.*

Bottoms, A. E. (1990). Crime prevention facing the 1990s. *Policing and Society, 1*(1), 3-22.

Bottoms, A. E., & Wiles, P. (1994). *Understanding crime prevention in late modern societies.* Paper presented at the 22nd Cropwood Round Table Conference: Preventing Crime and

Disorder: Targeting Strategies and Community Responsibilities, University of Cambridge, Institute of Criminology.

Box, S., Hale, C., & Andrews, G. (1988). Explaining fear of crime. *British Journal of Criminology, 28*, 340-356.

Bozinoff, L., & MacIntosh, P. (1990). *Canadians assess performance of community services* [Summary of survey]. Toronto: Gallup Canada.

Bozinoff, L., & MacIntosh, P. (1991). *Fully 78% of Canadians approve of police performance* [Summary of survey]. Toronto: Gallup Canada.

Braiden, C. (1988). Nothing new under the sun. In *Footprints*. East Lansing, MI: National Neighborhood Foot Patrol Center.

Brandl, S. G., & Horvath, F. (1991). Crime-victim evaluation of police investigative performance. *Journal of Criminal Justice, 19*, 293-205.

Buerger, M. E. (1993). The challenge of reinventing police and community. In D. Weisburd & C. Uchida (Eds.), *Police innovation and the control of the police*. New York: Springer.

Buerger, M. E. (1994a). The limits of community. In D. P. Rosenbaum (Ed.), *The challenge of community policing: Testing the promises*. Thousand Oaks, CA: Sage.

Buerger, M. E. (1994b). A tale of two targets: Limitations of community anti-crime activities. *Crime and Delinquency, 40*(3), 411-436.

Buerger, M. E., & Green, L. A. (1994). *Deviant persons, deviant places, and third-party policing*. Unpublished manuscript, National Institute of Justice, Washington, D.C.

Bursik, R. J., & Grasmick, H. G. (1993). *Neighborhoods and crime: The dimensions of effective community control*. New York: Lexington Books.

Byrne, J. M., & Sampson, R. J. (1986). *The social ecology of crime*. New York: Springer.

Capowich, G. E., & Roehl, J. A. (1994). Problem-oriented policing: Actions and effectiveness in San Diego. In D. P. Rosenbaum (Ed.), *The challenge of community policing: Testing the promises*. Thousand Oaks, CA: Sage.

Carter, D. L. (1985). Hispanic perception of police performance: An empirical assessment. *Journal of Criminal Justice, 13*, 487-500.

Carter, D. L., Sapp, A. D., & Stephens, D. W. (1988). Higher education as a bona fide occupational qualification (BFOQ) for police: A blueprint. *American Journal of Police, 7*, 1-27.

Chacko, J., & Nancoo, S. E. (Eds). (1993). *Community policing in Canada*. Toronto: Canadian Scholars' Press.

Charles, M. T. (1980). The utilization of attitude surveys in the police decision-making process. *Journal of Police Science and Administration, 8*(3), 294-303.

Chatterton, M. (1983). Police work and assault charges. In M. Punch (Ed.), *Control in the police organization*. Cambridge: MIT Press.

Chicago Community Policing Evaluation Consortium. (1995). *Community policing in Chicago, year two*. Chicago: Illinois Criminal Justice Information Authority.

Chicago Police Department. (1993). *Together we can: A strategic plan for reinventing the Chicago Police Department*. Chicago: Author.

Clark, M. (1994, January 7). Europe's hidden frontier. *Police Review*.

Clarke, R. (Ed.). (1992). *Crime prevention studies* (Vol. 2). Monsey, NY: Criminal Justice Press.

Cleveland Constabulary. (n.d.). *Force service plan*. Cleveland, UK: Author.

Cohen, B., & Chaiken, J. M. (1972). *Police background characteristics and performance*. Lexington, MA: D. C. Heath.

Cohen, L. E., & Felson, M. (1979). Social change and crime rate trends: A routine activities approach. *American Sociological Review, 44*, 588-608.

Cook, T. D., & Campbell, D. T. (1979). *Quasi-experimentation: Design and analysis issues for field settings*. Chicago: Rand McNally.

Cook, R. F., & Roehl, J. A. (1993). National evaluation of the community partnership program: Preliminary findings. In R. C. Davis, A. J. Lurigio, & D. P. Rosenbaum (Eds.), *Drugs and the community*. Springfield, IL: Charles C Thomas.

Couper, D. C. (1983). *How to rate your local police*. Washington, DC: U.S. Department of Justice, National Institute of Justice, Police Executive Research Forum.

Crank, J. P. (1994). State theory, myths of policing, and responses to crime. *Law and Society Review, 28*, 325-351.

Crank, J. P., & Langworthy, R. (1992). An institutional perspective of policing. *Journal of Criminal Law and Criminology, 83*, 338-363.

Crime wave boosts respect. (1993, July 25). *Sunday Times*, New Review Section, p. 6.

Critchley, T. A. (1967). *A history of police in England and Wales, 900-1966*. London: Constable.

Crook, S., Pakulski, J., & Waters, M. (1993). *Postmodernization: Change in advanced society*. London: Sage.

Cummings, T. G., & Worley, C. G. (1993). *Organizational development and change* (5th ed.). Minneapolis/St. Paul, MN: West.

Cunningham, W. C., & Taylor, T. (1985). *Private security and police in America*. London: Butterworth Heinemann.

Davis, M. (1992). *Beyond Blade Runner: Urban control: The ecology of fear*. Westfield, NJ: Open Magazine Pamphlet Series.

de Waard, J. (1993). The private security sector in fifteen European countries: Size, rules and legislation. *Security Journal, 4*(2), 58-63.

Decker, S. H. (1981). Citizen attitude toward the police: A review of past findings and suggestions for future policy. *Journal of Police Science and Administration, 9*, 80-87.

Deming, W. E. (1986). *Out of crisis*. Cambridge: MIT Center for Advanced Engineering Study.

DiMaggio, P. J., & Powell, W. W. (1983). The iron cage revisited: Institutional isomorphism and collective rationality in organizational fields. *American Sociological Review, 48*, 147-160.

DuBow, F., McCabe, E., & Kaplan, G. (1979). *Reactions to crime: A critical review of the literature*. Washington, DC: U.S. Department of Justice, National Institute of Justice.

Dunham, R. G., & Alpert, G. P. (1988). Neighborhood differences in attitudes toward policing: Evidence for a mixed-strategy model of policing in a multi-ethnic setting. *The Journal of Criminal Law and Criminology, 79*(2), 504-523.

Eck, J. E. (1984). *Using research: A primer for law enforcement managers*. Washington, DC: U.S. Department of Justice, National Institute of Justice, Police Executive Research Forum.

Eck, J. E., & Rosenbaum, D. P. (1994). The new police order: Effectiveness, equity, and efficiency in community policing. In D. P. Rosenbaum (Ed.), *The challenge of community policing: Testing the promises* (pp. 3-23). Thousand Oaks, CA: Sage.

Eck, J. E., & Spelman, W. (1987a). *Problem solving: Problem-oriented policing in Newport News*. Washington, DC: U.S. Department of Justice, National Institute of Justice, Police Executive Research Forum.

Eck, J. E., & Spelman, W. (1987b). Who ya gonna call? The police as problem-busters. *Crime and Delinquency, 33*(1), 31-52.

Eck, J. E., & Spelman, W. (1989). Problem-solving: Problem-oriented policing in Newport News. In R. G. Dunham & G. P. Alpert (Eds.), *Critical issues in policing: Contemporary readings*. Prospect Heights, IL: Waveland.

Eck, J. E., Spelman, W., Hill, D., Stephens, D. W., Stedman, J. R., & Murphy, G. R. (1987). *Problem solving: Problem-oriented policing in Newport News*. Washington, DC: U.S. Department of Justice, National Institute of Justice, Police Executive Research Forum.

Edelman, M. (1977). *Political language: Words that succeed and policies that fail*. New York: Academic Press.

Elias, R. (1993). *Victims still: The political manipulation of crime victims.* Newbury Park, CA: Sage.

Erez, E. (1984). Self-defined "desert" and citizens' assessment of the police. *The Journal of Criminal Law and Criminology, 75*(4), 1276-1299.

Ericson, R. (1994). The division of expert knowledge in policing and security. *British Journal of Sociology, 45*(2), 149-175.

Farrington, D. P., Sampson, R. J., & Wikstrom, P. H. (1993). *Integrating individual and ecological aspects of crime.* Stockholm: National Council for Crime Prevention.

Flanagan, T. J. (1985). Consumer perspectives on police operational strategy. *Journal of Police Science and Administration, 13*(1), 10-21.

Flavel, W. R. H. (1973). *Research into security organisations.* Paper presented at the 2nd Bristol Seminar on the Sociology of the Police, University of Bristol (unpublished).

Florin, P., Chavis, D., Wandersman, A., & Rich, R. (1992). A systems approach to understanding and enhancing grassroots organizations: The Block Booster Project. In H. E. Levine & R. L. Fitzgerald (Eds.), *Analysis of dynamic psychological systems* (pp. 215-243). New York: Plenum.

Fogelson, R. F. (1977). *Big city police.* Cambridge, MA: Harvard University Press.

Forde, D. R. (1992). *Winnipeg Area Study report no. 41: Public attitudes toward crime and police services: Survey findings for Winnipeg in 1989 and 1992.* Winnipeg: University of Manitoba.

Freedman, L. (1992). The concept of security. In M. Hawkesworth & M. Kogan (Eds.), *Encyclopedia of government and politics* (pp. 730-741). London: Routledge & Kegan Paul.

Friedman, W. (1994). The community role in community policing. In D. P. Rosenbaum (Ed.), *The challenge of community policing: Testing the promises* (pp. 263-269). Thousand Oaks, CA: Sage.

Fyfe, N. R. (1994). *Police user surveys in Scotland.* Edinburgh: Scottish Office, Central Research Unit.

Garofalo, J. (1977). *The police and public opinion: An analysis of victimization and attitude data from 13 American cities.* Washington, DC: U.S. Department of Justice/Law Enforcement Assistance Administration.

Gaskell, G., & Smith, P. (1985, August). How young blacks see the police. *New Society, 23,* 261-263.

Germann, A. C. (1969). Community policing: An assessment. *Journal of Criminal Law, Criminology and Police, 60,* 89-96.

Givens, G. (1993). A concept to involve citizens in the provision of police services. *American Journal of Police, 12,* 1-9.

Gladwell, M. (1996, June 3). The tipping point. *New Yorker,* pp. 32-38.

Goldsmith, A. (Ed.). (1991). *Complaints against the police: The trend to external review.* Oxford, UK: Oxford University Press.

Goldstein, H. (1963). Police discretion: The ideal versus the real. *Public Administration Review, 23,* 140-148.

Goldstein, H. (1967a). Administrative problems in controlling the exercise of police authority. *Journal of Criminal Law, Criminology and Police Science, 58,* 160-172.

Goldstein, H. (1967b). Grievance response mechanisms for police conduct. *Virginia Law Review, 55,* 909-951.

Goldstein, H. (1967c). Police policy formulation: A proposal for improving police performance. *Michigan Law Review, 65,* 1123-1146.

Goldstein, H. (1969). Governmental setting for police work. In G. E. Eastman (Ed.), *Municipal police administration* (pp. 2a/1-2a/16). (Reprinted 1971 by International City Management Association, Washington, DC)

Goldstein, H. (1977). *Policing a free society.* Cambridge, MA: Ballinger.

Goldstein, H. (1979). Improving policing: A problem-oriented approach. *Crime and Delinquency, 25,* 236-258.

Goldstein, H. (1987). Toward community-oriented policing: Potential, basic requirements, and threshold questions. *Crime and Delinquency, 33*(1), 6-30.

Goldstein, H. (1990). *Problem-oriented policing.* New York: McGraw-Hill.

Goldstein, H. (1993, August). *The new policing: Confronting complexity.* Paper presented at the Conference on Community Policing, National Institute of Justice, Washington, DC.

Goldstein, H. (1994). Foreword. In D. P. Rosenbaum (Ed.), *The challenge of community policing: Testing the promises.* Thousand Oaks, CA: Sage.

Gottfredson, M. R., & Gottfredson, D. (1988). *Decisionmaking in criminal justice* (2nd ed.). New York: Plenum.

Greene, J. R. (1989). Police and community relations: Where have we been and where are we going? In R. Dunham & G. Alpert (Eds.), *Critical issues in policing: Contemporary readings.* Prospect Heights, IL: Waveland.

Greene, J. R., Bergman, W. T., & McLaughlin, E. J. (1994). Implementing community policing: Cultural and structural change in police organizations. In D. P. Rosenbaum (Ed.), *The challenge of community policing: Testing the promises.* Thousand Oaks, CA: Sage.

Greene, J. R., & Decker, S. H. (1989). Police and community perceptions of the community role in policing: The Philadelphia experience. *Howard Journal of Criminal Justice, 20*(2), 105-123.

Greene, J. R., & Klockars, C. B. (1991). What police do. In C. B. Klockars & S. D. Mastrofski (Eds.), *Thinking about police* (2nd ed.). New York: McGraw-Hill.

Greene, J. R., & Mastrofski, S. D. (Eds.). (1988). *Community policing: Rhetoric or reality?* New York: Praeger.

Greene, J. R., & Taylor, R. B. (1988). Community-based policing and foot patrol: Issues of theory and evaluation. In J. R. Greene & S. D. Mastrofski (Eds.), *Community policing: Rhetoric or reality?* New York: Praeger.

Greenwood, P. W., Petersilia, J., & Chaiken, J. (1977). *The criminal investigation process.* Lexington, MA: D. C. Heath.

Grinc, R. M. (1994). "Angels in marble": Problems in stimulating community involvement in community policing. *Crime and Delinquency, 40,* 437-468.

Hall, S. (1992). The question of cultural identity. In S. Hall, D. Held, & T. McGrew (Eds.), *Modernity and its futures.* Cambridge, UK: Polity.

Hayek, F. A. (1960). *The constitution of liberty.* London: Routledge & Kegan Paul.

Hesseling, R., & van den Hul, H. (1993). Surveillance . . . A public or private concern? In P. Broadbent (Ed.), *Policing . . . Private or public?: Proceedings of a conference.* Manchester, UK: Metropolitan University Press.

HMSO. (1962). *Royal commission on the police 1962: Final report* (Command 1728). London: Author.

HMSO. (1993a). *Helping with enquiries: Tackling crime effectively* (Audit Commission Report). London: Author.

HMSO. (1993b). *Police reform* (White Paper). London: Author.

HMSO. (1996). *Streetwise: Effective policing patrol.* London: Author.

Holdaway, S. (1984). *Inside the British police: A force at work.* New York: Basil Blackwell.

Home Office. (1993a). *Police reform: A police service for the 21st century: The government's proposals for the police service in England and Wales.* London: Author.

Home Office. (1993b). *White paper on police reform* (Command 2281). London: Author.

Home Office. (1995). *Review of core and ancillary tasks.* London: Author.

Hoogenboom, A. B. (1989). The privatisation of social control. In R. Hood (Ed.), *Crime and criminal policy in Europe: Proceedings of a European colloquium* (pp. 121-124). Oxford, UK: University of Oxford Centre for Criminological Research.

Hoogenboom, A. B. (1991). Grey policing: A theoretical framework. *Policing and Society, 2*(1), 17-30.

Hope, T., & Hough, M. (1988). Area, crime, and incivility: A profile from the British Crime Survey. In T. Hope & M. Shaw (Eds.), *Communities and crime reduction*. London: H.M. Stationery Office.

Hopkins, N., Hewstone, M., & Hantzi, A. (1992). Police-schools liaison and young people's image of the police: An intervention evaluation. *British Journal of Psychology, 83*, 203-220.

Horne, D. G. (1992). Public opinion surveys: Implications for police organizations. *Canadian Police College Journal, 16*(4), 263-281.

Hornick, J. P., Burrows, B. A., Phillips, D. M., & Leighton, B. (1991). An impact evaluation of the Edmonton Neighbourhood Foot Patrol Program. *Canadian Journal of Program Evaluation, 6*, 47-70.

Hornick, J. P., Burrows, B. A., Philips, D. M., & Leighton, B. (1993). An impact evaluation of the Edmonton Neighbourhood Foot-Patrol Program. In J. Chacko & S. E. Nancoo (Eds.), *Community policing in Canada* (pp. 311-332). Toronto: Canadian Scholars' Press.

House of Commons. (1990). *Sixth report of the Defence Committee, Session 1989-90: The physical security of military installations in the United Kingdom* (HC 171). London: HMSO.

Institute for Law and Justice. (1994). *The Drug Market Analysis Project: Defining markets and effective law enforcement practices* (Report prepared for the National Institute of Justice). Alexandria, VA: Author.

Irving, B., Bird, C., Hibberd, M., & Willmore, J. (1989). *Neighbourhood policing: The natural history of a policing experiment*. London: Police Foundation.

Jacob, H., & Lineberry, R. L. (1982). *Government responses to crime. Executive summary* (Report to the National Institute of Justice, U.S. Department of Justice). Evanston, IL: Northwestern University, Center for Urban Affairs and Policy Research.

Jacobs, J. (1961). *The death and life of great American cities*. New York: Vintage.

Jefferson, T., & Walker, M. A. (1993). Attitudes to the police of ethnic minorities in a provincial city. *British Journal of Criminology, 33*(2), 251-266.

Johnson, C. A., Pentz, M. A., Weber, M. D., Dwyer, J. H., MacKinnon, D. P., Flay, B. R., Baer, N. A., & Hansen, W. B. (1990). The relative effectiveness of comprehensive community programming for drug abuse prevention with high risk and low risk adolescents. *Journal of Consulting and Clinical Psychology, 58*, 447-456.

Johnston, L. (1992). *The rebirth of private policing*. London: Routledge & Kegan Paul.

Johnston, L. (1993). Privatisation and protection: Spatial and sectoral ideologies in British policing and crime prevention. *Modern Law Review, 56*(6), 771-792.

Johnston, L. (1996a). Vigilance and vigilantism: Commercialisation and citizenship as crime prevention strategies. In T. H. Bennett (Ed.), *Preventing crime and disorder: Targeting strategies and responsibilities* (Cropwood Conference Series, No. 22). Cambridge, UK: University of Cambridge, Institute of Criminology.

Johnston, L. (1996b). What is vigilantism? *British Journal of Criminology, 36*(2), 220-236.

The Joint Consultative Committee. (1990). *Operational policing review*. Surrey, UK: Author.

Judd, D. R. (1988). *The politics of American cities: Private power and public policy* (3rd ed.). Glenview, IL: Scott, Foresman.

Kakalik, J. S., & Wildhorn, S. (1972). *Private police in the United States* (4 vols.). Washington, DC: U.S. Department of Justice, National Institute of Law Enforcement and Criminal Justice.

Kelling, G. L., & Moore, M. H. (1988a). The evolving strategy of policing. *Perspectives in policing* (No. 4, November). Washington, DC: U.S. Department of Justice, National Institute of Justice.

Kelling, G. L., & Moore, M. H. (1988b). From political to reform to community: The evolving strategy of police. In J. R. Greene & S. D. Mastrofski (Eds.), *Community policing: Rhetoric or reality?* New York: Praeger.

Kelling, G. L., Pate, T., Dieckman, D., & Brown, C. E. (1974a). *The Kansas City Preventive Patrol Experiment: A summary report*. Washington, DC: Police Foundation.

Kelling, G. L., Pate, T., Dieckman, D., & Brown, C. E. (1974b). *The Kansas City Preventive Patrol Experiment: A technical report*. Washington, DC: Police Foundation.

Kelling, G. L., & Wycoff, M. A. (1978). *The Dallas experience: Volume 1. Organizational reform*. Washington, DC: Police Foundation.

Kelling, G. W., & Bratton, W. J. (1993). Implementing community policing: The administrative problem. In *Perspectives on policing* (No. 17). Washington, DC: National Institute of Justice.

Kelling, G. W., & Moore, M. H. (1988). The evolution of the current strategy of policing. In *Perspectives on policing* (No. 4). Washington, DC: National Institute of Justice.

Kennedy, L. W. (1993). The evaluation of community-based policing in Canada. In J. Chacko & S. E. Nancoo (Eds.), *Community policing in Canada* (pp. 291-310). Toronto: Canadian Scholars' Press.

Kinsey, R., Lea, J., & Young, J. (1986). *Losing the fight against crime*. Oxford, UK: Basil Blackwell.

Kirby, G. (1993). Only one chance. *Professional Security, 3*(6), 22-24.

Klein, J. F., Webb, J. R., & DiSanto, J. E. (1978). Experience with the police and attitude towards the police. *Canadian Journal of Sociology, 3*(4), 441-456.

Klitzner, M. (1993). A public/dynamic systems approach to community-wide alcohol and other drug initiatives. In R. C. Davis, A. J. Lurigio, & D. P. Rosenbaum (Eds), *Drugs and the community* (pp. 201-224). Springfield, IL: Charles C Thomas.

Klockars, C. B. (1988). The rhetoric of community policing. In J. R. Greene & S. D. Mastrofski (Eds.), *Community policing: Rhetoric or reality?* (pp. 239-258). New York: Praeger.

Koenig, D. J. (1980). The effects of criminal victimization and judicial or police contacts on public attitudes toward local police. *Journal of Criminal Justice, 8,* 243-249.

Lab, S. (1988). *Crime prevention: Approaches, practices and evaluations*. Cincinnati, OH: Anderson.

Lambert, L. (1993). Police mini-stations in Toronto: An experience in compromise. In J. Chacko & S. E. Nancoo (Eds.), *Community policing in Canada* (pp. 183-192). Toronto: Canadian Scholars' Press.

Lane, R. (1992). Urban police and crime in nineteenth-century America. In M. Tonry & N. Morris (Eds.), *Modern policing*. Chicago: University of Chicago Press.

Lasley, J. R. (1994). The impact of the Rodney King incident on citizen attitudes toward police. *Policing and Society, 3*(4), 245-255.

Lavrakas, P. J. (1985). Citizen self-help and neighborhood crime prevention policy. In L. A. Curtis (Ed.), *American violence and public policy*. New Haven, CT: Yale University Press.

Lavrakas, P. J., Normoyle, J., Skogan, W. G., Hertz, E. J., Salem, G., & Lewis, D. A. (1980). *Factors related to citizen involvement in personal, household, and neighborhood anti-crime measures* (Final Report to the National Institute of Justice). Evanston, IL: Northwestern University, Center for Urban Affairs and Policy Research.

Lee, B. (1991). *Factors affecting citizen's cooperative attitude toward the police as perceived by Japanese, Chinese and Americans.* Unpublished doctoral dissertation, University of Michigan.

Leighton, B. N. (1988). The concept of community in criminology: Toward a social network approach. *Journal of Research in Crime and Delinquency, 25,* 351-374.

Leighton, B. N. (1991). Visions of community policing: Rhetoric and reality in Canada. *Canadian Journal of Criminology, 33,* 485-522.

Leighton, B. N. (1993). Community-based policing and police-community relations. In J. Chacko & S. E. Nancoo (Eds.), *Community policing in Canada* (pp. 245-250). Toronto: Canadian Scholars' Press.

Leighton, B. N. (1994). Community policing in Canada: An overview of experience and evaluations. In D. P. Rosenbaum (Ed.), *The challenge of community policing: Testing the promises* (pp. 209-223). Thousand Oaks, CA: Sage.

Lewis, D. L., & Salem, G. (1986). *Fear of crime: Incivility and the production of a social problem.* New Brunswick, NJ: Transaction Books.

Lilley, R. (1992). An international perspective on the privatization of correction. *Howard Journal, 31,* 174-192.

Linden, R., Barker, I., & Frisbie, D. (1984). *Working together to prevent crime: A practitioner's handbook.* Ottawa: Ministry of the Solicitor General of Canada.

Linguanti, F., & McIntyre, J. (1992). Public attitudes toward the police: Methodology and questionnaire. *Canadian Police College Journal, 16*(4), 251-262.

Lipsky, M. (1980). *Street-level bureaucracies.* New York: Russell Sage.

Long, N. E. (1968). The local community as an ecology of games. *The American Journal of Sociology, 64,* 251-261.

Lowi, T. J. (1969). *The end of liberalism: Ideology, policy, and the crisis of public authority.* New York: Norton.

Lurigio, A. J., & Rosenbaum, D. P. (1986). Evaluation research in community crime prevention: A critical look at the field. In D. P. Rosenbaum (Ed.), *Community crime prevention: Does it work?* (pp. 19-24). Beverly Hills, CA: Sage.

Lurigio, A. J., & Rosenbaum, D. P. (1994). The impact of community policing on police personnel: A review of the literature. In D. P. Rosenbaum (Ed.), *The challenge of community policing: Testing the promises* (pp. 147-163). Thousand Oaks, CA: Sage.

MacLean, B., & Milanovic, D. (Eds.). (1991). *New directions in critical criminology.* Vancouver, BC: Collective Press.

Maguire, E. R. (1997). Structural change in large municipal police organizations during the community policing era. *Justice Quarterly, 14,* 547-576.

Maguire, K., & Pastore, A. L. (Eds.). (1994). *Sourcebook of criminal justice statistics 1994.* Washington, DC: U.S. Department of Justice, Bureau of Justice Statistics.

Maguire, M. (1994). Crime statistics, patterns, and trends: Changing perceptions and their implications. In M. Maguire, R. Morgan, & R. Reiner (Eds.), *The Oxford handbook of criminology.* Oxford, UK: Oxford University Press.

Maltz, M. D., Gordon, A. C., & Friedman, W. (1990). *Mapping crime in its community setting: Event geography analysis.* New York: Springer.

Manning, P. K. (1977). *Police work: The social organization of policing.* Cambridge: MIT Press.

Manning, P. K. (1984). Community policing. *American Journal of Police, 3,* 205-227.

Manning, P. K. (1988). Community policing as a drama of control. In J. R. Greene & S. D. Mastrofski (Eds.), *Community policing: Rhetoric or reality?* (pp. 27-46). New York: Praeger.

Manning, P. K. (1992a). Information technologies and the police. In M. Tonry & N. Morris (Eds.), *Modern policing, crime and justice: A review of research* (Vol. 15, pp. 349-398). Chicago: University of Chicago Press.

Manning, P. K. (1992b). Technological dramas and the police: Statement and counterstatement in organizational analysis. *Criminology, 30,* 327-346.

Manning, P. K. (1994, July). Economic rhetoric and policing reform. *Police Forum, 4,* pp. 1-8.

Manning, P. K. (1995, April). TQM and the future of policing. *Police Forum, 5,* pp. 1-5.

Marx, G. (1987). The interweaving of public and private police in undercover work. In C. D. Shearing & P. C. Stenning (Eds.), *Private policing* (pp. 172-193). Newbury Park, CA: Sage.

Mastrofski, S. D. (1983). Police knowledge of the patrol beat: A performance measure. In R. R. Bennett (Ed.), *Police at work: Policy issues and analysis* (pp. 45-64). Beverly Hills, CA: Sage.

Mastrofski, S. D. (1988). Community policing as reform: A cautionary tale. In J. R. Greene & S. D. Mastrofski (Eds.), *Community policing: Rhetoric or reality?* (pp. 47-68). New York: Praeger.

Mastrofski, S. D. (1989). Police agency consolidation: Lessons from a case study. In J. J. Fyfe (Ed.), *Police practice in the '90s: Key management issues.* Washington, DC: International City Management Association.

Mastrofski, S. D. (1994). The police. In J. F. Sheley (Ed.), *Criminology: A contemporary handbook.* Belmont, CA: Wadsworth.

Mastrofski, S. D., & Greene, J. R. (1993). Community policing and the rule of law. In D. Weisburd & C. D. Uchida (Eds.), *Police innovation and control of the police.* New York: Springer.

Mastrofski, S. D., & Ritti, R. R. (1995). *Making sense of community policing: A theory-based analysis.* Paper delivered at the annual meeting of the American Society of Criminology, Boston.

Mastrofski, S. D., & Uchida, C. D. (1993). Transforming the police. *Journal of Research in Crime and Delinquency, 30,* 330-358.

Maxfield, M. G. (1988). The London Metropolitan Police and their clients: Victim and suspect attitudes. *Journal of Research in Crime and Delinquency, 25*(2), 188-206.

Mayhew, P., Elliott, D., & Dowds, L. (1989). *The 1988 British Crime Survey* (Home Office Research Study No. 111). London: Home Office.

Mayhew, P., Maung, N. A., & Mirrlees-Black, C. (1993). *The 1992 British Crime Survey* (Home Office Research Study No. 132). London: HMSO.

Mayhew, P., Mirrlees-Black, C., & Maung N. A. (1994). *Trends in crime: Findings from the 1994 British Crime Survey* (Research Findings No. 14). London: Home Office Research and Statistics Department.

McConville, M., & Shepherd, D. (1992). *Watching police watching communities.* London: Routledge & Kegan Paul.

McElroy, J. E., Cosgrove, C. A., & Sadd, S. (1993). *Community policing: The CPOP in New York.* Newbury Park, CA: Sage.

McGahan, P. (1992). Public awareness of policing initiatives. *Canadian Police College Journal, 16*(1), 24-46.

McIntyre, D. M., Goldstein, H., & Skoler, D. L. (1974). *Criminal justice in the United States.* Chicago: American Bar Foundation.

McIver, J. P., & Parks, R. G. (1983). Evaluating police performance: Identification of effective and ineffective police actions. In R. R. Bennett (Ed.), *Police at work: Policy issues and analysis* (pp. 21-44). Beverly Hills, CA: Sage.

Meindl, J. R., & Ehrlich, S. B. (1987). The romance of leadership and the evaluation of organizational performance. *Academy of Management Journal, 30,* 91-109.

Miller, J. P., & Luke, D. E. (1977). *Law enforcement by public officials and special police forces* (4 vols.). London: Home Office.

Miller, T. R., Cohen, M. A., & Wiersema, B. (1996). *Victim costs and consequences: A new look.* Washington, DC: U.S. Department of Justice, National Institute of Justice.

Mirande, A. (1980). Fear of crime and fear of the police in a Chicano community. *Sociology and Social Research, 64*(4), 528-541.

Mirrlees-Black, C., Mayhew, P., & Percy, A. (1996). *The 1996 British Crime Survey: England and Wales* (Home Office Statistical Bulletin, Issue 19/96). London: Home Office Research and Statistics Directorate.

Monkkonen, E. H. (1981). *Police in urban America: 1860-1920.* Cambridge, UK: Cambridge University Press.

Moore, M. H. (1992). Problem-solving and community policing. In M. Tonry & N. Morris (Eds.), *Modern policing, crime and justice: A review of research* (Vol. 15, pp. 99-158). Chicago: University of Chicago Press.

Moore, M. H. (1994). Research synthesis and policy implications. In D. P. Rosenbaum (Ed.), *The challenge of community policing: Testing the promises.* Thousand Oaks, CA: Sage.

Moore, M. H., & Stephens, D. W. (1991). *Beyond command and control: The strategic management of police departments.* Washington, DC: U.S. Department of Justice, National Institute of Justice, Police Executive Research Forum.

Morgan, R. (1986). Policing by consent: Legitimating the doctrine. In D. J. Smith & R. Morgan (Eds.), *Coming to terms with policing.* London: Routledge & Kegan Paul.

Morgan, R., & Maggs, C. (1985). *Setting the P.A.C.E.: Police community consultation arrangements in England and Wales.* Bath: University of Bath, Centre for the Analysis of Social Policy.

Morgan, R., & Newburn, T. (1994, August 5). Radically rethinking policing. *New Law Journal, 144*(6659), 1092-1093.

Muir, W. K., Jr. (1977). *Police: Streetcorner politicians.* Chicago: University of Chicago Press.

Munn, J. R., & Renner, K. E. (1978). Perceptions of police work by the police and by the public. *Criminal Justice and Behavior, 5*(2), 165-179.

Murphy, C. (1988). The development, impact, and implications of community policing in Canada. In J. R. Greene & S. D. Mastrofski (Eds.), *Community policing: Rhetoric or reality?* (pp. 177-189). New York: Praeger.

Murphy, C. (1993a). Community problems, problem communities and community policing in Toronto. In J. Chacko & S. E. Nancoo (Eds.), *Community policing in Canada* (pp. 193-210). Toronto: Canadian Scholars' Press.

Murphy, C. (1993b). The development, impact and implications of community policing in Canada. In J. Chacko & S. E. Nancoo (Eds.), *Community policing in Canada* (pp. 13-26). Toronto: Canadian Scholars' Press.

Murphy, C., & Lithopoulos, S. (1988). *Social determinants of attitudes towards police: Findings from the Toronto Community Policing Survey.* Ottawa: Solicitor General Canada/Ministry Secretariat.

Murphy, C., & Muir, G. (1984). *Community-based policing: A review of the critical issues.* Ottawa: Solicitor General of Canada.

Murray, R. (1991, May). The state after Henry. *Marxism Today,* pp. 22-27.

Murty, K. S., Roebuck, J. B., & Smith, J. D. (1990). The image of the police in black Atlantic communities. *Journal of Police Science and Administration, 17,* 520-527.

Nederveen Pierterse, J. (1995). Global system, globalization and the parameters of modernity. In M. Featherstone, S. Lash, & R. Robertson (Eds.), *Global modernities* (pp. 45-68). London: Sage.

Newburn, T., & Morgan, R. (1994). A new agenda for the Old Bill? *Policing, 10*(3), 143-150.

Normandeau, A., & Leighton, B. (1990). *A vision of the future of policing in Canada: Police-challenge 2000. Background document.* Ottawa: Solicitor General Canada, Ministry Secretariat, Police and Security Branch.

Ocqueteau, F. (1987). L'irresistible ascension des forces de securite privee. *Actes, 60,* 17, 19.

Office of Community Oriented Policing Services. (1994, October 15). *Accelerated hiring, education and deployment (COPS AHEAD) for populations of 50,000 or over.* Washington, DC: U.S. Department of Justice.

O'Malley, P., & Palmer, D. (1996). Post-Keynesian policing. *Economy and Society, 25*(2), 137-155.

Osborne, D., & Gaebler, D. (1992). *Reinventing government: How the entrepreneurial spirit is transforming the public sector.* Reading, MA: Addison-Wesley.

Ostrom, E. (1972). Metropolitan reform: Propositions derived from two traditions. *Social Science Quarterly, 53,* 474-493.

Parsons, T. (1960). *Structure and process in modern societies.* Glencoe, IL: Free Press.

Pate, A. M. (1986). Experimenting with foot patrol: The Newark experience. In D. P. Rosenbaum (Ed.), *Community crime prevention: Does it work?* (pp. 137-156). Beverly Hills, CA: Sage.

Pate, A. M., Wycoff, M. A., Skogan, W. G., & Sherman, L. W. (1986). *Reducing fear of crime in Houston and Newark: A summary report.* Washington, DC: Police Foundation.

Patterson, R. M., & Grant, N. K. (1988). Community mapping: Rationale and considerations for implementation. *Journal of Police Science and Administration, 16,* 136-143.

Pawson, R., & Tilly, N. (1994). What works in evaluation research? *British Journal of Criminology, 34*(3), 291-306.

Pease, K. (1994). Crime prevention. In M. Maguire, R. Morgan, & R. Reiner (Eds.), *The Oxford handbook of criminology.* Oxford, UK: Oxford University Press.

Pentz, M. A., Dwyer, J. H., MacKinnon, D. P., Flay, B. R., Hansen, W. B., Wang, E. Y., & Johnson, C. A. (1989). A multicommunity trial for primary prevention of adolescent drug abuse. *Journal of the American Medical Association, 261,* 3259-3266.

Percy, S. L. (1980). Response time and citizen evaluation of police. *Journal of Police Science and Administration, 8*(1), 75-86.

Peters, T. J., & Waterman, R. H., Jr. (1982). *In search of excellence.* New York: Warner Books.

Pinder, C. C. (1977). Concerning the application of human motivation theories in organizational settings. *The Academy of Management Review, 2,* 384-397.

Poister, T. H., & McDavid, J. C. (1978). Victims' evaluations of police performance. *Journal of Criminal Justice, 6,* 133-149.

Police Foundation/Policy Studies Institute. (1994). *Independent committee of inquiry into the roles and responsibilities of the police.* London: Police Foundation/Policy Studies Institute.

Police Foundation/Policy Studies Institute. (1996). *The role and responsibilities of the police: The report of an independent inquiry established by the Police Foundation and the Policy Studies Institute.* London: Police Foundation/Policy Studies Institute.

Pooley, E. (1996, January 15). One good apple. *Time,* pp. 54-56.

President's Commission on Law Enforcement and Administration of Justice. (1967). *Task force report: Crime and its impact—An assessment.* Washington, DC: Government Printing Office.

Prestby, J. E., & Wandersman, A. (1985). An empirical exploration of a framework of organizational viability: Maintaining block organizations. *Journal of Applied Behavioral Science, 21,* 287-305.

Punch, M., & Naylor, T. (1973). The police: A social service. *New Society, 24,* 358-361.

Reiner, R. (1989). The politics of police research. In M. Weatheritt (Ed.), *Police research: Some future prospects.* Aldershot, UK: Avebury.

Reiner, R. (1991). *Chief constables.* Oxford, UK: Oxford University Press.

Reiner, R. (1992a). Police research in the United Kingdom: A critical review. In M. Tonry & N. Morris (Eds.), *Modern policing.* Chicago: University of Chicago Press.

Reiner, R. (1992b). Policing a postmodern society. *Modern Law Review, 55*(6), 761-781.

Reiner, R. (1992c). *The politics of the police* (2nd ed.). Hemel Hempstead, UK: Harvester Wheatsheaf.

Reiner, R. (1994a). Policing and the police. In M. Maguire, R. Morgan, & R. Reiner (Eds.), *The Oxford handbook of criminology* (pp. 705-772). Oxford, UK: Oxford University Press.

Reiner, R. (1994b). What should the police be doing? *Policing, 10*(3), 151-157.

Reiner, R., & Cross, M. (Eds.). (1991). *Beyond law and order: Criminal justice policy and politics into the 1990s.* London: Macmillan.

Reiner, R., & Spencer, S. (Eds.). (1993). *Accountable policing: Effectiveness, empowerment and equity.* London: Institute for Public Policy Research.

Reiss, A. J., Jr. (1971). *The police and the public.* New Haven, CT: Yale University Press.

Reiss, A. J., Jr. (1992). Police organization in the twentieth century. In M. Tonry & N. Morris (Eds.), *Modern policing, crime and justice: A review of research* (Vol. 15, pp. 51-97). Chicago: University of Chicago Press.

Rizkalla, S., Archambault, S., & Cartier, B. (1991). La prévention communautaire du crime: Un programme novateur. *Revue Canadienne de Criminologie, 33*(3-4), 421-434.

Robinette, H. M. (1989, September). Operational streamlining. *FBI Law Enforcement Bulletin,* pp. 7-11.

Rose, D. (1994, September 18). Police forces face massive cut under secret Tory plan. *The Observer.*

Rose, N. (1996). The death of the social? Re-figuring the territory of government. *Economy and Society, 25*(3), 327-356.

Rosenbaum, D. P. (Ed.). (1986). *Community crime prevention: Does it work?* Beverly Hills, CA: Sage.

Rosenbaum, D. P. (1987). The theory and research behind Neighborhood Watch: Is it a sound fear and crime reduction strategy? *Crime and Delinquency, 33,* 103-134.

Rosenbaum, D. P. (1988). Community crime prevention: A review and synthesis of the literature. *Justice Quarterly, 5,* 323-395.

Rosenbaum, D. P. (Ed.). (1994). *The challenge of community policing: Testing the promises.* Thousand Oaks, CA: Sage.

Rosenbaum, D. P., Bennett, S., Lindsay, B., & Wilkinson, D. L. (1994). *Community responses to drug abuse: A program evaluation* (Research Report NCJ 145945). Washington, DC: U.S. Department of Justice, National Institute of Justice.

Rosenbaum, D. P., & Lurigio, A. J. (1994). An inside look at community policing reform: Definitions, organizational changes, and evaluation findings. *Crime & Delinquency, 40,* 299-314.

Rosenbaum, D. P., Wilkinson, D. L., Michener, A., Faggiani, D., Stemen, D., Anyah, M. A., Slovak, J., & Urbik, J. (1993). *Aurora/Joliet Neighborhood-Oriented Policing and Problem Solving Project: Impact on the police and the community.* Chicago: University of Illinois at Chicago, Center for Research in Law and Justice.

Rosenbaum D. P., Yeh, S., & Wilkinson, D. L. (1994). Impact of community policing on police personnel: A quasi-experimental test. *Crime & Delinquency, 40,* 331-353.

Rossi, P. H., & Freeman, H. E. (1985). *Evaluation: A systematic approach* (3rd ed.). Beverly Hills, CA: Sage.

Rothbard, M. N. (1978). *For a new liberty: The Libertarian manifesto.* New York: Collier Macmillan.

Rumbaut, R. G., & Bittner, E. (1979). Changing conceptions of the police role. In N. Morris & M. Tonry (Eds.), *Crime and justice* (Vol. 1). Chicago: University of Chicago Press.

Sacco, V. F. (1995, May). Media constructions of crime. *Annals of the American Academy of Political and Social Science, 539,* 141-154.

Sacco, V. F., & Johnson, H. (1990). *Patterns of criminal victimization in Canada.* Ottawa: Statistics Canada.

Sadd, S., & Grinc, R. (1994). Innovative neighborhood oriented policing: An evaluation of community policing programs in eight cities. In D. P. Rosenbaum (Ed.), *The challenge of community policing: Testing the promises.* Thousand Oaks, CA: Sage.

Sayre, W. S., & Kaufman, H. (1960). *Governing New York City: Politics in the metropolis.* New York: Russell Sage.

Scaglion, R., & Condon, R. G. (1980). Determinants of attitudes toward city police. *Criminology, 17*(4), 485-494.

Scarman, Lord. (1981). *The Brixton disorders* (Command 8427). London: HMSO.

Schorr, L. B. (1988). *Within our reach: Breaking the cycle of disadvantage.* Garden City, NY: Doubleday.

Schwartz, A. I., & Clarren, S. N. (1975). *Evaluation of Cincinnati's Community Sector Team Policing Program: A progress report—After one year* [Mimeograph]. Washington, DC: Urban Institute.

Schwartz, A. I., & Clarren, S. N. (1977). *The Cincinnati team policing experiment: A summary report.* Washington, DC: Police Foundation.

Scott, W. R. (1992). *Organizations: Rational, natural, and open systems* (3rd ed.). Englewood Cliffs, NJ: Prentice Hall.

Seashore, S., Lawler, E., III., Mirvis, P., & Cammann, C. (1983). *Assessing organizational change.* New York: Wiley Interscience.

Sechrest, L. B., White, S. O., & Brown, E. D. (Eds.). (1979). *The rehabilitation of criminal offenders: Problems and prospects.* Washington, DC: National Academy of Sciences.

Shaw, C. R., & McKay, H. D. (1942). *Juvenile delinquency and urban areas.* Chicago: University of Chicago Press.

Shea, S., & Basch, C. E. (1990). A review of five major community-based cardiovascular disease prevention programs: Part I. Rationale, design, and theoretical framework. *American Journal of Health Promotion, 4,* 202-213.

Shearing, C. (Ed.). (1981). *Organisational police deviance.* Toronto: Butterworths.

Shearing, C. D. (1992). The relation between public and private policing. In M. Tonry & N. Morris (Eds.), *Modern policing: Crime and justice. A review of research* (Vol. 15). Chicago: University of Chicago Press.

Shearing, C. D. (1994, November 2-4). Discussant's comments at *Workshop on Evaluating Police Service Delivery,* Minister of the Solicitor General of Canada/International Centre for Comparative Criminology, Montreal.

Shearing, C. D., & Stenning, P. C. (1981). Modern private security: Its growth and implications. In M. Tonry & N. Morris (Eds.), *Crime and justice: An annual review of research* (Vol. 3). Chicago: University of Chicago Press.

Shearing, C. D., & Stenning, P. C. (1987). *Private policing.* Newbury Park, CA: Sage.

Sheehy, Sir P. (1993). *Report of inquiry into police responsibilities and rewards* (Command 2280.I & 2280.II). London: HMSO.

Sherman, L. A., & Berk, R. A. (1984). The specific deterrent effects of arrest for domestic assault. *American Sociological Review, 49,* 261-272.

Sherman, L. W. (1986). Policing communities. What works? In A. J. Reiss & M. Tonry (Eds.), *Communities and crime, crime and justice: A review of research* (Vol. 8, pp. 343-386). Chicago: University of Chicago Press.

Sherman, L. W. (1992a). Book review: Problem-oriented policing. *Journal of Criminal Law and Criminology, 82,* 690-707.

Sherman, L. W. (1992b). *Policing domestic violence: Experiments and dilemmas.* New York: Free Press.

Sherman, L. W. (1993). Why crime control is not reactionary. In D. Weisburd & C. Uchida (Eds.), *Police innovation and the control of the police.* New York: Springer.

Sherman, L. W. (1995). The police. In J. Q. Wilson & J. Petersilia (Eds.), *Crime.* San Francisco: ICS Press.

Sherman, L. W., Gartin, P. R., & Buerger, M. E. (1989). Hot spots of predatory crime: Routine activities and the criminology of place. *Criminology, 27*(1), 27-55.

Sherman, L. W., Milton, C. H., & Kelly, T. V. (1973). *Team policing: Seven case studies.* Washington, DC: Police Foundation.

Short, C. (1983). Community policing: Beyond slogans. In T. Bennett (Ed.), *The future of policing.* Cambridge, UK: University of Cambridge, Institute of Criminology.

Skogan, W. G. (1978). Consumption of police and law enforcement policy. *Policy Studies Journal, 7,* 469-479.

Skogan, W. G. (1986). Fear of crime and neighborhood change. In A. Reiss & M. Tonry (Eds.), *Communities and crime* (pp. 203-230). Chicago: University of Chicago Press.

Skogan, W. G. (1990a). *Disorder and decline: Crime and the spiral of decay in American cities.* New York: Free Press.

Skogan, W. G. (1990b). *The police and public in England and Wales: A British Crime Survey report* (Home Office Research Study No. 117). London: HMSO.

Skogan, W. G. (1994a). *Contacts between police and public: Findings from the 1992 British Crime Survey* (Home Office Research Study No. 134). London: HMSO.

Skogan, W. G. (1994b). The impact of community policing on neighborhood residents: A cross-site analysis. In D. P. Rosenbaum (Ed.), *The challenge of community policing: Testing the promises* (pp. 167-181). Thousand Oaks, CA: Sage.

Skogan, W. G. (1995). Community policing in the U.S. In J. P. Brodeur (Ed.), *Comparisons in policing: An international perspective* (pp. 86-111). London: Avebury.

Skogan, W. G. (1996). Partnerships for prevention? Some obstacles to police-community cooperation. In T. Bennett (Ed.), *Preventing crime and disorder* (Cambridge Cropwood Series 1996; pp. 225-252). Cambridge, UK: University of Cambridge, Institute of Criminology.

Skogan, W. G., & Hartnett, S. M. (1997). *Community policing, Chicago style.* New York: Oxford University Press.

Skogan, W. G., Hartnett, S. M., DuBois, J., Lovig, J., Higgins, L., Bennett, S. F., Lavrakas, P. J., Lurigio, A., Block, R. L., Rosenbaum, D. P., & Dantzker, G. (1994). *Community policing in Chicago, year one.* Chicago: Illinois Criminal Justice Information Authority. (available on request)

Skogan, W. G., & Maxfield, M. G. (1981). *Coping with crime: Individual and neighborhood response reactions.* Beverly Hills, CA: Sage.

Skolnick, J. H., & Bayley, D. H. (1986). *The new blue line: Police innovation in six American cities.* New York: Free Press.

Skolnick, J. H., & Bayley, D. H. (1988a). *Community policing: Issues and practices around the world.* Washington, DC: National Institute of Justice.

Skolnick, J. H., & Bayley, D. H. (1988b). Theme and variation in community policing. In M. Tonry & N. Morris (Eds.), *Crime and justice: A review of research* (Vol. 10, pp. 1-38). Chicago: University of Chicago Press.

Smith, B. (1984). Rural victimizations and perceptions of police performance. *Victimology, 9,* 156-165.

Smith, D. J. (1991). Origins of black hostility to the police. *Policing and Society, 2,* 1-15.

Smith, J. (1994, October 16). Howard's reforms will kill community policing. *The Observer.*

Solicitor General of Canada. (1990). *A vision of the future of policing in Canada. Police-challenge 2000* (Discussion Paper). Ottawa: Ministry of the Solicitor General of Canada.

Southgate, P., & Ekblom, P. (1984). *Contact between police and public* (Home Office Research Study No. 77). London: Home Office.

Sparrow, M. K. (1988). Implementing community policing. In *Perspectives in policing* (No. 9). Washington, DC: U.S. Department of Justice, National Institute of Justice, Office of Justice Program.

Sparrow, M. K., Moore, M. H., & Kennedy, D. M. (1990). *Beyond 911: A new era for policing.* New York: Basic Books.

Spector, M., & Kitsuse, J. I. (1987). *Constructing social problems.* New York: Aldine de Gruyter.

Spelman, W., & Brown, D. K. (1984). *Calling the police: Citizen reporting of serious crime.* Washington, DC: Government Printing Office.

Spielberger, C. D. (Ed.). (1979). *Police selection and evaluation: Issues and techniques.* New York: Praeger.

Spielberger, C. D., Ward, J. C., & Spaulding, H. C. (1979). A model for the selection of law enforcement officers. In C. D. Spielberger (Ed.), *Police selection and evaluation: Issues and techniques.* New York: Praeger.

Spitzer, S. (1987). Security and control in capitalist societies: The fetishism of security and the secret thereof. In J. Lowman, R. J. Menzies, & T. S. Palys (Eds.), *Transcarceration: Essays in the sociology of social control* (pp. 43-58). Aldershot, UK: Gower.

Starr, P. (1982). *The social transformation of American medicine.* New York: Basic Books.

Stephens, M., & Becker, S. (Eds.). (1994). *Police force, police service.* London: Macmillan.

Suchman, E. A. (1968). *Evaluative research: Principles and practice in public service and social action programs.* New York: Russell Sage.

Sullivan, P. S., Dunham, R. G., & Alpert, G. P. (1987). Attitude structures of different ethnic and age groups concerning police. *The Journal of Criminal Law and Criminology, 78*(1), 177-195.

Surette, R. (1992). *Media, crime and criminal justice.* Pacific Grove, CA: Brooks/Cole.

Tarling, R. (1988). *Police work and manpower allocation* (Home Office Research and Planning Unit Paper 47). London: Home Office.

Taub, R. P., Taylor, D. G., & Dunham, J. (1984). *Paths of neighborhood change: Race and crime in urban America.* Chicago: University of Chicago Press.

Taxman, F. S., & McEwen, J. T. (1994). *Interagency workgroups: Using geographical tools to develop crime control strategies* (Report to the National Institute of Justice). Alexandria, VA: Institute for Law and Justice.

Taylor, F. W. (1911). *The principles of scientific management.* New York: Harper.

Taylor, R. B., Shumaker, S. A., & Gottfredson, S. D. (1985). Neighborhood-level linkages between physical features and local sentiments: Deterioration, fear of crime, and confidence. *Journal of Architectural Planning and Research,* pp. 261-275.

Thomas, C. W., & Hyman, J. M. (1977). Perceptions of crime, fear of victimization, and public perceptions of police performance. *Journal of Police Science and Administration, 5*(3), 305-317.

Thompson, J. D. (1967). *Organizations in action.* New York: McGraw-Hill.

Tien, J. M., Rich, T. F., Shell, M. C., Larson, R. C., & Donnelly, J. P. (1993). *Compass: A drug market analysis program, final report* (Submitted to the National Institute of Justice). Cambridge, MA: Queues Enforth Development.

Toch, H., & Grant, J. D. (1991). *Police as problem solvers.* New York: Plenum.

Travis, A. (1994a, September 20). Alarm over "patrolling by citizens" plan. *The Guardian,* p. 22.

Travis, A. (1994b, September 29). Howard switches street patrol plans to "walking with a purpose." *The Guardian,* p. 2.

Trojanowicz, R. C. (1986). Evaluating a neighborhood foot patrol program: The Flint Michigan Project. In D. P. Rosenbaum (Ed.), *Community crime prevention: Does it work?* (pp. 157-178). Beverly Hills, CA: Sage.

Trojanowicz, R. C. (1994). *Community policing: A survey of police departments in the United States.* Washington, DC: Federal Bureau of Investigation.

Trojanowicz, R. C., & Bucqueroux, B. (1990). *Community policing: A contemporary perspective.* Cincinnati, OH: Anderson.

Van Andel, H. (1989). Crime prevention that works: The case of public transport in The Netherlands. *British Journal of Criminology, 29*(1), 47-56.

van Dijk, J., & Mayhew, P. (1992). *Criminal victimisation in the industrialised world.* The Hague, The Netherlands: Directorate for Crime Prevention.

Van Maanen, J. (1983). The boss: A portrait of the American police sergeant. In M. Punch (Ed.), *The control of the police.* Cambridge: MIT Press.

Van Maanen, J. (1984). Making rank: Becoming an American police sergeant. *Urban Life, 13,* 155-176.

Van Maanen, J., & Dabbs, J. (1983). *Varieties of qualitative research.* Beverly Hills, CA: Sage.

Waddington, P. A. J., & Braddock, Q. (1991). Guardians or bullies? Perceptions of the police amongst adolescent black, white and Asian boys. *Policing and Society, 2,* 31-45.

Walker, C. R., & Walker, S. G. (1989). *The Victoria community police stations: An exercise in innovation.* Ottawa: Canadian Police College.

Walker, N. (1993). The international dimension. In R. Reiner & S. Spencer (Eds), *Accountable policing: Effectiveness, empowerment and equity* (pp. 113-171). London: Institute for Public Policy Research.

Walker, S. (1977). *A critical history of police reform: The emergence of professionalism.* Lexington, MA: Lexington Books.

Walker, S. (1983). *The police in America.* New York: McGraw-Hill.

Walker, S. (1989). *Sense and nonsense about crime* (2nd ed.). Pacific Grove, CA: Brooks/Cole.

Walker, S. G., Walker, C. R., & McDavid, J. C. (1993). Program impacts: The Victoria community police stations: A three-year evaluation. In J. Chacko & S. E. Nancoo (Eds.), *Community policing in Canada* (pp. 333-346). Toronto: Canadian Scholars' Press.

Walters, J. (1992, May). The cult of total quality. *Governing,* pp. 38-42.

Warner, K., & Havens, A. E. (1968). Goal displacement and the intangibility of organizational goals. *Administrative Science Quarterly, 12,* 538-555.

Watch schemes should mount street patrols, says Howard. (1993, December 10). *Police Review,* pp. 4-5.

Weatheritt, M. (1983). Community policing: Does it work and how do we know? In T. Bennett (Ed.), *The future of policing.* Cambridge, UK: University of Cambridge, Institute of Criminology.

Weatheritt, M. (1986). *Innovations in policing.* London: Croom Helm.

Weatheritt, M. (1993a). Getting more from less: Thinking about the use of police resources. In
     A. N. Doob (Ed.), *Thinking about police resources*. Toronto: University of Toronto, Centre
     of Criminology.
Weatheritt, M. (1993b). Measuring police performance: Accounting or accountability? In R. Reiner
     & S. Spencer (Eds.), *Accountable policing: Effectiveness, empowerment and equity*. Lon-
     don: Institute for Public Policy Research.
West, J. P., Berman, E. M., & Milakovich, M. E. (1995). Total Quality Management in local
     government. *Municipal yearbook, 1994* (pp. 14-25). Washington, DC: International City
     Management Association.
Wilkinson, D. L., & Rosenbaum, D. P. (1994). The effects of organizational structure on commu-
     nity policing: A comparison of two cities. In D. P. Rosenbaum (Ed.), *The challenge of
     community policing: Testing the promises*. Thousand Oaks, CA: Sage.
Wilkinson, D. L., Rosenbaum, D. P., Bruni, M., & Yeh, S. (1994). *Community policing in Joliet:
     Year 2 process evaluation*. Chicago: University of Illinois at Chicago, Center for Research
     in Law and Justice.
Williams, H., & Pate, A. M. (1987). Returning to first principles: Reducing the fear of crime in
     Newark. *Crime and Delinquency, 33*, 53-70.
Williams, W., Greene, J. R., & Bergman, W. T. (1992). Strategic planning in a big-city police
     department: The Philadelphia story. In K. E. Clark, M. B. Clark, & D. P. Campbell (Eds.),
     Impact of leadership (pp. 107-118). Greensboro, NC: Center for Creative Leadership.
Wilson, J. Q. (1968a). Dilemmas of police administration. *Public Administration Review, 28*,
     407-417.
Wilson, J. Q. (1968b). *Varieties of police behavior*. Cambridge, MA: Harvard University Press.
Wilson, J. Q. (1993). The problem of defining agency success. In *Performance measures for the
     criminal justice system* (pp. 157-165). Washington, DC: U.S. Department of Justice, Bureau
     of Justice Statistics.
Wilson, J. Q., & Kelling, G. L. (1982, March). Broken windows: The police and neighborhood
     safety. *The Atlantic Monthly*, pp. 29-38.
Wilson, J. Q., & Kelling, G. L. (1989). Making neighborhoods safe. *The Atlantic Monthly, 263*,
     46-52.
Wycoff, M. A. (1994). *Community policing strategies* (Draft Final Report). Washington, DC:
     Police Foundation.
Wycoff, M. A. (1995, November). Community policing strategies. *Research Preview*. Washington,
     DC: U.S. Department of Justice, National Institute of Justice.
Yarmey, A. D. (1991). Retrospective perceptions of police following victimization. *Canadian
     Police College Journal, 15*(2), 137-143.
Young, J. (1994). Recent paradigms in criminology. In M. Maguire, R. Morgan, & R. Reiner (Eds.),
     The Oxford handbook of criminology. Oxford, UK: Oxford University Press.
Young, M. (1991): *An inside job*. Oxford, UK: Oxford University Press.

INDEX

ABOUT THE CONTRIBUTORS

Trevor Bennett is currently Lecturer in Criminology at the University of Cambridge, Institute of Criminology and a Fellow of Wolfson College. He is also currently director of the M.Phil. program at the Institute of Criminology and also has overall responsibility for a new teaching program designed specifically for police officers. He has written widely on the topic of community policing and has recently completed a national survey of the community policing strategies in England and Wales. His publications include *Burglary in a Dwelling* and *Burglars on Burglary,* as well as *Evaluating Neighbourhood Watch* and work on the impact of police contact patrols on crime and fear reduction. (Address: University of Cambridge, Institute of Criminology, 7 West Road, Cambridge, CB3 9DT)

Jean-Paul Brodeur is Full Professor at the School of Criminology of the University of Montréal and was Director of the International Centre for Comparative Criminology at the same university. He has published *La délinquance de l'ordre* (Montréal, 1984) and several articles in French and English on policing. He is the author of several reports written for commissions of inquiry into policing.

Jack R. Greene is Professor of Criminal Justice and Director of Temple University's Center for Public Policy, where he conducts research and teaches on topics of organizational dynamics and the evaluation of police services. He has conducted research and published extensively on matters pertaining to police efficiency and effectiveness, police management, and community-oriented policing, most particularly in urban areas. His most recent coedited book, an anthology of readings, *Community Policing: Rhetoric or Reality?* (1988) examines a major institutional change occurring in American policing.

Les Johnston is currently Professor at the School of Human Studies at the University of Teesside in the United Kingdom. He has published *The Rebirth of Private Policing* (London, 1992) as well as many other works on private security.

Stephen D. Mastrofski is Professor of Criminal Justice at Michigan State University. He conducted research on a number of police-related topics, such as performance measurement, reform, agency consolidation, accreditation, and drunk driving enforcement. He has written several essays and articles on policing and is coeditor of *Community Policing: Rhetoric or Reality?* As a Visiting Fellow at the National Institute of Justice, he fielded a systematic observation study of patrol officers working under a community policing approach. He has provided technical assistance on community policing to a number of departments in the United States and Canada.

Jerome E. McElroy is currently Executive Director of the New York City Criminal Justice Agency. He was for a number of years Associate Director of the Vera Institute of Justice, during which time he directed numerous research projects dealing with police-related matters. He is presently also a faculty member of the John Jay College of Criminal Justice, Fordham College, and of Fordham University Graduate School of Social Work and serves as a member of the board of directors of the National Criminal Justice Association.

Robert Reiner is Lecturer in Criminology at the Department of Law of the London School of Economics and is coeditor of *Policing and Society: An International Journal* and review editor of the *British Journal of Criminology*. He is the author of *Beyond Law and Order: Criminal Justice Policy and*

Politics Into the 1990's (Great Britain, 1991) and of *Chief Constables: Bobbies, Bosses or Bureaucrats?* (Oxford, 1991).

Dennis P. Rosenbaum is Professor and head of the Department of Criminal Justice at the University of Illinois at Chicago. He is the former Director of the Center for Research in Law and Justice on campus. He has conducted a wide range of evaluations and research projects focusing on police and community efforts to *prevent* violence, drug abuse, and delinquency. These include studies of community mobilization, comprehensive interagency partnerships, media-based crime prevention, school-based drug education, crime prevention in public housing, and community policing. His books include *Community Crime Prevention: Does It Work?* (1986), *The Social Construction of Reform* (1988), *Drugs and Communities* (1993), and *The Challenge of Community Policing: Testing the Promises* (1994).

Vincent F. Sacco is Professor in the Department of Sociology at Queen's University. He has published extensively in the areas of fear of crime, criminal victimization, and crime and mass media. Recently, he coauthored *The Criminal Event: An Introduction to Criminology* with Leslie Kennedy of the University of Alberta.

Wesley G. Skogan is Professor of Political Science and Urban Affairs at Northwestern University. His publications include *Victims of Crime* (1989), which reflects his continuing interest in criminal victimization, and *Coping With Crime* (1990), which deals with issues of fear of crime and individual behavior. Sections of his 1990 book *Disorder and Decline* deal with community policing. His latest book (with Susan M. Hartnett) is titled *Community Policing, Chicago Style.* (Address: Center for Urban Affairs and Policy Research, Northwestern University, Evanston IL 60208 USA. skogan@nwu.edu)